MAN FROM MACEDONIA

my life of service, struggle, faith, and hope

Rev. Aaron Johnson

with Deb Cleveland

foreword by Chuck Colson

WestBow

PRESS

WestBow Press books may be ordered through booksellers or by contacting:

WestBow Press
A Division of Thomas Nelson
1663 Liberty Drive
Bloomington, IN 47403
www.westbowpress.com
1-(866) 928-1240

Because of the dynamic nature of the Internet, any Web addresses or links contained in this book may have changed since publication and may no longer be valid. The views expressed in this work are solely those of the author and do not necessarily reflect the views of the publisher, and the publisher hereby disclaims any responsibility for them.

ISBN: 978-1-4497-0028-7 (e)
ISBN: 978-1-4497-0029-4 (sc)
ISBN: 978-1-4497-0030-0 (hc)

Library of Congress Control Number: 2010920672

Printed in the United States of America

WestBow Press rev. date: 02/04/2010

To my wife, Mattie M. Johnson, who has been my life partner in both marriage and ministry; to our children, Dr. Dezette C. Johnson and Dr. Aaron Jamale Johnson, D.Min., who have been sweetly obedient to the call of God in their lives; and to our grandson, Tariq.

This book is also dedicated to the special memory of my mother, Cassie Henry Newkirk Johnson; my father, Willie Lee Johnson; my sister, Bernita West, and my brothers Tommy, James, Roscoe and Lennard. I am looking forward to our family reunion among the heavens.

A.J.

I humbly dedicate this book to all of those unsung heroes who refused to believe that God created them with less love and forethought. You changed a nation.

D.C.

Contents

ACKNOWLEDGEMENTS

"The steps of a good man are ordered by the Lord;
And He delights in His way." Psalms 37:23

These acknowledgements are very much incomplete. I regret that I am unable to include so many people who were and are involved in my life. They will forever live in my heart. I will always remain indebted to them.

I owe much to those who helped me recall my thoughts and refresh my memory of events that took place in the different stages of my life: my sister, Elma Delois Stephen, Vernell West and Denmark West, Sara Lee Johnson, Alice Everett, Nellie Mae Fields, and all my beloved extended family and Matthew Rouse.

I also want to thank those who allowed themselves to be interviewed for the purposes of this book: Fred Baker, Richard and Jo Ann Bishop, Benjamin Foster, Carolyn Gordon, Harlon and Lillie Gregory, Patricia Leach, Mary McAllister, Anne McNeil, Cardell Parks, and Claudia T. Simpson.

I am thankful for all the wonderful members of the Mount Sinai Missionary Baptist Church in Fayetteville, North Carolina. Our forty-five years together was a marriage put together in heaven. You were our strong support, faithful friends and passionate co-workers. We labored together in the service to mankind and the will of God. You were forever faithful to our motto: "We are trying because we care."

I will never forget the voters of Fayetteville who elected me four terms to the Fayetteville City Council, and the Council who elected me mayor pro-tempore during my last term. I was honored to be among you.

I am humbled by the life-long support given me by the residents and neighbors of *God's Country*—the Willard community in Pender County, North Carolina.

I am most grateful to the three former North Carolina governors who appointed me to work with the Human Relations Commission at a critical time in our state's history: Dan Moore, Robert W. Scott, and Jim Holshouser.

I thank them for their leadership as we worked together to transition our great state from a segregated society to an integrated society. And it is with deep gratitude that I must thank all those courageous volunteers who served tirelessly on local Human Relations Councils, building bridges of respect and dignity in their communities.

I was sincerely honored when Governor Jim Martin appointed me to a cabinet position in his administration. Only a man of courage and integrity could have appointed our state's first African-American and ordained minister to be Secretary of the Department of Corrections.

One of my highest joys was to partner in ministry with Prison Fellowship. I thank God for the friendship of my brother, Richard Payne. It is he who introduced me to Prison Fellowship and its founder, Charles Colson, and former president, Tom Pratt. Working with this ministry and with these exceptional men was a life-changing experience—one that will forever make my heart glad.

I am grateful to all those special people who lovingly called me to be their "spiritual father and granddaddy."

I am indebted to Dennis and Deborah Walsh for encouraging me to tell my story, and to Deb Cleveland for shepherding the writing of these printed pages. —Aaron Johnson

As for the writing of this book...

I must first express my gratitude to Dennis and Debbie Walsh. The phone call I received from them in 2005 asking me to write Aaron's story was pivotal for me. Thanks, guys, for your guidance and commitment to get this story told.

Thanks to all those who took the time to sit down with me and share how your stories converged with Aaron's. I especially want to thank former North Carolina Governor James G. Martin and Chaplain Michael Smith for the lovely afternoon spent reminiscing about your friend and mentor.

Jim Denney, thank you for mentoring me through those first couple of chapters. Your guidance made all the difference. Thank you, Lisa Watts and Julie Gilstrap, for your copyediting and your attention to detail. You've made us all look better.

As for my personal thanksgiving... I thank my parents, Ervin and Jane Doughty, who taught me to stand tall and love strong.

Thank you, Judy Truitt. You always thought I could do this writing thing, even when I didn't.

Thank you, Phyllis Nichols, for being a one-woman cheering section and for helping me through the writing of this book.

Thank you, my Oakhaven Family. I'm sure I'm not the preacher's wife you expected, but you've loved me unconditionally and hugged me at all the right times.

And finally, Nathan, Matthew and Joshua. No mom could be prouder. Thanks much for loving me, making me laugh, marrying sweet women and giving me grandchildren that are breathtaking. And then there's you, Gary Cleveland. You have always and forever believed in me. Thank you for buying me those first note cards and that little metal file box so many years ago with the admonition to "go write!" You've endured lonely nights and a crazy writer wife with unimaginable love and patience. Dearest family... you are my story.

And of course, thank you, Aaron and Mattie Johnson, for graciously allowing me to poke around in your lives. *Man from Macedonia* is your story, not mine, yet you've included me in its pages with much grace. I am humbled.
—*Deb Cleveland*

Man from Macedonia is a project of The Deborah and Dennis Walsh Foundation (www.walshfdn.org). The mission of the Foundation is to advance the gospel of Jesus Christ as a means to reconciliation, justice, and mercy. This includes supporting activities that proclaim the life-transforming power of the Christian gospel. A North Carolina nonprofit corporation, the Walsh Foundation is qualified to receive tax-deductible contributions.

FOREWORD

*A*aron Johnson is one of the most remarkable men I've been privileged to know. In 1985, when North Carolina Governor James Martin asked Johnson to become secretary of corrections, Martin told Johnson that he wanted him to be different from all the other corrections officials.

Governor Martin got what he was looking for.

Aaron Johnson was the first black man appointed to the position in North Carolina, the only ordained minister in the nation to hold the job, and the first official to throw open the doors of all the prisons of his state and challenge Prison Fellowship to do ministry like it's never been done before.

On his first day of work, Aaron Johnson walked into his large, gracious office and stared at the huge desk, the official insignia, the trappings of power. He dropped to his knees. "Lord," he prayed, "here I am. Use me however You want to."

And did He ever. From issuing an ordinance prohibiting cursing by employees and inmates to ending a practice of state-bought pornography for inmates, transforming the healthcare services and beyond, Aaron Johnson dramatically changed the environment of North Carolina's prisons.

Johnson came to our office at a time when the national economy was floundering. He came to do devotions and to tell us that he, like the man from Macedonia, was issuing a call for us to come into every one of the more than ninety North Carolina prisons, bringing in an evangelistic crusade. Tom Pratt, the president of Prison Fellowship at the time, was taken by the challenge. But by any objective measure, it was impossible to achieve. Our ministry was lacking funds, and what Johnson was calling for was a herculean administrative task. We didn't have the organization or the structure in place to do it.

In what became for our ministry a great leap of faith, we accepted that challenge. And God answered the fervent prayers of Aaron Johnson and many others. Over the course of the next year we managed to be in every prison in the state with great evangelistic crusades, many times with Aaron Johnson right there preaching with us. I've experienced nothing like it before in my ministry and nothing like it since.

When Aaron Johnson left his corrections post, he went back to the place where he has given most of his life—the pulpit. He is a great preacher, loved by all who have sat under his preaching, been beneficiaries of his counseling, or been associated with him in any way.

Just like me, Aaron could never get prisons out of his blood. He started going back with us time after time to visit prisons in North Carolina and in many other states. No matter how tired or ill he was, he would rise to the occasion and preach as few people can in the prisons.

Ever feel tired, worn out, maybe powerless to affect events around you? Read Aaron Johnson's story and do like he did. Here is a man of enormous faith, the kind that God responds to and does amazing things through.

Chuck Colson
Founder, Prison Fellowship

Part I: God's Country

ONE

The Lynching

*I*t's not every day that your neighbor is hunted, shot, beaten and lynched—even in Willard. But the day Sheriff Jack Brown knocked on my mother's door to warn us to stay inside, that's exactly what was going on. It was August 1933 and Sheriff Brown was making his rounds to the sparse houses scattered around the countryside of Willard, a piece of "God's Country" that lay in the northern half of Pender County, North Carolina.

Sheriff Brown had gotten wind of something and was trying to get us all to stay out of the way. He stood on our small front porch as the sweaty circles under the armpits of his khaki shirt slowly spread toward his back like lava; even the badge on his left shirt pocket drooped like a wilted daisy. One of our neighbors was going to die, and in 1933 a white, negro-friendly sheriff simply had no jurisdiction over men in white hooded sheets.

Willard was a segregated southern farming community of less than a thousand folks. Our neighbors the Wests, Murrays, Walkers, Gores, Wilsons, Pearsalls, Rogerses, Joneses, Powells, Brices, Rouses, Echoes, Boneys, Fillyaws, Johnsons and Olivers were a cereal mix of relatives and extended family. Down the highway a bit lived the white Wests, Murrays, Walkers, Gores, Johnsons, etc. At one time, the white ones owned the black ones, gave them their names and eventually their freedom—of sorts.

Several of the Negro families owned their own homes and small plots of land. Many of us blacks were sharecroppers by day and farmers at night. Potato pie and pound cake were our manna, collard and mustard greens our staples. Our faith poured out of us through hymns, shouts of glory and raised hands. But on this day, one of us was accused of getting out of his place. It would be Doc Rogers's last day on earth.

A black male, young or old, had to be careful in those days. Invisible lines and unspoken rules could silently circle you like a rabid dog and, before you knew it, your life would be on the line. I knew that danger from personal experience.

I was about sixteen years old. Every day, before and after school, I drove a school bus. The white schools would run their buses for about four or five years and then they'd give them to us—which meant our school buses were anything but reliable. One morning on the way to school, the bus that I was driving broke down, again. I had to pull to the side of the road, leave a bus full of children unsupervised, and walk half a mile back to the general store in Watha.

All of the little communities in Pender County had their own general stores where the white farmers gathered in the mornings for coffee. Most of the talk centered around crops, weather and how to keep Negroes in their place or how to use Negroes for profit. Usually these stores had the only telephone you could find in the community. My bus had broken down before almost in this exact spot. The white storekeeper in Watha had been nice enough to call the mechanics for me. I hoped he wouldn't mind calling for me again.

On this morning I ran smack dab into one of those unspoken rules. I walked in and noticed only the eight or nine white farmers standing around with their coffee. In my haste, I had failed to notice there was one white woman in the store. As luck would have it, I had stopped right next to her when I asked the storekeeper if he could make the call to the garage for me.

Suddenly one of the men walked up to me and said, "Nigger, don't you realize that you are standing next to a white woman?" Then he slapped me—hard. The blow knocked me off balance as I tried my best to back away. I dropped my chin to my chest, afraid to look up. My soul stung. I was mad. I was cornered. And those many sets of eyes bearing down on me turned me to stone. I waited for the next blow and was surprised when it didn't come.

"I-I-I apologize for having disrespected the lady," I said. "I'm so sorry." I hardly recognized my own voice as my apology soured in my throat like vomit. To my surprise the storekeeper went ahead and made my call for me. When I thanked him for his kindness, I backed out of the store then turned and started running toward the school bus. I kept looking back to see if anyone was following after me. I feared for the children on my bus and was trying to think, as I was running, how I would protect them if those men decided to come after me.

I climbed onto the bus, slammed the door and waited—never taking my eyes off the road toward Watha. The mechanic arrived and began working on the bus as I kept glancing down the road. Black boys were being strung up all over the South for less than I had done that morning. I looked around at the children crowded together on the seats yawning and talking amongst themselves, unaware that the shadow of death had just passed over them because of my foolish mistake.

Like I said, you had to watch out for those cloaked rules. No standing too close to a white woman. No speaking to her or making eye contact. And any black man who thought he was worthy of the love of a white woman was just going to get himself killed.

The fiery torches thrown into Doc's house were hungry for dry wood and began licking up every splinter they touched. The men in dingy white hoods danced around his yard like hungry demons. There wasn't a court in North Carolina that would convict these law-abiding citizens for simply protecting their own.

Tears spilled down Mama's face as she looked across the field in front of our house. She held me in her arms as my brothers Tommy and James and sister Bernita clung to her skirt-tails. Black smoke billowed out of Doc Rogers's house.

While the wooden frame flared up all around him, Doc pulled up some floorboards and dropped to the dirt below. He crawled from under his back porch through the cover of thick smoke and clawed through the tall grass behind his house—carrying his rifle.

Doc might have escaped but, for whatever reason, he stood up and began firing his rifle at the Klansmen. The white men quickly pounced on him and then shot him until their guns were empty. As the mob encircled his body, they took turns kicking his head and stomach until their hate needed to get a breather. By the time they had put a noose around his neck and tied him to the bumper of their truck, no one could be deader.

A little bit later, the truck full of hooded men calmly drove past our house. They drove by as if on a Sunday drive; in tow behind them was the body of Doc Rogers bouncing down the dirt road like an old string of tin cans—his skin now chalky, his face unrecognizable. The men drove Doc all through Willard as a warning to those of us who might be thinking we were better than we were. Then they drove all the way to Burgaw, eleven miles from Willard, with Doc tied to their bumper.

Once they arrived at the county seat, the men circled the courthouse with what was left of Doc's peeled and bloodied body trailing behind them. There was one last deed to be done. With a fresh noose around his neck, Doc—a man with whom we had shared meals and a church pew—was lynched from a tree and left on display like a gutted deer.

Now, I tell you this story as the truth. If you look up in the library or on the Internet you will find Doc Rogers's name listed among those lynched in the state of North Carolina. You might even find some old newspaper clippings telling you a slightly different story—that Doc shot someone and that a "deputized posse" of about two hundred men chased him into his house and that the house mysteriously caught on fire. But if you lived in Willard in 1933, you knew the truth.

Another thing you'll notice is that Doc was murdered on August 27, 1933. I was born on March 6, 1933. I was only five months old when they dragged Doc by our house. I was stunned to learn that. My brother Tommy was nine years old. James was three years old and my sister, Bernita, was six. Yet I can still smell the smoke bellowing from Doc's house. In my mind's eye I can actually see the rope around his neck.

You see, Doc Rogers's story has been told over and over again throughout Willard for seventy-six years now. It is as old as I am. It is embedded in me so deeply that my mind has always held it as memory—not a story. This catastrophic event seared into Willard's collective memory like a weld. If you were an infant like me, it eventually caught up with you like a nasty north wind forcing you to choose one of two paths—hatred or forgiveness.

Needless to say, I grew up in a dangerous time for a colored child. I could have easily chosen a life of fury and rage because it was all around me, but my mama wouldn't have it. She was determined that Doc's death would mean something, that the lesson learned here was not going to be vengeance or fear or loathing. Her children, and eventually there would be seven of us, were going to learn courage, compassion and the challenge of a life well lived for God. I must tell you that my mama, Cassie Henry Newkirk Johnson, had a lot of praying to do.

TWO

The Promise

My mother was thirteen years old when she married my father. She had only a fourth-grade education, yet she mothered her brood like a scholar. God entrusted to her and my father, Willie Lee Johnson, seven children for safekeeping. My mother thought it was her calling to raise Tommy, Bernita, James, me, Roscoe, Lennard and Delois to be faithful to God.

My father, Willie, was seventeen when he and my mother married. His third grade education was pretty typical for a black man in the south at that time. He was a strong worker who sharecropped most of his life for the Johnson family—the white family who once owned my people as slaves. They stole our strong backs but left us with their name.

Over the generations my family has worked hard to claim the Johnson name as our own. As each son passed it down, the name took on more strength, boldness, and courage. With each generation the stripes on our backs became less and less until today my children and I bear them no more.

We lived in a three-bedroom bungalow with no plumbing, running water or electricity. Seven children slept in three beds. I know I should tell you that my raising was meager at best and depressed. After all, I was born during the Great Depression. At that time there were white men starving, and many more little black boys missing meals. Yet, I don't remember it that way. Despite our poverty, our cook stove never sat cold. With sweat running down her back and on her brow, Mama spread our table with fried chicken, fried okra, mashed potatoes, sweet potato pie, ham, bacon, creamed corn, blackberry cobbler, biscuits, gravy, black-eyed peas and much, much more. Mama and Bernita would cook and us boys would keep the wood stoked under the stove. Just the promise of Mama's pound cake kept us happily on task.

Aaron Johnson's parents, Cassie H. and Willie Lee Johnson.

Our smokehouse stayed stocked with canned stringed beans, beets, corn, sweet pickles and salted meat—all kinds of meat from beef to squirrel. We owned some chickens, a cow, a mule and a pig. In the 1930s and '40s, I don't know about the white Johnsons, but the black Johnsons in Willard, North Carolina never missed a meal.

Cassie Johnson believed in the mighty power of prayer. Every Sunday morning for as long as I can remember, the tiny hammer on the alarm clock felt like it was hitting my head instead of that little bell next to it. The sound scattered around the room like buckshot. Five boys sandwiched together on two beds jumped collectively. An arm flung up, someone rolled over, another groaned. Whosever turn it was to make the fire in the stove had to leave his warm spot for the good of the others. If it was you, that clanging clapper vibrating on the bed stand instilled extreme dislike for every other sleeping family member at that moment.

"Aaron! It's your turn. Get up!" hissed Tommy.

"I'm going," I said as I sat up. The minute I pulled the quilt off of me, the cold air made huge goose bumps pop up on my legs. I hopped across the floor like it was jet hot instead of the icicle cold it was. I hobbled into the kitchen on the sides of my feet trying to touch as little of me to the floor as possible. At least the night before I'd had the good sense to bring in the firewood and stack it next to the stove.

I ripped up paper and stacked kindling with my eyes closed, willing myself into thinking I was still asleep and not freezing my behind off in that chilly, dark room.

By the time I got the fire going, Mama was in the kitchen, the iron skillet placed on the stove—a clang here, a ding there, the familiar sounds of Mama cracking open the day.

Before my mother entered the kitchen she had gone around to the children's bedrooms and awakened each child. Slowly all my siblings began joining me in the room and gathered around the stove. My two sisters came wrapped in their quilt and waddled together close to the heater.

With everyone accounted for, my mother began to sing.

"I know the Lord will find a way somehow. I know the Lord will find a way somehow. If I walk in heaven's light, shun the wrong and do the right. I know the Lord will find a way somehow . . ."

Mama's voice was a purr. As she sang, we children began to sway underneath its spell. "Babies, don't rely on just yourselves. God will make a way for you somehow. Look here what He's already done for this family. A house. Food. Clothes. We're not wantin' for nothin'," she said.

The stove was starting its red glow when its heat finally reached my feet. I knew what was coming next. As Mama talked, I tried my best to summon my weekly Bible verse—the one I was supposed to have committed to memory by this morning. We each were given a scripture to recite and mine was messing with my head. To my annoyance, the Bible verse that scrolled through my memory wasn't the verse my mother was expecting to hear in a few minutes.

Mama had various ways of making us children feel special. One of her ways was giving us each a "life verse" when we were little. Mama would meditate and hunt scripture for just the right verse. I don't even remember when she gave me mine. It just seems like I've always been able to recite it. Sometimes it would pop up in my head at the oddest times—like when I was brushing my teeth or chopping wood: *"Seek ye first His kingdom and His righteousness and all these things shall be added unto you." (Matthew 6:33 ASV).* Or when I couldn't get to sleep at night because the summer heat was trapped inside our house, boiling me and James together in bed like two clams. I'd lay still and repeat over and over again like a hypnotist, *"Seek ye first His kingdom and His righteousness and all these things shall be added unto you."* It worked... usually. I'd drift off to sleep and dream about cowboys or boxers.

Mama held her Bible in her hands as she preached. "Those children of Israel saw no way out that day," Mother said. "Moses had led them to the edge of the Red Sea and Pharaoh was a-coming after 'em. They was doomed!"

I knew I was doomed as well if I could not recall that verse. What was it?

"And then it happened," she said. "Moses sl-o-o-o-wly raised his staff." Mother lifted her arm dramatically over her head and held it there. "Then All-Mighty God, hisself, opened the waters! He made a way for his children even when it all looked hopeless." The smile on her face made me believe every word.

When Mother was done with her preaching we got on our knees. "Who'd like to go first?" she asked.

Delois raised her hand. She was our baby. She was the youngest one of us and we all looked after her. For good or bad, Delois could do no wrong. We all protected her. She was our little darling. And this morning I was hoping she'd distract Mama long enough for me to recall that verse.

One by one my brothers and sisters fumbled through their own verses. "Okay, Aaron you're the last one. Go ahead, baby," she said.

I was fourteen years old and as scrawny as a broom handle. I took a breath and was just about to confess that I didn't have a clue when suddenly there it was, *"Trust in the Lord with all your heart and lean not on your own understanding, in all your ways acknowledge Him and He shall direct your paths."(Proverbs 3: 5-6)*

I'm not sure the Lord saved my skin that morning, but I sure gave Him credit for it.

Then Mother got on her knees with us and started to pray. "Lord, thank you so much for these children. Thank you for my son Tommy and my daughter Bernita. Thank you for James and Aaron and for . . ." Mama named us all one by one starting with the oldest on down. If there was one thing I could always count on my whole life while Mother was alive, it was that my name would be laid at God's feet every Sunday morning.

Once we got up off our knees, Mother gathered us close and said, "Now your Mama is going to die before ya'll, but I want each one of you to promise me that you'll meet me in heaven one day. Go ahead. Promise."

Heaven? How could we promise something so big and unimaginable? Heaven seemed about as impossible to get to as the Rocky Mountains did back then. But we did it. I did it. I promised her. I truly believe it is one of the reasons I am still a Christian today.

Our breakfast that morning and just about every Sunday morning that I can remember was salmon, grits, eggs, and gravy and biscuits.

"You children go get your church clothes on, you hear? Bernita, help me with the biscuits please," Mama said.

Bernita was the second oldest child and the second mom in the house. She helped Mama with the cooking and the cleaning. "Yes, Mama," she said.

"Don't forget to do the special ones, sweet girl," said Mama.

Another way Mama made each of us feel unique was that we all had our own biscuit, a distinctive shape that was just ours. Mostly they went by size. The oldest got the biggest biscuit and then on down.

"Mama, can't I help with the biscuits too?" I asked, reluctant to go back into that cold bedroom.

"You can help me later, Aaron, when I start to put the cover on the new quilt. It'll be too cold tomorrow to work outside, so you can help me inside. You'll never have to be cold, son, if you learn how to make a quilt."

I was thinking that quilt-making wouldn't be quite as much fun as making biscuits.

"Mama, when can I start to work at one of the white people's houses? I can help bring in money then," asked Bernita.

"Baby, you'll never work for white folks—not at this age. It's too dangerous. No sister, that will not happen," said my mother.

My parents were very particular with our sisters and kept close tabs on them. They just could not take a chance of some of the monstrosities that had happened to other young black girls happening to our sisters. Mother would never let one of them go around whites if she could help it. It had to be two or all of us together when the girls went anywhere. As children, our only dealings with whites came either from riding on the bus with them to Wallace or when we'd work their farms. And even then, on the farms we worked as a family. None of us ever worked alone.

Bernita did a lot of the looking out for us younger ones too. In fact, she did more whipping than Mama did. And what beats all—Mama gave her permission to do it!

Mother kept switches in the house at the ready. At our first offense, we'd get a lecture about what we had done—but no whipping. Then if we did it again, we'd get a whipping and a lecture. Sometimes, we'd get both at the same time. Mama'd say, "I'm whipping this time so I won't have to whip no more." Then she'd give us a few licks. Next she'd say, "And now I'm whipping you to keep you out of jail!" And, we'd get more licks. Nothing can sting a set of dancing, prancing legs worse than a hickory switch.

But I'll tell you, I would have much rather gotten a whipping, especially from Bernita, than what Mama would do sometimes instead of whipping. Depending on how severe the crime, Mama would make us get on our knees and put God on us.

One summer afternoon while my mother had gone to work for some white folks doing housework and Bernita was watching us, my younger brother RV (Roscoe) and I accidentally killed all of Mama's biddies.

Biddies were baby chicks that Mama would buy at the feed store to raise. Once grown, those chicks were sometimes what stood between us and going to bed hungry. RV was about six or so at the time and I was about nine. He was my responsibility while Bernita got supper on. We started wrestling around in the yard and it wasn't long before we had tangled ourselves in the clothesline, trampled what buds were in the flowerbed and tumbled our way toward the back shed knocking and banging everything in sight. I knew we had gotten close to where the box of chicks was because I could hear them peeping and chirping like crazy. The box was kept by the shed. Inside it with the chicks was a water dish and feed.

RV and I kept pulling, tugging, grabbing and slapping at each other like bulldogs fighting over a bone. We had kicked the box of biddies a couple of times and I had almost pushed RV over into it at least once. And then it happened. I pushed RV just once too hard and, to gain his balance, he grabbed onto anything he could—including a full can of kerosene sitting by the side of the shed next to the box of chicks. RV managed to regain his balance; the can of kerosene didn't and toppled over into the box of biddies.

"Look what you made us do, RV!" I said. "Mama's gonna kill us."

"I didn't see no box! It ain't my fault!"

"It is your fault, too. You're the one who wanted to wrestle."

"Whatta we do, Aaron?" asked RV, bobbing up and down like a cork in water.

I looked into the box and knew there was nothing to be done. My stomach started to sour as panic got the best of me. "Run!" I yelled.

RV and I ran down the road a piece and then jutted off into the woods. I didn't know where we were going—I just knew we needed to get there fast.

When my mother got home and discovered all fifty chicks dead in the box, she knew somebody had been up to no good. When RV and I didn't show up for supper that evening, we gave ourselves away. Finally our stomachs betrayed us and dragged us home to eat. As I walked up the back steps, I couldn't help but glance over to where the box of biddies had been. It was gone. And for just a second I actually thought that maybe it had all been a dream. I had made it up in my mind like a story you'd tell to be witty and charming, a story with a happy ending with baby chicks marching out of the barn two-by-two, peeping and alive. But when I walked into the kitchen and met my mother's eyes head on, I knew there was no happy ending.

As the blood drained from my head, my courage left with it. I confessed to my mother right where I stood. "Mama," said I, "RV done it."

Of course, she knew better. The lecture I received rivaled any hellfire and brimstone sermon ever preached. That small kitchen disappeared before my eyes and in its place sprouted a church altar and a wailing bench.

It got worse when Mama told me to get on my knees. Here it comes! Mama put God on me big time. My carelessness, my cowardliness and my thoughtlessness were handed over to God like rocks piled into a sock. My mother's heart was wailing and broken as she laid her hands on me and told God so.

"Lord, I've done all I can do with this boy," prayed my mother in a throaty, low voice that told me she was having a hard time talking. Mama inhaled and exhaled slowly several times. I waited in silence with my head bowed, not daring to open my eyes. My knees protested being flattened out on the floor like mud cakes on gravel. I sensed her arms move and heard the rustling of her apron. She was wiping her eyes, I was sure of it. "I need you to take him, Lord, and help him be more responsible to you and to this family," Mama pleaded.

As Mama continued to pray, she placed her palm on my forehead. The warmth of it, her thumb gently rubbing my temple, shamed me. I had caused my mother pain. And, for the first time in my young life, I felt the cruel wrench of regret that comes with thoughtless action—the first crowning of sin.

As I was growing up I got the impression that Mama felt time was pressing her like a cloud threatening rain. She didn't feel she could waste a minute when it came to the instruction of our hearts or souls.

13

"Never forget the bridge that brought you over the water because you just might have to go back over that same bridge someday," she'd say. Or, "Be kind to everybody because you never know who will give you your last drink of water." And, according to Mother, being wasteful was the eighth deadliest sin—a downright insult to God's mercy and grace. Because of her frugality, we'd find ourselves replacing the soles on our own shoes over and over again until the shoelaces were long gone and the toes worn clean off.

We never lacked for blankets. It wasn't unusual to find old dresses, shirts, pants and even old socks incorporated into a quilt at our house. We also never lacked for meat. We'd eat some critters down to their ears, snout and feet.

In Mother's lifetime, besides Doc Rogers, twenty other black men or boys were lynched in surrounding North Carolina towns and communities. The threatening cloud of hatred hovered, and Mother had five sons who needed to be taught the dangers lurking just outside of her protective reach. If we ever did anything that would put us into the white man's court or at his mercy, she feared the worst would happen to us.

Mama meant for us to behave, have manners and be courageous. She wanted us to live long lives and give her grandchildren. But mostly, Mama fully intended to one day see us march toward her through those Pearly Gates for that much-anticipated family reunion. And so she disciplined, corrected, nurtured and stood guard over us—trying her best to coax the best out of her skittish, imprudent, reluctant children.

She wasn't much older than her children, but Mama raised us on bended knee with the help of the Holy Spirit, some homespun wisdom, and occasionally, with a good piece of hickory.

THREE

The Relatives

And then there were the relatives. Aunt Annie, my cousin Ottie's mother and my mama's eldest sister, was my favorite aunt. Turning the other cheek was all well and good; however, we didn't have to get ridiculous with it is what Aunt Annie thought. She taught us children to fight for ourselves if we had to—I mean with balled up fists and all. Aunt Annie wasn't quite as God-fearing as Mama.

I remember my mother and her sisters sitting out front at our house under the shade tree snapping beans. They were laughing and fussing and cutting up when Aunt Annie said, "I'm telling you, if people step on your toes, get them off any way you can!" Aunt Annie would go to church on Sunday mornings and shout and *Amen* the preacher, then march directly out the doors and cuss you if she thought that's what you deserved. Cross Aunt Annie and she could go a whole year and not speak to you. It wasn't at all a surprise when she outlived all of her sisters.

My mother's brothers, the Newkirk men, were mostly hard workers, decent, and they provided for their families. They'd often come by and get us boys and take us out. My brothers and I would listen to them argue about which was better, a Ford or a Chevy. They'd also brag about who could drink the most liquor. And on those outings they taught us what it was to be a man—at least their version of it.

Sundays were always like a holiday with my family. We'd take turns going to each other's houses for dinner. The men would never drink liquor around the women, but after a little while, my uncles would slip out and go meet up with friends. It was an unspoken arrangement—the women would gather and gossip and the men would meet out under a shade tree somewhere—usually in someone's yard or out in a field someplace. We had no shortage of shade trees in Willard. Many a Sunday, after the fried chicken and pecan pie were nothing more than leftover crumbs on a plate, the uncles would gather the boy cousins and go off to find a shade tree.

I remember one Sunday afternoon us "men" were scattered under a live oak in the scrub out behind our school building. Trucks, cars and bicycles were circled around the tree as we sat on the grass or on the hoods of cars.

"A man is one who can drink his liquor and not get drunk," said Uncle Willie Newkirk with a firm nod of his head. Unfortunately, Uncle Willie and liquor were a bad mix—he was just the only one who didn't realize it.

"I say a man is one who doesn't lick his ice cream cone after it's dropped in the dirt," said my Uncle Aaron Newkirk, winking at his son, Kevin, and me.

Uncle Aaron was remembering the time he'd taken us to get ice cream. We were age six or so. It was one of those hot, summer afternoons that could melt the rubber right off your re-treads. I had never anticipated anything as much as my first lick of that vanilla cone.

Uncle Aaron gave us each a nickel and sent us into the Rose Hill general store to buy the cones. Coming out of the store, I'd no sooner stuck out my tongue when the ice cream fell off the cone and into the dirt. Of course, I did what any self-respecting six-year-old would do—I picked up the ice cream and put it back on my cone, grass, grit and all.

Immediately, Uncle Aaron yelled at me to throw it away, but I wouldn't. I didn't mind licking a little bit of dirt. He got out of his car, pulled the cone from my hands and stomped it into the ground.

"You look just like a fool eating dirt! Here's another nickel. Go in there and get you another one," he demanded.

I did—so I was happy. But Uncle Aaron rarely missed a chance to remind me about that dirty ice cream cone.

"You are a man if you can carry a two-hundred-pound sack of fertilizer on one shoulder," said Uncle Robert Newkirk. He was leaning against the oak tree holding a bottle of beer in one hand and swatting flies with the other.

"Yeah, but you're a *real* man if you can carry one on *each* shoulder," said Uncle Aaron. He was the supervisor at the mill and knew a thing or two about carrying heavy loads.

"Come here, boys," said Uncle Robert. He was leaning on a truck with one foot up on the bumper. "If you're going to be men someday, you just as well better get acquainted with this taste." Uncle Robert grabbed a brown jug he had placed at his feet and pulled the cork out with a pop. One after another, each of the cousins lined up to take a swig. When it was my turn, I swallowed hard and stepped forward.

The stink that crawled out of the jug knocked my head back like a punch. The liquid oozed over my tongue and detonated in the back of my throat, causing me to cough and hack my way back to where I was sitting.

"Now your mamas aren't to know nothing about this, ya'll hear?" said Uncle Henry to all of us boys. Even though our eyes were watering like the falls at Niagara and our tongues burning like hell fire itself, our lips would remain sealed.

Proving you were a man came up a lot where I grew up. It seems from the time I was six years old I had to be proving to somebody or another I was one. At the time, Joe Lewis was the heavyweight champion of the world. Joe was every young black boy's hero. One of the things boys did in Willard to prove their manhood was box like Joe. We'd square off with naked fists and whoever was left standing was the winner.

As our skinny, shirtless bodies sparred around each other, we'd talk smack and warn, "I'm gonna put a Joe Lewis on you; you better watch out now!" I am amazed that I came out of my childhood with both eyeballs intact and earlobes still attached.

Saturday afternoon was our only playtime. After lunch we'd either walk the three miles to Wallace or take the train for ten cents. Of course, if you took the train, before you could sit down it was time for you to get off. We'd go to Wallace just to walk around and see our schoolmates or buy an ice cream cone.

The main street around the courthouse in Wallace was for white folks only. We colored folks would hang out on the back streets or near the railroad tracks where Negro shopkeepers welcomed our business.

The only place we'd mingle with the whites was at the movie theater, and even then they made sure there was no real mingling. Coloreds lined up outside while whites lined up inside. Coloreds even had their own ticket window where we'd pay our fifteen cents. After purchasing our popcorn, we were herded up the back stairs to the balcony where a few rows of squeaky seats awaited us.

Hopalong Cassidy or just about any Western movie packed us in by the dozens. It did not matter that there were no Negro cowboys. The fancy saddles, twirling pistols and gunfights around the corral made up for it. Portrayed on that big screen were dreams, not reality. Nobody would pay to see reality—not back then.

"Stop that, RV. You're going to get us thrown out!" I said as we settled into our seats. We had no more gotten seated in the balcony when he and some others started tossing popcorn over the balcony ledge.

"Don't have to!" he said.

Then my cousin Ottie did it. A kernel of popcorn shot out of his mouth like a cannon ball and lofted over the balcony rail. Everyone laughed—including me. It wouldn't be long before someone else would muster up the courage to loft a few kernels of corn down toward the white seats.

"I dare you," said RV.

"Stop it." I said to my younger brother.

"Chicken!" he whispered, just loud enough for Ottie and others to hear. They looked over at me like I was a disgrace or something.

I couldn't have that. So I showed them. I not only tossed popcorn over the ledge, but just as Hoppy twirled himself backwards in his saddle, I spit over the rail with the same precision as one of Hopalong's flying bullets. A scream came from somewhere below. Bull's-eye!

RV's eyes got as big as tractor wheels. Ottie just stared at me with his mouth open. Our eyes met and went from merriment to terror in less than a second. What had I done?

I flattened myself into my seat as far as I could go. The whole bunch of us sat up and stared straight ahead at the movie screen, barely breathing. Our pounding hearts drowned out the raging gunfight on screen. We waited. We expected to hear the manager's footsteps on the stairs at any moment. We waited some more . . . finally nothing.

I was a hero, however not necessarily a noble one. I do not know why we never got into a fight or were thrown out of the theater, because we acted up every time we went. I guess it's true that God looks out for fools and children.

FOUR

School Days

*M*y cousin Ottie and I were the same age and went all the way through school together. We were fortunate to even have a school to go to in Willard. Had we been born during our great-grandfathers' era, children like us wouldn't have been allowed to go to school. After the Civil War, the public school system in North Carolina made no provisions to educate black children. Most of our schools were begun by the kindness and vision of the Negro Baptist Association in the late 1800s and early 1900s. By the late 1930s when my cousin and I enrolled in school, the state had already taken over our black schools and had proceeded to ignore them regularly.

Willard Elementary School went from first to eighth grade—four rooms with two grades in each room. One teacher was assigned to each separate room and had to teach two grade levels. Second graders would help teach first graders. Fourth graders would help teach third graders, and so on. Sometimes it seemed like we learned more from each other than we did from our teachers.

We received only second- and third-hand materials. We had no library. Our schoolbooks were hand-me-downs at best and in short supply. We had no janitor, and our parents supplied the only heat we had. Our families would donate wood and our fathers would take their Saturday afternoons to chop it up for the school.

The school had a strong PTA and parents worked hard together to try and get the students what was needed. Along about my third grade year, a decision was made to convert from wood heat to coal. White schools had had coal heat for some time.

The PTA knew the county school district would not pay for the coal, so our parents organized a fundraiser. It was decided that a play put on at the end of the school year by the students would be a perfect way to raise money for the coal. Each grade was to perform a play that included a song and a recitation. Parents, grandparents and others would pay to come see their children and grandchildren perform. These plays lasted all week as the grades took turns in the evenings performing in the multipurpose room.

The entire student body worked for months preparing and practicing for this important event. Most of our school day was spent learning to read and write—the usual. At the end of the day, we'd spend time learning our lines for the play or the poems we were each going to recite. Memorization was a huge part of my education, not just for the play. The lack of books made it necessary to memorize what we'd read, because chances were we'd have to pass the book along to someone else the next day.

On the evening of our play, you would have thought the president of the United States himself was paying our little community a visit. Our grandmothers were showing up in their Sunday best complete with fancy hats and matching purses. The men showed up in their suits and ties. Our mothers, most of whom had helped pull this all together, were standing in small clusters in pretty dresses—dresses they'd all made themselves in the middle of the night while their children slept and weary husbands snored. They had done all they could do. It was now up to the teachers and their students.

I remember peeking out the door of my classroom and seeing all the folks starting to arrive to watch us third and fourth graders perform. They filled up the multipurpose room pretty fast. That night the stage in front of the room looked like a guillotine as far as I could tell.

"Ottie! Look at this!" I said.

Ottie glanced out the door and sighed. He didn't like this any better than I did. We were used to memorizing things, but reciting in front of our teacher, Miss Leon Johnson (not related), was very different than reciting in front of the whole world.

"Let's go home, Ottie," I said.

"What? Are you crazy?" said Ottie.

"We could slip out back and no one would notice," I said.

"Our mothers would kill us," he said.

He was right. Aunt Annie would do it, too.

"Sit down, children! They're going to call the third and fourth grade out in just a few minutes," said Miss Johnson.

I can't remember how old Miss Johnson was, but it was a good bet that she was barely out of high school. In the early days, black children graduated from high school after the eleventh grade. After that, you'd either become a teacher, a housekeeper, join the military, or you'd work in the fields.

After what seemed an eternity, the third and fourth grade classes were brought into the multipurpose room and paraded in front of the onlookers. Then we climbed the stairs to the stage.

"Aaron, it's like a big birthday party. Look, there's decorations," whispered Ottie.

"I think the older kids made them," I whispered back, remembering Tommy complaining about cutting out stuff until his fingers hurt.

The crowded room got still as Miss Johnson made her way to center stage. "Good evening. I'd like to thank ya'll for coming to our first annual Closing Plays. As you know, all of this year's proceeds will go to help the PTA purchase the heating fuel for next winter."

And so it began. We sang the national anthem and "God Bless America" and even threw in a few spirituals. There was no worry about separation of church and state back then in Willard. We'd have thought you a fool to even say something as nonsensical as not mentioning God in school. What kind of fool thing was that? We didn't take God out of anything; to do so only courted disaster. As far back as could be remembered, every school morning started out the same—all the grades met in the multipurpose room for a devotional with a prayer and a hymn. If you tried to mess with that you'd be run out of town.

That evening our third and fourth grade class was going to recite from the Jack and Jill rhyming books.

"Ottie, I can't breathe," I said as I saw my mother sitting over on the side with Aunt Annie. They were both smiling at Ottie and me like we had already done something good.

I don't remember too much more of that evening except for all the laughter that came next. When my turn came, I stepped forward and stood center stage where Ottie had just been before me. I cleared my throat and began my recitation:

> *Mama killed a chicken*
> *She thought he was a duck.*
> *She put him on the table*
> *With his heels cocked up.*

I didn't think I was doing stand-up comedy. It was a simple recitation of a poem I had learned. But I guess I turned out to be the highlight of the evening or the laughing stock of the school, depending on who was telling it. I tried hard not to cry.

I don't know how much money we raised, but we had coal enough for the next winter. That following year when it was time to begin rehearsals again for our play, my stomach started to ache.

It went without saying that in colored schools we had no money for janitors. The school children had to do all the work inside and outside the schoolyard. We'd take turns getting the fire going in the potbelly stove or later, bringing in the coal to keep the classrooms warm.

I remember once, Ottie and I were sent outside at our first recess in the morning to bring in the coal for the stove. We took the bucket and ran to the coal pile. I held the bucket while Ottie used the small shovel to fill it with coals. We returned to class, emptied out the coal and went back out for another load.

Wild Bill Hickok was one of our favorite cowboys and every chance we got we boys would play like we were a part of Buffalo Bill's Wild West Show. It wasn't long until we had forgotten our purpose of bringing in the coal and proceeded in our imaginations to be cowboys of the most notorious kind. Before we knew it, the second recess had let out and Miss Johnson came outside gunning for us. We had probably spent an hour and a half outside playing. We were in big trouble.

Our punishment for missing most of our classroom instruction was to stand in the corner on one foot. By today's standards, that would be considered cruel and unusual punishment. I thought it was back then as well.

When my mother came into the school house that day to have her piano lesson with another teacher, I heard her down the hall as I stood on my one foot. I quickly developed a plan.

"Mr. Aaron, what are you doing?" asked Miss Johnson.

"I'm not standing on my one foot no more," I answered.

Ottie looked over at me from his punishment corner like I had lost my mind, like I had sealed my own death like those people who accidently drink arsenic.

"Excuse me, Sir?" said Miss Johnson.

"I'm not doing it anymore. It hurts and it isn't right. You shouldn't be making us stand on one foot like this. It's mean," I said.

"You'll turn back around there, right this minute, and put that foot up, if you know what's good for you," warned Miss Johnson.

My mama was in the building. There wasn't any way that my teacher or anybody else was going to punish me like a common criminal. Not with my mama around.

"I will not!" I yelled. "You're mean!"

Miss Johnson and I began yelling back and forth. I became more confident and cockier the louder we both got.

By this time, Ottie had had a complete nervous breakdown over in his corner and had his face in his hands crying.

When my mama entered the room I just smiled. This crazy teacher was going to get hers now.

"Aaron, you please come here," Mama said.

I strutted over to her in front of Miss Johnson like a dandy. Mama loved me and I was convinced I was her favorite. This poor ole' teacher probably would be let go and never be able to teach again. I smiled.

Then my mother grabbed me around the neck and had me over her knee faster than a rattlesnake could bite. As she whipped me in front of the entire third and fourth grade classes at Willard Elementary School, I knew my plan had gone terribly wrong.

"Mama, you don't understand! She was making me . . ."

"No!" Mama roared. "It's you who don't understand. You never, ever," and then for emphasis she said it again, "you *never, ever* talk to your teachers or any other adult with disrespect. Not while I'm your mama!"

When my mother got through with me, she marched me back to my corner. As she left the room she apologized to Miss Johnson for disrupting class. "Oh, and I'm sure that *Mr.* Aaron will not be giving you any more trouble. But if he does, please let me know. Thank you very much."

Pender County had only one colored high school. It was located in Burgaw and approximately five hundred students from around the county attended it. When I was a student at Burgaw High School, which by then was renamed C.F. Pope High School, we had four teachers, a principal and a librarian who juggled teaching English, social studies, math and science between them.

Burgaw High School's beginning was a source of pride for the black community of Pender County. At the opening of the fall term of 1907, two buildings were erected — one for schoolrooms that also had space for a dormitory for girls, and the other a dormitory for boys. It was a boarding school, built by the Middle District Baptist Association, where the blacks sent their children to complete their secondary education. Burgaw High School's first principal, Mr. J. A. Fennel, was an unassuming and energetic man who fought for the advancement of the high school. After the state took over the school several decades later, it was with pride that every student was still taught about the school's religious foundation and how it all began.

I drove the school bus my last two years in high school. I'd leave the house at 5:30 a.m., walk to the field next to our house where I parked the bus, meet up with Ottie, who always rode along with me, and then get to the high school at 9 a.m. just in time for my first class. Would you believe I was able to get seventy-five to eighty kids at a time on my bus? That certainly wouldn't be allowed today. I drove seventy-five miles a day round-trip hauling students to and from school.

My school experiences were a collective thing—everyone helping out in one way or another. While my school buildings were ill equipped and supplies were sparse, the experience as a whole was a good one. We learned to depend on each other and we picked up survival skills that would last a lifetime.

FIVE

Summer Days

When I was in high school, the Negro students had a shorter school year than the whites. When the warmer months hit, we'd have to go help in the fields instead of going to school. It's how our families survived.

Summer days were long, but lazy days simply did not exist in Willard. If your family was going to survive, it had to work. Once my siblings, cousins and I were old enough, our parents sent us to the fields. If we wanted school clothes, we'd work the fields. If we wanted supper on the table, we'd work the fields. If we wanted a roof over our heads, we'd work the fields.

Every summer morning before four a.m., my father, brothers and cousins would head to the tobacco fields. Usually my cousins Ottie and George worked side-by-side with James and me. From sun up to sun down, we'd hack away at those mule-sized tobacco leaves until our bent and aching backs resembled those of old men.

Long about six a.m., my mother and Aunt Annie would bring around our breakfast.

"I can't believe it," grumbled George. "Mama only brought me fifteen biscuits. How am I going to get through the morning with only fifteen biscuits?"

"How can anybody eat that many biscuits at once?" asked James.

"George could eat a buffalo by himself if we could find him one," said Ottie, George's younger brother.

"Where d'ya put all that food?" I asked.

"I dunno," said George, as he began slathering honey on his first biscuit.

James and I had pancakes and sausage. Mama also brought us a small crock of butter that Bernita had churned and some strawberry preserves to top them with. As we sat among the rows of tobacco and ate our breakfast, Ottie and I would begin our first Bible reading of the day.

Ottie reached inside his shirt and brought out a small, tattered New Testament. Its corners were lop-eared and its pages smudged with dirt and sweat. "Where'd we leave off yesterday?"

"I think we're starting the book of James today," I said.

"James! Must be a page turner," teased my brother James. James was my next eldest brother. I don't know if he took me on to watch after on his own or if Mama made him do it. He saved my life once though—at least that's how I looked at it.

It was a hot July day and I was about twelve or so. Our house was a field away from the juke joint in Willard. As I was walking past it, my Uncle Willie looked out the door and saw me.

"Hey, Aaron! Come on in here, boy!" he yelled. I could tell by his slurred words that he had a good start on getting drunk.

I looked behind me to make sure that no one at the house saw me. My mother would have my hide if she were looking. I walked in quickly and immediately the smell of sweat, cigarette smoke and liquor assaulted my clothes and pores. In the dark coolness of the bar, several men sat lined up on stools like buzzards on a dead branch.

My Uncle Willie had his problems with liquor, and stump hole liquor was a real demon for him. "Are you ready to be a man, son?" asked Uncle Willie as he put his heavy arm over my shoulder and pulled me further into the building. I knew I shouldn't go anywhere near Uncle Willie when he was drunk, especially when none of his brothers were around to help him out.

"A real man can drink a pint of stump hole without stopping," he said. The men sitting up at the bar laughed and poked each other. "Naw, this here boy ain't no man!" one of them taunted.

Growing up, my arrogance got the best of me more than once. Of course, I wanted to prove myself in front of these men—men I had known all of my life. The most I had ever had of stump hole was just the little tastes my uncles would give us on the odd Sunday. But a pint? "Sure. I can drink it," I said. I practically thumped my chest and crowed.

"Without stopping?" asked Uncle Willie. He tilted his head and pushed his sweaty brown felt hat off of his forehead.

"Uh-huh," I said.

Before I knew it, the buzzards on the stools were holding me down while Uncle Willie poured a jug of stump hole down me. I slobbered and swallowed as my own funeral passed before my eyes. My chest started burning; my throat was seared clear through and my head felt like someone had suddenly slammed it into a door.

When they had thoroughly soaked me inside and out, I remember my uncle laughing and pointing at me like I was a zoo animal. I stumbled and weaved for their entertainment for several minutes until I could find my way out of the juke joint. Once out the door, I weaved toward the back of the building and the woods while my uncle's taunting rang in my ear: "Ain't no man, that's for sure!"

Next thing I knew, James was holding me up and had one hand over my forehead. I vomited until I felt like I had no inside organs, just a burning hole where my stomach and liver once were. Had James not been there, I probably would have died in my own puke.

"What were you thinking, Aaron?" asked James. "Uncle Willie is as mean as a twisted snake when he's drunk—you know that!"

"Don't tell Mama! Please don't tell Mama!" I begged.

"Come on. Let's go home, Aaron."

"Please!" I said.

"It's alright," said James. He wrapped his arms around me and slowly started walking me to the house. "Mama's not home right now, so let's get you fixed up." James took me to our bedroom, put cold rags on my head and sat with me the rest of the afternoon. As far as I know, Mama never found out. It took me two or three months to get my stomach back right though. James never mentioned it to me again.

"Okay," said Ottie. "The first chapter and first verse of James reads, '*James, a bondservant of God and of the Lord Jesus Christ, to the twelve tribes which are scattered abroad: Greetings...*' "

Ottie and I had vowed to read the entire New Testament through that summer. I even carried a little dictionary in my shirt pocket. We'd begin every work day reading a verse or two from the Bible and then commit ourselves to learning how to spell the words we read and to learn what they meant. We'd discuss them all day in the fields.

Later that morning as Ottie started to cut off the bottom leaf of a stalk, working his way up the tobacco plant, he asked, "What does 'bondservant' mean again?"

"Umm, it said in the dictionary, 'one who gives himself up to the will of another.'" I had just cut a tobacco leaf and placed it onto a drag. The sun was rising now and already the day showed promise of a scorcher. "I think it's saying that even though James was the actual brother of Christ, he wasn't acting haughty about it," I said. "James saw himself more as a slave to Jesus than anything else."

"A slave?" asked Ottie.

"I guess," I said. "Ottie, you've had me look up just about every other word we've read this morning. At this rate it's going to take us twelve years to finish reading the whole thing."

27

"I'm just trying to understand it all, that's all. Hey, I think we should get the rest of these leaves on the drag and get the mules to haul them up to the barn. We've got a pretty good load right now," said James.

By the time we got the tobacco to the barn and got them on the ties, I spotted Bernita, my little sister Delois, and Aunt Annie walking towards us with their arms full.

"How'd ya'll know to come up here with our lunches?" I asked her.

"I saw ya'll walking across the field with the mules and figured this was where ya'll were headed. Good timing, eh?" Bernita said.

The women had fixed fried chicken, cornbread, coleslaw and butter beans for lunch and had brought a couple of jugs of iced tea along. Nothing can squelch a thirst on a hot day better than sweet iced tea. I still believe that.

Day after summer day, we'd stay in the tobacco fields past dark. Once we'd tied all the tobacco up in the barn, we'd start drying it with the fire we had stoked in the middle of the barn. On those late nights, my whole family would join us to help us finish out the drying. Only God and Satan knew how hot those tobacco barns got.

During those summers, with the aid of Aunt Annie's teacakes and my mama's pound cake, not to mention the iced tea, the tobacco got cropped, tied, dried and ready to sell.

A Johnson daughter and a son-in-law by the name of Mr. Chrub headed the generation of white Johnsons that my family had to contend with. Miss Johnson had inherited the land—the land that my daddy sharecropped on—and once she married Mr. Chrub, he started running the general store in Willard. For the most part, Mr. and Mrs. Chrub treated my family with nonviolent deceitfulness. They never physically harmed us—because they didn't have to. My father kowtowed to them and allowed them to lie and cheat us out of our share of the profits year after year.

The deal between them and my father was supposed to be fifty-fifty. We'd work three days a week sharecropping on white Johnson land, and the other two days of the week Daddy would hire us kids out to other farms by the hour. As sharecroppers, we were supposed to split the cost of the fertilizer and seed with Mr. Chrub. Of course, we had to buy the fertilizer and seed from *his* store—on credit. Mr. Chrub did the bookkeeping and supposedly recorded who spent what between us. However, between his bookkeeping and Mrs. Chrub's steely-eyed management of the fields, the split came out at an unbalanced thirty-seventy when all was said and done.

When Daddy would come home from his dealings with Mr. Chrub, he'd be disappointed but accepting of the way it was. "Daddy, you can't let Mr. Chrub do that to you. He's robbing us," I said.

"Shah, boy!" said my father. "Don't worry about it. Mr. Chrub is doing the best he can. The white man has to have his way. There isn't no other way to do it," he said as he hung his hat on a peg on the back door.

"But Daddy!" said Tommy.

"That's the end of it, I said. It is what it is!" With that my father walked into the living room and left us standing in the kitchen, duly silenced.

My brothers and I were ashamed of our father because he didn't haggle with the Chrubs. To our way of thinking, he was a coward and we despised him for it. We didn't understand then how much our father feared what haggling with the Chrubs could cost us. My daddy was only two generations from being born a slave. It was his grandfather's back that was whipped and scarred. As a child, my father had actually touched those scars with his own hands; his fingers would disappear down into those jagged ruts across his grandfather's back—mentally, those scars became his.

My father knew something else his sons didn't know at the time. Doc Rogers's body was riddled through with hundreds of bullets that fateful day in August 1933—bullets supplied by Chrub's General Store in Willard, bullets that were supplied free of charge. Like I said, we simply didn't understand the cost haggling could have. My daddy did.

While our father embarrassed us, left to our own devices, us boys could wrangle with the best of them—especially when bad weather and ruined produce was on our side.

"Okay now once we get there, we just sit there, ya'll hear? Do nothing until I tell ya'll to," said Tommy. "You hear me, James? Aaron? Ottie? George?

"I know. We hold out," said James

"What if she tells Daddy on us?" I asked.

"He'll whip us all, even us," said cousin Ottie.

Ottie's older brother George said, "Ya'll's daddy will not be whipping me over nothing, ya hear!"

"Don't worry about it. Daddy won't be whipping anybody who gets five cents a quart instead of three," said Tommy.

The rectangular packing shed on the Johnson property was about twenty feet long and fifteen feet wide with no sides. The tables lined up on the inside were where the packers would cull through the quart baskets the pickers brought in. They'd then separate the ripe strawberries from the rotten or green ones. I'd swear those berries would almost ruin the minute you took them out of the field—so picking and packing had to be done fast.

Like all the fields on Johnson land, Mrs. Chrub oversaw the packing shed. She was tall and gangly and always wore a flowery dress. From the last weekend in April through the whole month of May, she'd sit up under the shed in her comfortable, cushioned chair and preside like she was a screaming

Queen of Sheba. However, Mrs. Chrub was at the mercy of her pickers and packers, and she knew it.

The five of us got to the shed and sat down right in front of Mrs. Chrub.

"Ya'll go to work!" she barked.

"No, Ma'am. Not until we get five cents a quart," said Tommy.

"Mrs. Chrub, we're not gonna work for a measly three cents—not today," said George, who acted braver than I'd ever seen him. Tommy gave him that look that meant for him to shut up.

Her face immediately scrunched up at us like we were spiders or something else distasteful. As I sat there holding my breath, I could see azaleas and some yellow orchids over by the gate just starting to bloom. If Mrs. Chrub did not give in, I feared my father would not let me live long enough to see another flower open up.

"Ya'll go to work, ya hear!" she shouted again. We sat as still as a day with no breeze. After a few long air-sucking-out-of-you minutes she grunted and asked, "Ya'll not gonna work?"

The five of us shook our heads. Mrs. Chrub left us sitting out in the morning sun as long as she dared. She knew there were strawberries rotting every second we sat on our behinds. Finally, after what seemed like hundreds and hundreds of years, the wall crumbled around Mrs. Chrub's resolve. "Alright, ya'll go out there and pick, but don't ask for no more."

"Yes, Ma'am! Let's go boys," said Tommy. We jumped up like we'd been pinched. Running out into the strawberry fields that morning, I got my first taste of power and justice. It felt good.

That day no harm was done. We got our five cents a quart and were able to buy school clothes come fall. But our childish bravado could have cost us dearly. Many years prior, my grandparents had the good fortune to be able to buy fifteen acres of land. The property purchased was just down the road from the white Johnson farm where my daddy and his daddy before him sharecropped. My family still owned that land, which provided us with our home, and it couldn't be taken away from us out of spite.

Some of our neighbors weren't as fortunate. Many did not own their own land. They lived in houses supplied by the white farmer. So, if one of them held out for the better wage, they may have eventually gotten it—but it would have cost them. It wouldn't be long before you'd see them moving out of their house—evicted by the farmer who owned it. We lost many good neighbors that way.

SIX

Redemption

As soon as I learned to read, the Bible intrigued me. I'd come home from school and, instead of going outside to play, I'd rush to my room, open my Bible, and read. Huddled up on my bed with pillows stacked behind me, I'd read it out loud.

"Aaron, sweetie, who are you talking to in here?" asked Mama one day. She had been in the kitchen starting supper and must have heard me.

"I'm just reading my Bible, Mama."

She came into the room and sat down on the bed with me. "You're not sick are you?"

"No, Mama. I just . . . well . . . it's just that *it* talks to me."

"What talks to you?" she asked.

"The Bible. When I read it out loud, it's as if God himself is talking straight to me."

"I'm so glad to hear that, sweetie. You keep listening and God will tell you some amazing things," she said.

As she got up off the bed to leave, I asked, "Mama, why did you name me 'Aaron'?"

I had found the name "Aaron" in the Bible a few days before and got excited. At that time, the only other person I knew with that name was my Uncle Aaron, my mother's brother. So to find it in the Bible thrilled me. I was Biblical and didn't even know it!

Mama sat back down on the bed and stared at me hard, not like she was mad or anything, but more like she was trying to decide something. She took the Bible I was holding into her own hands and began turning the pages gently like they were made of angel wings or something else holy. She carefully closed the cover on the book and laid it beside her.

"I wanted to see what would happen in your life before I told you this," she said. "I wanted to wait until you were a little older. But since you've asked me now, I guess now is the time."

Mama was a larger woman, so when she scooted over beside me and wrapped her bulky arm over my shoulder, I felt like I was being swallowed up by a giant cloud. That's always how Mama's hugs felt too, like you were being squeezed right inside her.

She tucked me up next to her like a blanket she was tucking in around herself on a cold winter's day. Then she said, "Before you were born, before you were even conceived, I had read about the mother of Jesus and how she gave her son to the world for the good of others. I decided that I wanted to give something back to the world, too."

The house was starting to get shadowy as we sat together on the bed. The smell of cornbread in the cook stove began drifting into the room, promising another good supper.

Mama cleared her throat and continued, "So, I began to pray that God would give me a son who would become a minister." Mama looked down at me and squeezed me a little bit more. "When you came along, I just knew that God had answered my prayers, so I named you 'Aaron' from the Bible in hopes that you would one day hear the call to ministry."

"Well, then why didn't you name me 'Moses' instead?" I asked feeling a little disappointed. After all, from what I had read, Moses was the hero, not his brother Aaron.

"Oh, baby, Aaron did all the talking," she said smiling. "Aaron was God's voice to the people." We sat there together a minute quietly while Mama let what she'd told me sink in. She squeezed me again and said, "Now come on, cornbread's ready."

While Mother left me to tend to our supper, I sat there alone for a bit more. I remember thinking that something was different now, that I was different from when I started out that morning.

Sitting on the bed that I shared with my brothers, I bowed my head and committed my life to God—as much as a six-year-old can, anyway. In the shadows of that late afternoon, as my mother told me the story of how I got my name, something right in the middle of me woke up. It stood and stretched and inhaled for the first time. The *core* of who I am had just been spoken into existence by my mother's words, spoken just like in the beginning when God uttered, "Let there be light," and light just was.

Sundays in Willard meant two things: food and church. My mama hosted Sunday dinner every third Sunday. That was the Sunday the Baptist preacher came to town. We'd walk to Sunday School and walk back home. Then an hour later, we'd walk back up to the church house for service at eleven o'clock to hear the traveling pastor. As soon as the "Amen" was said, we'd all walk back home together—my mother and father, my brothers and sisters, my aunts, uncles—walking, fanning ourselves with our King Jameses, children being told to stop fussing, and my uncles trying not to upset my aunts with their foolish talk. We'd walk together like sheep being herded home to rest.

My mother did not believe in working or cooking on Sundays, so she'd cook all Saturday evening while us boys would keep the woodstove stoked at the perfect temperature. All Saturday night as I slept, I could smell fried chicken, creamed corn or a big old pot roast, and I'd wake up hungry enough to eat the sheets.

It was unthinkable to be invited to a home on a Sunday and there be fewer than two meat dishes and three or four vegetables and at least two pies to choose from. And of course, every other woman in attendance brought her share of goodies as well.

"Cassie, where you want me to set my cakes?" asked Aunt Annie.

"Over yonder on the dry sink," Mama answered. "Willie, how about you and the others setting the sawhorses up and getting those tabletops ready so we can get the food on?"

Mama would point, nod and direct all of us around until she had the food spread out before us like a garden that had never known a weed. Nobody spread a table like my mother. She was a true Southern lady.

The other Sundays in the month, we'd just go to Sunday School at the Baptist church and then head on over to either the Methodist, or what we'd call the Holiness church. You see, whatever preacher came traveling around on that particular Sunday, that's where we'd go. The same folks went to each other's buildings and services—that's just the way it was in Willard.

And then, every third week in September, there was a Revival. Everybody went to church during Revival, even the drunks. It was like a festival that every church in Willard took turns hosting. Church buildings would fill up and spill over; pews would hold twice their limit and windowsills doubled as benches. The wood floors in those modest buildings would creak and sway under the weight like a tiny footbridge under a heavy wagon.

Then there were the preachers. They came in all sizes—tall and skinny, short and round, and big and bigger – and dressed in suits that were shiny from use and white shirts bleached and starched so many times they were the color of ghosts, white but fading.

However, once they stood up to preach, they all became the voice of God. They were mighty messengers sent to deliver us from the clutches of Satan— or from ourselves. With shouts, shaking, sweating and singsong cadence, these men could coax a congregation into a holy frenzy with a raised hand, a bellowing "Amen" and a melodic hum.

"JE-sus! He IS the Son of the Almighty God, mmm?" the preachers would shout.

"Uh-huh!" "Yes sir!" "Amen!" "Go on!" the congregation responded back.

"JE-sus! Was the conqueror of DARK-ness. Am I right, mmm?" asked the preachers.

"Amen." "Go on!"

"Then why are some of ya'll still in-FI-dels, the Lord wants to know?" The preachers shouted as if some deacon had plugged their coat tails into an electrical socket.

"Oh, Lordy!" "That's right!" "Yes sir!"

"Repent! I say."

"Yes sir!"

"Repent! says the Lord!"

"That's right!"

"YOU yonder, repent! And YOU over there! Repent!" implored the preachers, culling sinners out like those packers did with blemished strawberries.

During Revival, there was so much crackle in the air it was impossible to keep children still. Fortunately, being still wasn't what was required. After the choir would welcome us in with hymns and spirituals as comforting as a pot roast and as stirring as hot peppers, the preacher would step up on the podium—the signal for parents to bring their children down to the mourner's bench right in front for all to see.

As boys, my brothers, Ottie and I would sit in the back of the Holiness church and watch the Charismatics get the Spirit. The Holy Ghost would hit someone and they'd start jerking and moving and prancing in place like they were so tickled to be alive.

Preaching, testifying, praying and shouting—yes sir, that was Revival— whether you were a Baptist, Methodist, Presbyterian or Pentecostal, it was all so exciting.

However, when the Revival was at the Baptist church, Mama would hunt us up and haul us to the front before the choir could put an "amen" on its first hymn.

Reverend C.C. Underwood was the preacher who impacted me the most. He had this way about him that would make you want to get up and shout sure enough. If by the end of his sermon there was still a child or two who hadn't jumped up and shouted and got religion, as we'd say, our parents would make us all get back down on our knees to sing and pray and have the pastor preach at us some more.

"Get down on your knees, Aaron. You too, RV," whispered Mama who was sitting right behind us.

"Ottie West! You get yourself on those knees and pray to the Good Lord for your salvation, do you hear me!" That was Aunt Annie.

RV scooted over to me and practically climbed up on my shoulders. "What are you doing?" I whispered.

"I'm scared of hell, Aaron."

"Then jump up and shout, RV," I said as I pushed him off of me.

"Uh-uh. I'm more scared of that preacher," he said.

"Just jump up. Go on. It ain't scary or nothing," whispered Ottie. "Come on, we'll do it together."

"Praise God! Halleluiah! Thank you, Jesus!" shouted Ottie and RV as they hopped up from the mourner's bench. Not to be left alone to be toyed with by the devil, I too got religion that night. Depending on how we behaved in school or at home that particular year, a lot of us kids were made to get religion every time the preacher gave the invitation.

During the week of Revival, the principal at the elementary school would have the visiting preacher come in during the school day and teach us kids. He'd hop up on the stage in the seventh and eighth grade classroom and, more times than not, we'd hear the exact same sermon we'd heard the night before. I guess the grown-ups were determined to get the Holy Ghost after us a-coming and a-going.

When I was eleven years old, I was baptized in a creek in the northeastern part of the Cape Fear River. It was Revival time and Pastor C.C. Underwood had just preached about the Prodigal Son that Saturday night. It was on a Sunday morning about nine o'clock, before the eleven o'clock service. Standing behind the pulpit, Pastor Underwood started to pace back and forth shaking his head. "Naw sir, it wasn't right!" he said. "This here boy had a good father and a good home life and still he didn't appreciate what he had!" boomed Pastor Underwood.

I was older now and had begun to actually hear those dramatic sermons rather than just be entertained by them. The words I had read in the Bible myself were starting to come together for me, so much so that when C.C. Underwood stepped into the pulpit that year, my heart did a little jump and shout of its own.

"The boy left his family," said Pastor Underwood nodding and wringing his hands, "He drifted away and began a life of sin that had no value to anyone."

"It ain't right!" "No sir!" wailed the congregation.

"The boy wallered in the mud with swine!" shouted Pastor Underwood as he stepped from behind the pulpit and started to pace back and forth.

"No sir!" shouted our fathers.

"Slop for his supper, I mean to tell ya'll!" he preached on.

"It ain't right!" wailed our mothers.

That evening our little Baptist church was a sea of people smashed into the pews like sardines. Women tried rustling a breeze with the church's cardboard fans that advertised Williams Funeral Home. The men tried to get comfortable standing in the aisles or leaning against the walls. But all were intent on the words of Brother Underwood as he called the prodigals home.

Sitting up front on the mourners' bench again with Ottie, I could feel the heat of Pastor Underwood's sermon scorching my soul. I was that ungrateful son. I was that wayward boy. I needed to be saved.

"That son disgraced his family!" bellowed Reverend Underwood as sweat began to bead on his forehead. "Disgraced his family! Do ya'll hear?"

"Yes sir!" "Lord have mercy!" responded the crowd sitting behind me.

I couldn't sit in my seat a moment longer. I jumped up, raised my hands and shouted, "Save me, Jesus!"

I had almost forgotten why Mama had named me Aaron. But on that Sunday morning, as the whole congregation walked together toward the banks of the river, I felt the calling once again that God had on my life.

About ten or twelve of us, mostly children, were baptized that day. White robes made by the deaconesses were slipped over our heads before we walked out into the water.

"I feel silly in this," whispered Ottie.

"Me too. I've never worn a dress before," I said and giggled.

"We all look like we just blew off of a cottonwood tree," said James as he flapped his arms around.

As we stepped into the water, our bodies shivered from the excitement and the cold of the river. Our white robes ballooned around us as the Cape Fear River swished by. The sun was already high in the sky and bright enough to make you squint. The ever-present humidity was wasting no time wilting our clothing, making it stick to us like a licked postage stamp.

Those of us in white robes gathered in the water around Pastor Underwood. From the shore, we must have looked like white corks bobbing in the water as we waded up to our waists.

One-by-one Pastor Underwood heard our confessions and baptized us in the name of the Father, the Son and the Holy Spirit. The chilly waters prompted us not to dilly dally or have second thoughts.

My whole family stood on the banks and watched the baptisms. The last of the summer dragonflies buzzed around my father's head as he leaned close to Mother. My mama stood at the edge of the water as straight as a rake.

She smiled at me and bowed her head. I knew she was thanking Jesus as she handed me over to Him.

Oh, how I wish I could tell you that from that day on I lived a life my parents were proud of. If it had been up to my mama's prayers alone, the angel Gabriel himself would have been summoned as my guardian. But free will and rebellion has enticed more than one teenager to play too close to the flames of hell.

Stump hole liquor could steal your moral compass before you even took the second drink. By age fourteen, I had discovered its seductive and destructive powers. And for two years I danced with the devil, ignoring all I knew to be right.

"If you aren't careful, Aaron, that stump hole brew will strike you blind and take the use of your legs from you," warned my Uncle Robert one Sunday afternoon during one of our manly shade tree gatherings.

Other wives tales and stories of mice being found in the homemade brew had no effect on me. Ottie and I and some of our buddies became regular customers who bought our refreshment out of car trunks and foggy woods.

It didn't help that the local juke joint was only about five hundred yards from my house. It wasn't unusual to sit in our living room and be able to hear the Piccolo whine out twenty-five-cent tunes from Duke Ellington's band or from Louis Jordan, Albert King or Skeets McDonald.

Once Ottie and I crossed the line with moonshine, the next step was to wander just a little ways down the road to the joint. By the time we were sixteen, my cousin and I were regulars. We'd even go on weeknights, which meant our homework wasn't getting done and I was missing my curfew more than I was making it.

While my mama didn't believe in dancing, I was a true convert. The juke joint had a large dance floor where folks were moving and shaking at all hours of the night. One of my favorite dance moves was the split. I'd fight all the way down to the floor and then shoot back up like a cannon ball shot across a circus tent.

At the joint, a game of pool combined with too much alcohol consumption could get you into a fight faster than anything.

"Come on, Aaron, let's go. He's not worth it," said Ottie.

"But he's cheating. I know he is," I said as I stumbled over my own feet.

"It doesn't matter. Let it go," said Ottie.

I glared across the pool table at the guy who had just beaten me in a game. "Yeah, but…"

"Come on. It's getting late," said my cousin as he took my arm and started directing me to the door.

"Quit pushing me!" I protested. I pulled my arm away from Ottie but, in doing so, I lost my balance and tumbled to the floor—knocking a rack of pool cues over on top of me. The crash was loud and the fall was not graceful.

"What is going on here? I want you two out now," said the bartender, who had rushed into the back room to check things out.

"I didn't do anything. It's his fault," I said pointing to Ottie.

"Just get yourself up and get out," he said. "And I don't want to see either of you around here for a while."

When the bartender left, Ottie started picking up the pool cues and stacking them back in the rack. As I struggled to get up on my feet, I felt sick.

Ottie and I didn't speak to each other as we stumbled outside. Out in the parking lot, we stood for a minute looking at each other. "Can you get home alright?" Ottie asked.

I nodded.

"Then see you tomorrow," he said, and turned and started walking across the sandy parking lot.

I stood there unsure if I could make it the five hundred yards to my house.

My parents were distressed by my behavior to say the least. They kept after me to stop hanging around with those boys who were influencing me. They didn't realize that I was as much of a troublemaker as my friends.

I liked my nightlife with its smoking, drinking, dancing and foul-mouthed talk. Those behaviors were like fingers tugging on the buttons of my shirt calling me to dark ways. There was something uncomfortable about it, yet I wouldn't stop. My mother kept telling me my behavior wasn't respectful to the Lord. I didn't want to hear it. I had all but forgotten my promise to her. Any thoughts of me meeting up with her in heaven some day were banished from memory—exiled to the desert of broken promises.

Then one night not long after my sixteenth birthday, I stumbled into our yard missing my curfew once again—liquor running through my veins like blood. The next day was a school day and I was expected to be up and driving my bus route by 5:30 a.m. I was trying to quietly open the front door when Mother suddenly pushed the door open herself. As she stood there with the kerosene lamp from the dining room silhouetting her body, her shadow fell across my face like a shovel. She was crying. Her face was puffy, her eyes were red and swollen and the anguish on her face couldn't have been sadder than if someone close had died. Never had my mother looked at me with such sorrow. It stung me and sobered me up a bit.

"Aaron, you're not supposed to be like this," she said, holding her voice as solid as she could. "I didn't want you to come into the world to be a child of the devil. I wanted you to be a child of the Lord. Don't you understand that God has something important for you to do?"

As I stood before my mother, the distress on her face made my stomach turn on me as my last drink began a fiery boil back up my throat. The lines on my mother's forehead were so deep they reminded me of muddy ruts carved into a rain-soaked dirt road. Her eyes drooped so far down her cheeks I was afraid they might slide off her face. Mama looked old. Then it hit me—I had done this to her. I had aged her with worry.

Next, the memory of what Mama had told me about my name and where it had come from dangled behind my eyelids as tears burned my eyes. I felt myself sag and flatten like a tire. From down deep inside, I felt a sickened groan bubbling up my chest—rattling and banging and clanging its way up.

"If you keep going on like you're doing, you're going to kill me, Aaron. You're supposed to be God's child."

My mother's voice seemed like it was coming from the back of the house, but as the meaning of her words began to sink in they got louder and burned so hot the alcohol in me evaporated like water on hot pavement.

I couldn't think of anything to say. Even if I could have, I don't think I had enough air in me to push the words beyond my lips. I turned away from my mother. Looking into her face felt like a slap, and this time I knew I deserved it. I staggered past her and went into my bedroom. I closed the door and collapsed onto my knees.

I don't know where my brothers were that night. I think my mother may have sent them to sleep over at one of my aunts', anticipating my bad behavior. For the first time in my life, I had the bedroom all to myself. I usually slept in the middle between Tommy and James. But that night I was alone.

My knees began to press into the wood floorboards, crunching and sobering me up even more. Kneeling in the dark, I began to remember things: Mama kneeling, small folded hands, bowed heads, a promise made.

I had not prayed since, when? At first I didn't know where to start. I fidgeted a while trying to get comfortable, trying to muster up the courage to speak. I concluded that night that we're not supposed to be comfortable on our knees, not really. It's a posture of contrition, not comfort.

All alone in that dark room something inside of me nudged and I knew it was now or never. I took a deep breath and began, "God, I don't want to kill my mama. She's the most precious thing in the world to me. Please, God! I don't want to kill her."

Uttering those words unplugged something in me and the next ones tumbled out like marbles spewed onto the floor. "Jesus, if you are real, I want you to come into my life and I want you to save me. I don't know who you are—not really. I've read about you and been told about you, but I don't know you."

I was surprised at my own honesty. I truly didn't know God, even though I had grown up in His camp, so to speak. It had all been words and stories and as natural for me as buttering bread at supper, but until that moment I had not felt His power. I had been sitting on top of a spiritual volcano with my hands placed on its hot, bubbling heart. The rumblings, the shaking of the earth and the held-back power of the eruption made me quake and sway—and then yearn. I was suddenly hit with this forceful appetite for all things spiritual. I was starving for Jesus when I laid my face on the floor and prayed, "I want to know you for myself and I give you my life."

As I say these words now, they come easily off my lips. But they were not easy that night. In fact, I really don't know how long it took me to get them all out, but they eventually did come. Afterwards I was left with just enough strength to crawl into bed on top of the covers.

The next morning when I got up for school, it was still dark, but the minute I opened my eyes I was greeted with lightness. I felt like I could float right off of the bed. I felt super. I came out of the bedroom smiling like I'd eaten up all of Aunt Annie's teacakes myself.

Mama was up fixing my breakfast and said, "Why are you smiling like that?"

I grinned real big and said, "I was saved last night, Mama."

"What? Have you lost your mind?" I'm sure she was thinking to herself that I certainly didn't smell saved.

"No, Mama. I'm saved."

I went on to tell her what I had prayed and that I really wanted to know Jesus. Mother stopped what she was doing and just stared at me as if I was a goat that had just eaten the kitchen curtains. She searched my face looking for clues that would tell her if I was just messing with her or if I was telling her the truth.

Mama stood there wrestling between hope and fear. But once convinced that her wayward son Aaron had indeed come home and broken the grip of Satan, my mother pulled me to her and held me like the long lost child I was— the child who had finally crawled out of the pig pen and wandered home.

When I got to the school bus that morning, Ottie was waiting for me. He usually met me at the bus and rode with me while I made my rounds. As we climbed on the bus, I told him, "Ottie, I've got something to tell you. Last night I gave my life to Christ. I'm changed. I won't be drinking anymore."

At first, Ottie just stared at me like I was speaking French or something. After a second or two, he got this big ole grin on his face and said, "Then I will too. I want to give my life to Christ too."

So right there in the early morning on a dilapidated school bus, my cousin Ottie confessed Jesus as his Savior. As I picked up the children at their various stops, he and I talked about what we would do now and promised each other that our juke joint days were over. We both wanted this to be real.

After I got to school, I asked my teacher in my first class if I could make an announcement. She seemed a little reluctant, but when I told her it was important, she allowed me to stand up and speak. "I just want all of ya'll and the teachers here at school to know that last night I gave my life to Jesus. I won't be drinking any more or hanging out in the wrong places. I want to live for Jesus and spend the rest of my life trying to do the right things." I figured I needed to say these things out loud right away before the devil could get another grip.

You could have heard sweat drop. I didn't know if the kids in class were going to make fun of me or what, but I didn't care. I knew I needed to announce my change in behavior as quickly as I could. I had already wasted a lot my time behaving badly. I didn't want to waste any more.

To my surprise, a few of my buddies, some of whom had been out at the juke joint with me the night before, decided that they too wanted to repent and be Christians. They confessed right there in the classroom that they were turning from their old sinful lives as well.

My teacher really didn't know what to do. Repentance and confessions of faith were not an everyday occurrence in the classroom. "And Miss Johnson, I want to apologize to you for the way I've been acting in school with disrespect and all. That's all going to change," I said.

It was a good day. I was happy. I was clean once again. It was like God reached inside of me and thumped my core, waking it from a bleak, long winter's nap.

Not long after graduation, I left "God's country" for the first time. Oh, I didn't leave alone, of course. I took with me parts of everyone and anyone who had taught me something. When the sands of Willard were no longer under my feet, my decisions got harder. When I'd have to choose between loving all the people God created or hating the white ones, or sticking up for what I believed or backing down, or reaching my hand out either to get help or to give help, I'd think, "What would Mama do?" Or, "What would Bernita do?" Or James, or Ottie. And if I needed some grit, I'd even think about what Aunt Annie would do.

The answer would come to me just like that: *"Aaron, seek first His kingdom and His righteousness and all these other things... will take care of themselves...."*

Part II: Leaving Home

SEVEN

Leaving Home

*A*s I stood in front of the building that held the registrar's office, the three hundred and three dollars folded deep in my pants pocket felt like it was leaping around in there like jumping beans. Circled around me were several other buildings with students walking in and out and meeting and greeting each other after the Christmas break. It was January in Raleigh, North Carolina, and Shaw University was about to register a new student for spring semester: Me.

Inside, I carefully counted my money out onto the countertop in front of the business manager. He watched me, trying his best not to laugh out loud. "Two hundred ninety-nine. Three hundred. There, that ought to do it," I said, wiping my sweaty palms on my pants. I took a deep breath, hoping the spring tuition for Shaw hadn't gone up since I'd last inquired about it.

"Looks good to me, son," replied the business manager. "Do you have a place to live while you're here?"

"Yes, sir. I'll be staying with my cousin and his wife about five miles out of town."

"Do I know your cousin?"

"No, sir. But you might know my other cousin, Ottie West. Ottie came here last semester on full scholarship."

"Ottie West, you say?"

"Yes, sir."

The business manager looked at me and rolled his head back and forth like he was trying to picture Ottie and me being related. I was sure hoping my first cousin hadn't done anything stupid since he'd enrolled at Shaw, making this man dislike me right off the bat.

"Oh, yes, young Mr. West. I do believe I've seen him around campus. Nice fellow."

"We're both staying at our cousin's house."

"That'll be fine. Just make sure you can get here on time for your first class in the mornings. Punctuality is important."

"Yes, sir." I kept watching as the registrar scooted my money into a pile. It sure didn't look like much lying there, barely a half-inch thick if that. Yet that little bundle of money represented months of twelve-hour days and three-hour bus rides. I had swept, dusted, stocked and clerked my way to this very spot. Parting with that three-hundred-dollar tuition fee was one of my proudest moments—also one of my hardest. I had worked so hard for so long and dreamed about this day so much that finally being here and emptying my pockets was anticlimactic. I stood there dumbfounded. *Now what?*

The business manager probably had seen this a million times—a wide-eyed, bewildered, incredulous student paying for his first semester of college. All the sweat and early mornings, all the harvested tobacco and cotton, and all the strawberry picking it took to get them there—all of it finally paying off. It was enough to bring them to their knees. No doubt many a student did just that. However, I felt a bit silly—just standing there unable to move.

The registrar, seeing that I was stuck where I stood, left his post behind the counter and walked over to me. He slapped me on the back, probably to jump-start my heart, and told me I'd never regret spending my money on education. "Think of it as an investment in yourself, my boy. You've done good."

I left the business office and started my five-mile walk to my cousin's— with three measly dollars left for rent, food, clothing, and books. Those three bills weren't quite hopping and jumping around in my pocket the way the three hundred had done. Weeping? Yes. Hopping? No. The registrar told me to have faith. Walking through the streets of Raleigh that day, faith was the only thing I felt I did have left.

During my life, God has generously, yet cleverly, placed in my path folks who would help me along the way to become the person He intended me to be—no doubt a result of my mother's prayers. Some of those folks I met at just the right time and in just the right place. I believe God truly excels at that—this converging of lives to meet at the ends of a pinpoint. However, there are other folks we never actually get to meet face-to-face, but God intertwines our lives with them so beautifully that the weaving almost seems orchestrated to music. The meeting of the two becomes a symphony of lives, days, struggles, accomplishments and events. They become people who can profoundly touch each other's lives and who can sometimes even live decades or centuries apart from each other, yet through God's timing and God's will, become connected. One such person in my life was Dr. Henry Martin Tupper.

Imagine a country whose landscape is pock-marked by cannonballs, muskets and blood. The southern half of her received the worst end of the beating with plantations and homes in ruins—tobacco crops tromped, cotton trampled, corn ravished—while one-legged soldier/farmers and widowed mothers are forced to beg for their existence like today's bag ladies.

Once gun barrels were laid down and the Southern surrender was completed, the prize was finally bestowed. Slaves were given their freedom only to discover that once they walked away from the plantation, they had no job, no home, no food, no prospects—all the things that slavery, despite its cruelty, provided.

Late in 1865, Raleigh, North Carolina, was trying to reinvent herself and readjust to a South she no longer knew. Although Raleigh had remained unscathed throughout the war, in the spring of 1865 the city and her state capitol building began to finally experience the Civil War firsthand. When General William T. Sherman's army, led by Judson Kilpatrick's Third Cavalry Division, marched into town, Raleigh became occupied by the Federal Army. Eleven days after that invasion, a Union officer relayed a coded message to troops outside the city, from on top of the capitol rotunda. Using fire and torches the message translated: "Peace on earth, Good will toward men."

General Sherman, who had been waiting on the outskirts of Raleigh, smiled at the message relayed and quickly marched the rest of his troops into the embarrassed and sorrowful city. Turned upside-down, and not unlike most Southern cities at the time, Raleigh had to figure out what was next. It is into this chaos and rebuilding that Dr. Henry Martin Tupper entered.

Dr. Tupper was as Yankee as they come. Born in Monson, Massachusetts, he had been a private and a chaplain in the Union Army. He spent most of his three years of service ministering to Yankee soldiers on Southern soil and saw more than his share of the ugliness and brutality of a war bent on killing its own. But in the midst of the mayhem around him, the chaplain's heart was captured by the plight of the slaves his army struggled to liberate.

At the end of the war and after an honorable discharge, the thirty-year-old Tupper immediately moved his young bride, Sarah, to Raleigh only six months after General Sherman made his entrance. Supported by the American Baptist Home Mission Society and the Freedmen's Bureau, Dr. Tupper became a missionary to freed slaves. His plan was to preach salvation and promote education to whomever he could muster up to listen.

The day after Henry Tupper arrived in Raleigh, he paid a call to the pastor of the Baptist church to introduce himself and announce his mission to the freed slaves. He had hoped that his ministry would be met with pleasure and support from his white brethren in the South. However, with Union soldiers still camped inside the capitol rotunda and Reconstruction being forced upon

Raleigh citizens like strained peas on a crying baby, Dr. Tupper's mission did not find much favor with the local Baptist minister or his humiliated congregation.

Upon that first meeting, it became clear to Henry that a ministry focused on ex-slaves wasn't going to be popular or welcomed. So without waiting for any further approval, Dr. Tupper began his work among the colored people of Raleigh. What he found broke his heart.

The freed slaves were the poorest of the poor. They were refugees who had followed the Union Army around and now congregated in Raleigh looking for the triumphant federal soldiers to care for them. They had no ruined homes to salvage, no distressed land to work, and currency—Confederate or otherwise —was not socked away in a family hiding place. Henry found it hard to teach a man to read the Gospel of Christ when his children were literally starving.

So the pastor attended to the most urgent of things first. To do that, he turned for help from the Freedmen's Bureau and his connections to the Union Army. Using his influence as a former Union officer and chaplain, the missionary was able to assist with the procuring of food and clothing for the ex-slaves and their families. Since he had been in the army himself, he was able to approach the right people for help. At one time, it was reported that Dr. Tupper had one hundred and seventy-five colored persons over the age of seventy-five whom he regularly assisted in obtaining rations.

Once starvation was less of a threat, Dr. Tupper began religious instruction in earnest for his colored parishioners. For those who could not read, he taught them how, using scripture as their primer. The Freedman's Bureau also had its own "reader" that was sent out to groups wanting to educate slaves in white communities. This reader, while better than nothing, was a thinly veiled booklet of behavioral expectations for slaves entering a free society. Chocked full of carefully selected scriptures on forgiveness, piety, humbleness and temperance, the reader was aimed at teaching freed slaves to forgive their enemies—mainly their former masters—even though it never exactly used the words *slave* or *master*.

For those ex-slaves who could read and expressed a desire to learn more, Dr. Tupper began a theological class. In the beginning, he was unable to find a consistent meeting place for this class so he would alternate assembling his little band of students under neighboring trees or the low, dark, comfortless cabins the colored people in Raleigh were beginning to inhabit on the outskirts of town.

In December, 1865, two months after Henry and Sarah's arrival in Raleigh, Dr. Tupper entered into his personal journal: *"December 1st. Visited six families; held a prayer meeting; heard my theological class."* This date is recorded as the humble beginnings of what is now known as Shaw University.

In just a few short months, Dr. Tupper founded the Second Baptist Church of Raleigh. His first theological class had grown to six colored men. Eventually they moved their classroom from under the trees and sparse cabins to the old Guion Hotel, where today the State Museum stands.

Of course, I'm leaving out quite a bit of history here. Henry and Sarah's lives were threatened many times. There's even an account of their spending one night behind their cabin because someone had warned them of an over-heard plot to burn it down while they slept. The deep, white South was not ready en masse for equality for the black people. Too many wounds and deaths, and the loss of a prosperous way of life, had left the white citizens of Raleigh feeling threatened. That earnest signal from the rotunda may have proclaimed *peace and good will toward men*, but not exactly *all* men would have that peace or good will—not overnight.

Yet, a gauntlet was thrown down that day and, thanks be to God, Henry Tupper and many others like him took it up and sacrificed much for it. They would not be the last to do so, of course. It was a beginning.

I've often wondered how it must have felt to be one of Henry Tupper's first students—an ex-slave handed his own Bible for the very first time.

"Go, ahead, this one's yours," said Henry Tupper.

"Naw, sir, dat's alright. I's sit here n' lis'en."

"Everyone gets a Good Book for himself, Brother Joshua. And no one just sits and listens. This is a theological class—a place of thought and discussion."

Dr. Tupper handed Joshua a Bible and continued down the row of students. Thanks to the American Baptist Home Mission Society, a shipment of Bibles had just arrived and Henry was only too thrilled to be able to personally hand them out to his first students.

The Guion Hotel allowed the missionary to move his unconventional theological class into one of their back rooms. After the darkness of mud-chinked log cabins, the back storeroom of the hotel was a treat. The transom over the door gave the room an open-air feeling, while the tiny window looking toward the hotel latrines was almost like a garden view…almost.

"Thank ya, kindly, sir. I's b'most proud ta hold da Wurd of Gawd fer ya," said Joshua, as he shifted and squirmed on the bench.

"Oh, it's not mine. This is yours—yours to keep. Bring it with you every time we have lessons," said Dr. Tupper as he patted the burly shoulder.

Joshua bit his bottom lip and concentrated hard on the gold imprinted title embossed on the cover. The words Holy Bible seemed to shimmer as tears stubbornly forged a gully over Joshua's cheeks like a rain-flooded river. The unassuming former slave tried his best to catch the run-off with his sleeve before it dripped off the tip of his nose.

"Ain't nobody ever gives me a Bible b'for," he said. The rest of the men in the room seemed to be fidgeting as well and could only nod in agreement. They kept their heads low—bowed over their own new leather-bound books.

Dr. Tupper stood back and caught his breath. Sitting before him were six colored men, all of them with uncontrollable tears streaming down their faces. He cleared his throat a bit and said quietly, "Gentlemen, we are going to be sharing many books together through our studies. This is only the beginning."

"Yessir, but dis'en's da bestest one dey is," answered Joshua softly.

Henry felt his own throat swell and after a few moments said, "You're right, friend. You are so right."

After a few minutes, Dr. Tupper announced the first scripture to be pondered and opened the class with a question. "Who wants to read first?"

With his new Bible balanced awkwardly on his lap, Joshua slowly raised his hand.

"Fine. Begin when you're ready, Brother Joshua."

The freed slave stood up from the bench as straight as his six-foot frame could muster. Held up by a belt of jute rope, his threadbare pants dropped their tattered cuffs just above his ankles. The sleeves of his white shirt, yellow with age—wrinkled but clean—strained to reach his wrists. Joshua pushed his shoulders back, coaxing the ill-fitted shirt to release its rub on the healing wounds that were rutted deep into the slave's back. Clearing his throat, Joshua prepared to read for the first time in his life—in front of a white man. Trying his best to make his dry mouth obey, Joshua boldly read "In da b'gin'n wus da Wurd, and da Wurd was wid Gawd, and da Wurd was Gawd. Da same was in da b'gin'n wid Gawd ... "

Can you imagine!

In January 1866, Dr. Tupper began admitting women into his theological classes. It wasn't long before that tiny back room was bulging. Using his own money—five hundred dollars he had saved while in the Army—Dr. Tupper purchased a vacant lot at the corner of Blount and Cabarrus streets.

After a day of study, Tupper and his students would tromp out to the nearby woods and chop down trees. Those trees were used to construct a two-story structure on that corner plot. When completed, the bottom of the building became The Second Baptist Church and the top floor became The Raleigh Institute—where colored men and women, all ex-slaves, studied side by side to become ministers, missionaries or teachers.

The Raleigh Institute was renamed the Shaw Collegiate Institute in 1872 after a benevolent donation from Mr. Elijah Shaw, a New England philanthropist from Wales, Massachusetts, no doubt a friend of Dr. Tupper.

Those charitable funds purchased the acreage where Shaw University stands today. In 1875 the school was incorporated and chartered by the State of North Carolina under the name Shaw University.

I thank God for making Dr. Henry Martin Tupper's heart tender toward a race of people that was not his own. He looked at the black man and saw children of God instead of property. He was convinced that while the war gave the black man his physical freedom, education would truly free him. Today, Shaw University is one of the oldest African-American universities in the American South.

Of course, my road to Shaw University was not a straight one. I wanted to go to college right after my high school graduation, but in those days, the odds of a poor, black sharecropper's son doing anything except following in his daddy's footsteps were highly unlikely. If college was going to be in my future, God and my stubborn will would need to be in cahoots.

While Ottie's family was just as poor as mine, he had something I didn't: straight As. Ottie became the valedictorian of our class, and when Shaw University offered him a full scholarship in Biblical Studies, he jumped at it.

As you may well imagine, Aunt Annie was busting with pride. Her boy had heard the call to ministry and was going on to college. Can't you just hear Aunt Annie on the day that scholarship letter arrived? "Praise, the Lord! Glory Halleluiah! Thank you, Jesus!"

I don't think there is anything sweeter to a mother who has spent diligent years correcting, hounding, protecting and watch-dogging the ways of her children than to see them have a chance at something better than she had. It was true then. It's still true now.

But for me, watching my cousin take off for college and leaving me behind was like being whipped. Ottie and me. Me and Ottie. He'd sneeze and I'd wipe my nose on my sleeve. I'd stub my toe and he'd limp. And, once we began living the Christian life in earnest, there wasn't a day that went by that we didn't pray together. Playtime was worship for us.

As I watched the Greyhound bus leave from the corner in front of our house that fall morning, I tried waving to Ottie from my front porch, but my right arm betrayed my sorrow. It was a pitiful wave, and my arm couldn't have hurt more if someone had ripped it off and tossed it into the Cape Fear River. I not only lost my best friend, my best friend was getting to do what I'd only hoped to do. As the bus drove out of sight, my heart sank into the muddy creek right alongside my arm. Ottie deserved that scholarship. But I sure wished it had been me.

While my cousin packed his bags for Shaw University, God was getting ready to sit me on top of that pinpoint once again with the most unlikely person.

If I was ever going to afford college, I needed to get paid more than five cents per quart for strawberries. When I heard that Camp Lejeune Marine Corps Base in Jacksonville, North Carolina, was hiring janitors, I jumped at the chance. At age nineteen, I took my first job outside of Willard. The base was only fifty miles or so from my home, but it might as well have been on the moon. That hour and a half bus ride was the furthest I'd ever been away from home.

For sixty-five cents an hour, I stocked, swept and mopped my hopes into a frenzy at the Camp Lejeune PX. Never in my life had I wanted to please someone as much as I did the Master Sergeant, my new boss.

The first time I saw him I was star struck. He was a tall, slender, beautiful man. In Willard, when we worked tobacco or picked strawberries, we were either shirtless or wore overalls. Even our Sunday clothes would have looked shabby next to the Master Sergeant's khakis. The white farmers who gathered in the mornings at the general store drinking coffee from stained cups didn't even come close to the starched, creased, tucked-in, buttoned-up look of my Master Sergeant. He belonged up there on the movie screen with Gary Cooper—not a hair out of place, no dirt under his fingernails. He was as strong as a tractor. I'm sure those two-hundred pound bags of fertilizer my uncles always talked about would have been like sacks of turkey feathers heaved on his shoulder. If he had wanted to, he could have picked me up with one hand and set me up on the top shelf with the pot lids.

What this fine, uniformed white man must have thought the first time he saw me walk through the low doorway of the PX, I can only imagine.

I left for work every morning at five o'clock. Still sleeping between two brothers and being fed breakfast by my mother, I'd catch the bus to Jacksonville, basically right out my front door. Before the roosters could give a second crow, I'd be settling down into my bus seat. I'd get home after dark, tired but pleased. Something was happening. I could feel it.

Every job the Master Sergeant gave me, I'd hear my mother in my head saying, "Now, Aaron, if someone is willing to pay you this wage, you work in such a way that he'd think the smartest thing he ever did was to hire you." So I did.

It wasn't long at all until the Master Sergeant took a liking to me and started to trust me with more work and more responsibility. One morning after I opened the PX for the day, Master Sergeant called me into his office at the back of the store and said, "Aaron, I have never seen anyone work as hard as you. And you're smart, too. You should be doing more with yourself. If it's alright with you, I'd like to give you a twenty-five cent raise."

Well, it was alright with me! It was also alright when he gave me three more raises the next month. I had never had a white man treat me that way—

like he saw something else when he looked at me, like my skin color, dark eyes and crinkled hair weren't something to fear or hate. He treated me like I was, well, for lack of a better word—*white.*

When the Master Sergeant offered his hand to me like he meant it, I took it. In four months time, I had earned $303. It was time to go to college!

When I got ready to leave home for my first semester at Shaw, my mother walked me to the end of our yard to wait for the bus. She had slipped her housecoat on over her apron and needed to hurry back in to finish up breakfast for the others.

"I'm going to miss you, baby."

"Yeah, I'm going to miss you too, Mama, and the others."

Lifting her face toward me, I saw pride in her eyes. I was the first in our family to go to college. Of course, Aunt Annie let it be known often that I wasn't the *very* first one of the cousins to leave for college. But Mama was proud of me all the same. My success would be hers, too.

"Aaron, son, God provides for the faithful and when He does, like He's done with you, it's best not even to think of it as coincidence or luck. You hear what I'm saying?"

I did. I surely did.

At Shaw my world exploded. Colorful wrapped bits of knowledge and experiences fell around me like candy spewing from a piñata. Students from all over the United States and Africa walked the campus grounds. College-educated teachers, both white and black, taught my classes. My professors were prepared; they were people who had succeeded and were where I wanted to go with my life. All of them became mentors. President W.R. Strassner, Dean Brown, Reverend McCray, Mr. Morrison, Miss Arson, Mrs. Verquoy and many others. They welcomed us, motivated us and expected great things from us. I was a kid dropped down in a vat of honey.

After a lifetime of being told how worthless we were by white men who slapped colored children for fun, men who lynched black boys to make a point, or by women who hired our mothers to clean their toilets just because they could—here on these hallowed grounds we were not only told we mattered, we were convinced we could change the course of the nation, maybe even the world.

I walked into my classroom that first Monday morning and sat at a sturdy wooden desk. My new books smelled like ink and oiled leather. It was the first time I ever held a new book in my hands. The halls of the auditorium glistened with floor polish and varnish. Window panes sparkled with not a single pane missing or patched with cardboard. I felt like I had stepped into a dream, but like no dream I'd ever had before. In this dream, I mattered. I floated. I had to bite the insides of my cheeks just to keep from weeping out loud.

During those four years at Shaw, I found summer work in New England cutting down brush for an electric company, thanks to Dean Brown. Ottie and I went to New England together as wide-eyed as they come, but we earned enough tuition money for the next two semesters.

During the school year, I worked several jobs to earn my board and keep. I was a janitor for the dorms and I took orders at a whites-only drive-in burger joint in Raleigh. While working that job, I was determined to show the white college students from nearby North Carolina State College the best face of a black man. No matter how they treated me, my return response would be courteous. If they'd say their burger was too raw, I'd replace it with a smile. If they'd say their Coke was too watery, I'd give them another one without so much as a grunt.

I wanted those students to see me as the same as them, a student making his way. I also wanted them to see what an educated black man looked like.

Another job I had, which convinced me that God indeed showed attention to detail, came about one day while I was working as a substitute bellhop at a Raleigh hotel for a friend who was sick. As I stood outside the big doors of the hotel, a white woman who had just eaten at the hotel started up a conversation with me. It didn't take us long to realize we were related—so to speak. She was a Johnson relative of the white family in Willard. Right there on the spot, she offered me a job as a gardener at her home in Raleigh. That turned out to be a good job and helped me finish out my undergrad years without too much financial worry. Like Mama had told me, "Aaron, be kind to everybody because you never know who will give you your last drink of water." Well, Miss Johnson didn't give me my last drink, but she did help make sure I had enough to drink—and eat and to pay rent. Had I been too mean to old Mrs. Chrub back in my strawberry bargaining days, I dare say I might not have gotten that job.

My mother's simple homemade shirts, my re-soled shoes and my wide-eyed face would have been dead giveaways that a poor boy was on campus. But the fact that a good many of us looked that same way was a credit to our upbringing. While college wasn't exactly an experience common among my race in the 1950s, times were changing. Dr. Henry Martin Tupper's call for Christ and humanity had reached out through the decades and was ringing true for a whole new generation.

In 1953, I became a freshman at Shaw University. A few short years later, during my last semester of seminary at Shaw, a young pastor was getting ready to walk onto campus with a preacher's zeal and a king's heart. He would quickly empower us with a dream—a dream of mountaintops and peaceful revolution. In the meantime, God was preparing me for the rest of my life.

EIGHT

Mattie

When the introductions were done, Mattie Miller, chairperson for the Winston-Salem Baptist Church Youth Day, turned and walked up to the podium as I followed her. She sat on one side and I sat on the other. That's it. That's how I met my wife. The earth didn't quake underneath my feet or anything. However, I'm not sure when I started breathing normally again.

I was taken with her to say the least.

She was to lead the opening prayer to begin Youth Day. I was the guest speaker, a first-year seminary student from Shaw University Divinity School. The year before, I had graduated with my undergraduate degree in religion and social studies. When we met, Mattie was a sophomore at Winston-Salem Teacher's College.

"Mr. Johnson, we are so pleased that you have agreed to be our devotional speaker for Youth Day. Shaw has always been so wonderful to send us such marvelous young seminary students," said the youth director, who had just introduced me to Miss Miller and several others who were taking part in the event that Sunday afternoon. I kept glancing over to get another look at the tall, slender young lady who had with one word changed all of my expectations for the day.

"*Hello,*" was all she said. Yet, she must have said more, right? She must have said something to make me notice her like I did. Something witty? Charming? Something pious? But, no. Just *hello*. Yet, all of a sudden everything had changed.

When the program finally began, Mattie Miller stood and walked the few steps to the podium and invited us to pray with her and ask God's blessing on our event. If she had not had my attention already, the prayer she offered moments later grabbed my heart and shook it good. I'd heard no prayer like it before—especially from a woman. She brought us before our Father with such humility and grace that the room where we sat became a holy place. This young woman was in touch with God in a way I'd only hoped to be. Her petition that afternoon wasn't long or showy, but it was every bit Mattie—insightful, humble and confident in who she was and in who *He* is.

After the service came to a close, I casually maneuvered myself in Mattie's direction. At the dinner that evening, I made sure I was sitting next to her. We visited together and when I asked for her address and phone number, for some reason she gave it to me without question.

I don't remember what my lesson was that day but later, once we started getting to know each other, Mattie told me, "I was impressed with the message and the delivery of the message and how passionate you were for the Lord. And I liked the way you expounded the scripture." I just wanted to know if she thought I was cute.

Thus began a three-and-a-half-year long-distance courtship. We got to know each other through correspondence and phone calls, when I could afford them, and the occasional visit. I proposed one evening while we sat on a porch swing where she was living. I asked her to marry me and told her I wanted to spend the rest of my life with her. Shortly after that, I gave her a ring. We were married June 17, 1960, just a couple weeks after our graduations.

As outgoing and center-stage as I was, probably still am, Mattie was the complete opposite. As the oldest child with four younger brothers, she knew how to hold her own, no question. However, Mattie's strength was and still is her intelligence—second only to her faith. While I felt called to a civic ministry that made use of my bumbling, stumbling loud ways, Mattie was called to a quieter service, yet one whose leadership was graced with wisdom and a velvet, anvil-like will. I am a bear in a suit that carries The Word in a big paw. Mattie Miller Johnson filled her role as First Lady of Mount Sinai Missionary Baptist Church by my side for more than forty-five years with pure, elegant grace. Her purr is more effective than my growl will ever be.

Here's how she tells her story. "My mother was a homemaker," Mattie says. "My father was a professional chef in our hometown, Spartanburg, South Carolina. I grew up in the city. It looked rural because the houses were farther apart than they are today, but it was in the city limits all the same.

"My mother didn't garden much, but once we got a freezer, she did freeze a lot of vegetables and things of that sort.

"Our home was modest, but had the comforts of electricity and indoor plumbing. I had a very good upbringing. My life was easy and good, and I grew up as a happy child.

"I'd say my life growing up was different from Aaron's, but to hear him tell it, his childhood was as rich and nurturing as mine. I believe it is all in what you have known and are familiar with. But we really did experience the 'country boy meets city girl' scenario and had to get used to each other's ways.

"I went to city schools that were well-equipped—for colored schools that is. I do remember that each student had his own required books, but I don't remember if they were secondhand or not. They probably were, but we did have enough of them.

"My elementary years were from first to sixth grade. Each grade had its own classroom and teacher. We didn't share teachers and no two classes were crowded together like Aaron's were. My junior high school was seventh and eighth grades only and high school was ninth through twelfth. All of my schools had libraries.

"I chose Winston-Salem Teacher's College because my grandmother had a niece who lived in the city. It was a black co-ed school and I majored in primary elementary, grades one through four. I taught in public schools in and around Fayetteville for over forty years."

If you didn't know better, you'd almost think my beautiful wife grew up in another era than me. The differences in our upbringing were stark. Of course, Mattie and her family, while not as impoverished as my own, still contended with what just about every African-American family confronted before the Civil Rights Movement began in earnest—prejudice, fear, malice and injustice. Her brothers had to be just as careful as mine did. The unspoken rules weren't just for black boys and men in rural areas. South Carolina had the tenth-highest recorded number of lynchings from 1880 to 1947 in the nation.

Mattie was only ten years old when a Mr. Willie Earle was dragged from his Pickens County jail cell by a mob of unmasked white men and lynched. He was shot twice in the face, cut, stabbed and beaten to death. It was 1947, and Mr. Earle had the unfortunate distinction of being South Carolina's last lynching victim. No one escapes the effects of that kind of violence.

At the time Mattie and I met, race issues were beginning to heat up and statewide headlines brought attention to the rolling boil of unrest. I was at a Baptist college, a college that was training its young people, especially its ministers, to become leaders in the struggle. I was being drawn into civic ministry and taught by my professors as much how to lead my future parishioners into community activism as I was taught the power of the twenty-third Psalm.

Shaw University was becoming a hotbed of civil rights activity. Raleigh was the capital of North Carolina and hosted several colleges and universities. Because of that, the pulse of racial activism beat strong there. Then along came Dr. Martin Luther King, Jr., himself, stirring the pot on Shaw's campus.

As for Mattie, she was a student at a public, co-educational college in Winston-Salem, a college with no religious connections. Winston-Salem Teacher's College, later renamed Winston-Salem State University, was the first African-American institution in the United States to grant degrees in elementary teacher education—thus making the majority of its student population women.

"We had a few radicals on campus at the time, but it wasn't until after I graduated that the college got more active in civil rights and demonstrations," says Mattie.

However, those few radicals, as Mattie calls them, made history when they helped stage a nonviolent sit-in at a Woolworth's in neighboring Greensboro on February 1, 1960. The protest ended 107 days later with the successful signing of a desegregation agreement by city officials and local businesses. Mattie, however, was not involved. "It just wasn't part of my personality," she says.

Still, she never complained nor asked me to stop my involvement. And more importantly, her faith saw us both through it. "I can honestly say that fear never gripped me. I knew that Aaron was called to civic ministry, and I just figured that God would take care of him. Maybe if I had not been so young or been more knowledgeable I would have been more nervous or concerned for him."

Mattie's activism came in the classroom. She has given her entire adult life to teaching children and instilling in them a strong heart. She's given them a clear sense of who they are and all that they can accomplish.

During our entire marriage, Mattie has endured my absence with stoic grace. Her role as a pastor's wife, mother to our two children, and educator has been performed through her confidence in a God she serves—not because of my support.

My one regret is that I was gone from her so much. Saying "yes" to one thing almost always means saying "no" to another. I wish I had learned that sooner. I chose to follow the call I sincerely felt to minister to God's church and the community at large. But by doing so, my wife suffered. If you listen to her long enough, you'll hear the hurt.

"Whatever Aaron got involved in, he gave it his all. He was dedicated to the cause—whatever the cause may have been at the time. And I was proud of him for it. He was a country boy with humble beginnings who worked his way up to college and seminary. He proved that through hard work and study and with the help of others, and naturally with the help of God, you can do what you want to do if you set your mind to it," says Mattie. "As a result, he has a compassion for other people and a willing desire to learn and share with others. Whatever he was involved in, he gave it a sense of dedication and loyalty—and he still does. Even now, people seek his advice and opinion whether it be politics or religious matters."

Don't you hear a big "but" coming? I do.

"*However*, I just didn't see the need for both of us being out there. I've never been involved in political activities. It's just not the kind of thing I wanted to be a part of. It was always something Aaron enjoyed, though, and I didn't object to it. With that said, I don't want to give the impression that I approved of his outside activities all of the time. I just didn't complain about them—I'll put it that way. It kept him away from home a lot. I just had to learn how to deal with it. I knew it was something important he was doing and was going to do regardless, whether I complained or not."

Did you hear what she said? She had to learn to *deal* with it. I'm not proud of that.

Since my retirement in December 2005, I have apologized to Mattie many times. I did not give her the kind of time and attention a husband should give a wife. A lot of the time, because of my ministry, she was out there by herself. I wasn't there to pick the kids up from school. I was in Raleigh, or at a church meeting, or trying to get a sermon out. She was the one helping with their homework and carpooling them to band practice. I have said through the years that a pastor is always on the cross. That may be, but a pastor's wife has her own cross to bear. I pray that God will forgive me for being one of the ones who hammered the nails on Mattie's cross at times.

My wife's service has been in missions and benevolence. But her calling has been one of a pillar, a strong, straight, trustworthy fortress. Our children, Dezette and Jamale, our brothers and sisters at Mount Sinai Missionary Baptist Church, and me—none of us would be who we are now if Mattie Miller Johnson had not been who she is. I thank God for the days ahead in which she has my full attention. I am also very thankful that after all of these years, she still wants it.

NINE

MLK and SNCC

Statement at Founding Conference of Student Nonviolent Coordinating Committee

" *We affirm the philosophical or religious ideal of nonviolence as the foundation of our purpose, the presupposition of our belief, and the manner of our action.*

Nonviolence, as it grows from the Judeo-Christian tradition, seeks a social order of justice permeated by love. Integration of human endeavor represents the crucial first step towards such a society.

Through nonviolence, courage displaces fear. Love transcends hate. Acceptance dissipates prejudice; hope ends despair. Faith reconciles doubt. Peace dominates war. Mutual regards cancel enmity. Justice for all overthrows injustice. The redemptive community supersedes immoral social systems.

By appealing to conscience and standing on the moral nature of human existence, nonviolence nurtures the atmosphere in which reconciliation and justice become actual possibilities.

Although each local group in this movement must diligently work out the clear meaning of this statement of purpose, each act or phase of our corporate effort must reflect a genuine spirit of love and good-will. "

- Student Nonviolent Coordinating Committee Founding Statement-
April 1960, Raleigh, North Carolina, Shaw University

The blackjack hit my ribcage with a force that knocked the wind right out of my lungs. The Raleigh city police officer yanking on my arm was red faced, and even though it was a pleasant spring day outside, inside at the Fayetteville Street F.W. Woolworth's lunch counter the air was filled with sticky perspiration and the smell of hot soup running down my face and melding my white Sunday shirt to my chest.

"They've kindly asked you to leave, boy! Now move!" snarled the officer as his blackjack once again found its mark.

Just moments before, the white waiter behind the counter had actually taken my order. It was a Friday afternoon in April. The year was 1960, and I had a fire in my belly hot enough to consume the whole state of North Carolina. Dr. Martin Luther King, Jr. had just been on Shaw's campus the week before, holding one of his nonviolent workshops. We students had organized ourselves with the help of Dr. King, the fearless Ella Baker, Ralph Abernathy, and many others of the Southern Christian Leadership Conference.

That Easter weekend, as two hundred students representing twelve states gathered on Shaw's campus, we organized and gave ourselves a name—the Student Nonviolent Coordinating Committee (SNCC). We pronounced it *Snick*.

A couple of months before Easter, on February 1, 1960, the student sit-ins at the Woolworth's lunch counter in Greensboro had ignited an indignation while black pride lit like a fuse across the South. North Carolina A & T State University freshmen Franklin McCain, Ezell Blair, Jr., Joseph McNeil and David Richmond—all on academic scholarships—inked themselves forever in history books by bravely walking into the downtown Woolworth's and sitting down at the segregated lunch counter.

Only in the South were black patrons prohibited from sitting at lunch counters. This particular Woolworth's had a separate blacks-only stand-up counter, but only whites were allowed to sit at the regular counter. Of course, African-Americans were welcome to purchase merchandise at the store any time they pleased.

These four students had had enough. Within a week, their righteous indignation had spread to hundreds of students, mostly black, throughout North Carolina. Like an itch that wouldn't be satisfied, college students across the Deep South began scratching at the humiliation of segregated lunch counters, bus stations, theaters, water fountains and bathrooms with fervor.

I was nervous that April afternoon as I walked the protest line with hundreds of students from Shaw's campus to downtown—but I refused to be afraid. We had taken careful precautions as we trained ourselves to disobey the law with the blessings of Dr. King, our teachers, our pastors and even some attorneys and elected officials.

On February 10, 1960, Aaron Johnson and fellow Shaw University
students begin protesting at lunch counters in downtown Raleigh,
N.C. Here students stage a sit-in at Woolworth's on Fayetteville
Street. Courtesy of the North Carolina State Archives; reprinted
by permission of The News & Observer of Raleigh, N.C.

On February 13, 1960, police arrest student protesters at Cameron Village shopping center in Durham, N.C. Johnson chauffeurs the protesters back and forth from campus while black Raleigh attorney George Greene bails them out of jail. Courtesy of the North Carolina State Archives; reprinted by permission of The News & Observer of Raleigh, N.C.

Shaw University students take turns picketing and protesting segregated lunch counters in front of downtown Raleigh dime stores, February 16, 1960. Courtesy of the North Carolina State Archives; reprinted by permission of The News & Observer of Raleigh, N.C.

For the past couple of years, Martin Luther King, Jr., had come to Raleigh several times and begun discipling seminary and college students toward the nonviolent movement. Of course, he was not the only one talking about these things. Our teachers and professors were already leading us students, especially us ministerial students, toward the non-aggressive protest mindset. By the time Dr. King gathered a small group of us seminary students together in a classroom at Shaw in 1959, we were ripe to hear his theology of deliverance. Our minds had been conditioned to receive the mission of integration. Dr. King simply came along at the right time and defined it for us. He made it a reality.

As I crossed Fayetteville Street that bright spring day toward the five and dime store, Dr. King had already plucked the fear from me. In its place he planted seeds of boldness, commitment and a hot, smoldering righteousness to put an end to segregation. My assignment was the Woolworth's dime store while another twenty students in my group walked on toward Walgreens and another group headed out toward Kress. Fayetteville Street in Raleigh was loaded with five and dime stores—all with segregated lunch counters.

Dressed in my best suit and tie that day, I was confident in my schooling in civil disobedience strategies perfected by Martin Luther King. I was determined to carry out my own peaceful resistance with dignity. I would not give in. I would not leave the lunch counter when asked. I would not oblige officers who tried to arrest me, and I would not retaliate either by my speech or actions when arrested. And I would be arrested. That was our goal—to fill up the jails and plug up the system and to draw attention to the evils of segregation. Anything less would be failure.

As I took up my place in line along with my fellow foot soldiers, a protest sign was passed to me that read, "How Do We Get Invited To Lunch?"

"Here ya'll go," said the girl who handed me her sign. "It's my turn to go in." She smiled but looked a little nervous. Dressed in her best skirt and blouse and a white felt ladies hat, the girl seemed determined to do her part. About thirty of the students holding signs passed them out to our new batch of picketers and began filing into the front double doors of Woolworth's, entering directly in front of several disgruntled police officers. I began to walk down the sidewalk carrying my sign behind the student in front of me. The thirty or forty of us walked up and down the line in front of the dime store like a zipper opening and closing.

Our strategy, as taught to us by Dr. King, was to try our best to keep white customers away from the lunch counters by intimidating them from even entering the store. And what was more intimidating to white people than a bunch of black folks in one place, dressed in our Sunday best, singing victory hymns and carrying signs that read, "Black is not a vice, nor is segregation a virtue," and "Temporarily closed. Why? Just a cup of coffee. Shame!" and "Do we eat today?" or "We pray for our southern brothers. No kidding."

The Montgomery bus strike in 1955 had been a relentless and dangerous instructor for Dr. King in the best tactics of civil disobedience. Combining those insights and the philosophies of King's hero, Mahatma Gandhi, the strategies of nonviolent demonstration were hammered out on the anvil of persecution and death threats.

According to Dr. King, a successful attack on segregation depended on several simultaneous battlefronts: purchasing boycotts, picketing, and then the sit-in itself. When all took place at the same time, the havoc they caused for law enforcement, city officials, and store managers and owners meant a better chance for our success.

That afternoon as I marched with my sign, I kept silently repeating Dr. King's Seven Steps to Nonviolent Actions in my head: "*Remain calm and gather information... Education—it is essential to inform others about your issues... Personal Commitment—eliminate hidden motives and prepare to accept suffering... Negotiation—use grace, humor, intelligence to confront... Direct Action imposes a creative tension into the conflict... Reconciliation—we seek to not defeat the opponent, but to seek his/her understanding, and... Final Preparation—prepare yourself to live each day using techniques of nonviolence.*"

At one point the undergrad picketing behind me tapped me on the shoulder. "Did you tie your own tie? Could you help me?" he asked.

"I can't believe you don't know how to tie a tie! Here, turn around and let me do it for you," I said as I stuck my protest sign between my knees. Other students in line had to walk around us as they continued their march in front of the store.

"I can't do it without a mirror," my friend said. Taking his wadded up tie from his suit coat pocket, he dangled it in front of me. "I can't believe how many people have shown up! Can you?"

Standing behind him with the picketers walking all around us, I placed his tie over his head and around his neck. "You want a big knot or a little knot?" I asked.

Our turn to become sit-in protesters came more quickly than expected. As my group prepared to pass off our signs to a new batch of picketers who had arrived to relieve us, the sudden shouting, cursing and movement from the front of Woolworth's had us all craning to see what was happening.

Police officers had pulled a black girl through the doorway of the dime store and practically heaved her—on the count of three—onto the already full paddy wagon. Her skirt was torn and her nose appeared to be bleeding. While tears were smudged over her face, she flashed a brave half-smile toward us.

As the paddy wagon doors slammed shut, I was just able to see her trembling hands return her white felt hat onto her head.

"Okay, it's our turn," I heard myself say to the group. Passing off our signs like batons, we started walking toward the front doors as an empty paddy wagon pulled up to the curb beside us.

Back in February, just a month before this protest, Dr. King and Reverend Ralph Abernathy had come to Raleigh and Durham to present another of their nonviolent workshops. Since the Greensboro Four had spurred the sit-in protests, students from Shaw University and St. Augustine College had joined forces in Raleigh and Durham and had organized several sit-ins of our own.

As a seminary student at Shaw, I had become a part of what was called the Intelligence Committee, which organized the protests.

On Wednesday, February 10, 1960, we started protesting both downtown drug stores and the F.W. Woolworth's out at Cameron Village—a model shopping and apartment center at the time on the 500 block of Woodburn Road. It was an exciting three days.

Then on February 12, Shaw University and St. Augustine students had the distinction of having the first protesters to be arrested in the state. On that particular day, I was one of the drivers. It was a cold, cold February day and not fit for anyone to be out.

The Intelligence Committee had decided to target the Cameron Village Woolworth's store for a protest demonstration that afternoon. My duties were to provide transportation for students from Shaw's campus to the shopping center. My $250 green Chrysler sure came in handy during this time. I don't remember the model and year of the car, but I do know it was old when I got it. However, it did what I needed it to do. It got me to my preaching assignments during my seminary years in one piece, so that was something.

The students I let off at Cameron Village were doing what we had normally been doing, picketing on the sidewalk in front of the stores and sitting down at the whites-only lunch counter and refusing to leave. But on this particular day, the vice president of Cameron Village, Mr. William Worth I believe his name was, had had enough. He flagged down a passing police officer and asked him to arrest the students—because he said they were loitering on private property. That's exactly what the officer did. He arrested forty-one students in all and had them paddy-wagoned to the county jail. All forty-one students were booked and fingerprinted for trespassing on private property.

Never in my wildest dreams had I thought that the same boy who had picked strawberries for five cents a quart would one day be a member of a college fraternity. But here I was—a bona fide member of Phi Beta Sigma. Our adult advisor was Dr. Greene, a professor of religion. I mention his name because his son, George Greene, became a lifesaver that day to the jailed students. George was one of the few young black attorneys in Raleigh and when the students were arrested, Professor Greene called his son for help.

Either Attorney Greene paid the students' bail set at $50 each or he rounded up enough supporters from churches, both black and white, and sympathetic businesses owners and city leaders to help pay the arrested students' bail.

It wasn't hard to find supporters who encouraged the sit-in participants. In fact, one of the largest and most progressive white Baptist churches in Raleigh publicly supported the sit-ins from their very beginning.

Pullen Memorial Baptist Church was the first white church I had ever attended. I started Sunday School there in my freshman year and was made to feel very welcome, first by Pastor E. McNeill Poteat, who was a strong theologian, and then by his successor, Pastor W.W. Finlator, a strong social activist.

It was at Pullen where I first heard Dr. King speak. He was invited to preach at Pullen Memorial several times throughout my college career. After the student arrests that February, it was Pastor Finlator who was quoted in *The News and Observer* as saying, "The demeanor of self-discipline of the students has been exemplary. The only unusual thing in their action is that they're behaving like American citizens. The students are doing in our day what we honored our forefathers for doing in their day and that is struggling for liberty. There is one exception—the students are doing it by absolutely peaceful means."

Pastor Finlator was also quoted in *The News and Observer* as saying, "The action of the students has been termed a 'sit-down strike.' This seems to be to be a misnomer. Actually, the students are sitting down for service, not for purposes of striking. The strike has been behind the counter... They will be less than American citizens never to challenge, never to protest such a deprivation of citizenship."

However he did it, Attorney George Greene spent the whole evening advocating for the students at the county jail and did not rest until all of the students were released. Attorney Greene was also quoted in the Raleigh paper as saying, "This incident is shameful and is a violation of the students' constitutional rights. We'll carry it to the highest court in the land if necessary."

That same night about ten p.m. after a basketball game between Shaw and St. Augustine College, about seven hundred of us met in the Shaw gymnasium. Can you imagine seven hundred students who didn't really care what the outcome of the ball game was? In fact, I have no recollection of who won the game. The important event that evening was meeting together to talk about what had happened that day. Those who were arrested were all present and treated like heroes. The Intelligence Committee helped the undergraduate students plan our next move. By now, almost every student on both campuses was committed to the cause. And if they weren't, what happened next cinched it for them.

Dr. Martin Luther King, Jr., came to Durham that following Tuesday, February 16, 1960. First he conducted a nonviolent workshop for about one hundred students from Shaw, St. Augustine, Winston-Salem Teacher's College, Bennett College and several others. That evening at a rally at White Rock Baptist Church, Dr. King spoke to more than twelve hundred people—after being run out of an F.W. Woolworth's store himself in Durham by the store manager that afternoon.

In his charismatic and unflappable manner, Dr. King stood up behind the grand pulpit at White Rock and bellowed, "Let's not fear going to jail! We must say that we are willing and prepared to fill up the jailhouses of the South…Our ultimate aim is not to humiliate the white man but to win his understanding…with a little song on your lips keep saying we just want to be free!"

We just want to be free… We just want to be free.

Anticipation of what was coming next that April afternoon on Fayetteville Street made my insides flutter like a rollercoaster ride. Failure was not an option. And I knew that whatever happened next, our lives, my life, would be changed forever.

As my group of students walked through the large glass front doors of F.W. Woolworth's, the first thing I noticed was the huge sign posted just inside that read, "Lunch Counter Closed in the Interest of Public Safety." A white student from the University of North Carolina walked past me and started toward the lunch counter—ignoring the sign.

Another one of our strategies was to use white students who were sympathetic to the struggle to gain us entry to the counters. Once a white student sat down and the wait staff started to serve him, the black students would join him.

As I glanced toward the white student who was now placing his order, I couldn't help but notice the long line of dropped lighting just above the lunch counter. At least the lights were still on. Sometimes, the management would try to intimidate students and make the situation even more menacing by killing the lights and making us sit in the dark.

As I sat down next to the undergrad whose tie I had tied earlier, twenty or thirty other students joined me. At first, it was so quiet you could have heard the soda fountain drip. Looking out the large plate-glass window, I could see the picketers marching up and down the sidewalks with their signs.

Looking straight at the waiter in front of me I said, "I'd like to order, please." The waiter I spoke to was leaning up against the prep counter with his arms crossed over his white apron. His white paper cap pushed back on his head gave him that boy-next-door look. He didn't acknowledge me. The three other waiters behind the counter weren't moving toward their customers either.

"I'd like to order, please," I repeated.

After a long moment of silence, the waiter pushed himself from the prep counter and stepped in front of me. "All we have today is soup," he said.

"Fine. That'll be just fine. I'll take soup." I was surprised. I had not counted on this response.

My waiter slowly smiled at me and said, "Hot soup coming right up."

I felt my stomach knot up like a giant, spiky pretzel. Nervously licking my lips, I started looking around. Several police officers had walked up near the lunch counter and were now standing behind us. The waiter had his back turned to me as he began dishing out my soup. Something was not right. I could feel it in my bones.

"Here ya are, boy. Some nice, hot soup!" Before I could move out of his way, the waiter splashed the bowl of soup directly in my face. My eyes started burning as the salt, pepper and other ingredients seeped under my eyelids. My face blistered up in seconds. I fumbled for the napkin dispenser but found it empty. Behind me, the officers were laughing. Never leaving my stool, I yanked off my suit coat and tried wiping my face with its lining.

"We don't serve niggers here, boy!" shouted the waiter. "Now git outta here!"

Then someone I could only suppose was the store manager walked up behind me and yelled, "The lunch counter is closed, nigger. All of you get out!"

None of us moved.

Taking a deep breath I sat up as straight as I could, placing my hands firmly on the white Formica counter. My burnt face felt like it was shrinking and sizzling off my cheekbones. My shirt was stinging and sticking to my chest like a horde of angry bees. And if I had let it, my heart would have probably jumped straight through my soiled shirt and rolled under the stool I was sitting on.

Some of the soup had also spilled on my thighs, but I wouldn't dare touch them or pull at my pants leg. I refused to give my persecutors the satisfaction of seeing any more of my discomfort than possible. My waiter stepped back like a proud rooster and once again leaned on the prep area. Behind him the orange juice dispenser was stirring the pulpy liquid as it sloshed around its plastic dome. The chrome milkshake machine stood gleaming by his side, mocking me with its silence.

"Okay, that's enough now. You boys need to move on out. Ya'll made your point. Now move!" barked one of the officers from behind me.

Again, no one moved.

"Don't make us do it the hard way. Move! Now!"

"I'm sick and tired of being sick and tired." When forty-five-year-old civil rights activist Fannie Lou Hamer, a field representative for SNCC, spoke those words later in 1962, she voiced the sentiments of every weary civil rights foot soldier in America. Even though she had not yet spoken those words by my seminary years, they were gushing through my veins as the police officer, store manager and my obliging waiter glared at me with enough hatred to poison the air for decades.

Had it only been a few days before that I had sat on the second row at Pullen Memorial Baptist Church and listened to the inspiring words of Dr. Martin Luther King, Jr.? It seemed like a hundred years ago that he and Ella Baker, Ralph Abernathy and several other notables from the Southern Christian Leadership Conference, CORE, Fellowship of Reconciliation, the National Student Association, Students for a Democratic Society and the National Association for the Advancement of Colored People stood before us and inspired us by saying, "Segregation is wrong because it assumes God made a mistake."

It was those heroes who came to Shaw's campus on Easter weekend, April 15-17, 1960. Baker, executive secretary to the Southern Christian Leadership Conference, and Dr. King had organized a three-day nonviolence workshop to help student protesters get ourselves organized. It was three days that propelled the course of my life.

Vernon Malone, J.C. Harris and I maneuvered our way toward the front of the Pullen Memorial Baptist Church sanctuary. It was Friday evening on the first day of the workshop—a day highly charged with protests, arrests and injuries.

"Are you sure Jeremiah is alright, Aaron?" asked fellow seminary buddy J.C. Harris. A few student protesters had gotten hurt earlier in the day and had quickly become local heroes.

"Yes. I talked with him just a while ago. He got shoved around this afternoon quite a bit, but he's okay," I said.

"That student from Colgate-Rochester got the brunt of it from what I hear. I think they said he got seven stitches in all," added Vernon, another friend and Shaw Divinity School student.

"Punched right across his chin, I think. It didn't matter that he was white and not even from here; it was just that he was protesting for our side that made that other boy so mad. I guess if someone disagrees with you, violence doesn't know color or state lines," I said.

"Or nationality lines. Jeremiah Walker is from Liberia," said Vernon.

"Black is black, my friend," I said. Finding three spots right in front on the second row, the three of us wiggled our way into the pew, making several students scoot and shuffle to make room for us. The church was just about full with students and workshop participants from twelve states and nineteen northern colleges—all primed to be inspired.

From what I remember, Ella Baker had to convince Dr. King that coming to Shaw during the sit-in demonstrations was a good idea. Once committed, Dr. King drained SCLC's meager funds by providing eight hundred dollars to finance the conference for student sit-in leaders. Ms. Baker, in a letter signed by herself and Dr. King, promised students that they would be heard as she said, "Understanding your desire for independence, the call to conference states that although 'adult freedom fighters' will be present for counsel and guidance, the conference will be youth centered." It's funny now when I think about it because Dr. King, the most prominent adult to attend that weekend, was only thirty-one years old at the time. I was twenty-seven.

As the three of us settled in our seats, a hush came over the sanctuary as our speakers walked up on the podium. In front of us sat Ms. Baker, Dr. King, Rev. Abernathy, Rev. Fred Shuttlesworth from Birmingham, Alabama and a few others. Dr. King's face was already burrowed deep with lines.

Only five years before, Dr. King and Rev. Abernathy had put their lives on the line upholding Rosa Parks's right to sit anywhere she wanted on a city bus. And now here they were looking back at us *kids*. We must have looked naïve and freshly plucked out of the fields. Yet they looked out over us like we mattered, like we were doing something important. My heart whirred like an engine. What would Mama say, I wondered? Of course, I hadn't told her anything about all of this. I didn't want her to worry, and I wasn't sure how Daddy would take it all. My father had seemed so content with the status quo back in Willard; I couldn't imagine that he would be pleased with me being part of such a stir in Raleigh.

Before Dr. King spoke, several speakers pumped us up like a spiritual rally. We sang several hymns and songs. "We Shall Overcome" was becoming our anthem as words were slightly changed to fit our weekend. The crowd in that church building that night fervently prayed together—reminiscent of a revival at Willard. All that was missing was Aunt Annie standing up and shouting, "Praise God! Glory Hallelujah!" then inviting us all to eat her teacakes.

Rev. Abernathy spoke right before Dr. King. I remember him saying, "The problem for the Negro is to lift the stigma of black. As long as the Negro is not free in Mississippi, he is not free in Africa, and vice-versa."

Being at Shaw those seven years broadened my world view considerably, but that night suddenly the world around me grew yet smaller. This time, I saw the world not as this global entity where thousands of miles separated us. Instead, I saw this new world filled with neighbors and friends. The blacks in Africa were fighting for the same thing we were. Gandhi died for the same thing I was picketing for on Fayetteville Street. Dignity, respect and understanding were universal. Without them, none of us could really be free.

When Martin Luther King, Jr., finally took his place in the pulpit, the crowd breathed as one. Our heartbeats became an organic metronome pounding out the powerful rhythm of equality and liberty.

"This is an era of offensive on the part of oppressed people," began King. He encouraged us to organize, to strategize for victory and to be ready to sacrifice for the cause of integration. "We are in an era in which a prison term for a freedom struggle is a badge of honor!"

I sat in my seat mesmerized as any fear I harbored faded away. Dr. King praised the student who had received stitches from his arrest. He congratulated my friend, Jeremiah Walker, for his example of leadership under pressure. The room went wild when those two stood up before us—singled out by Dr. King. Spontaneously, the auditorium erupted into song. *"We shall overcome...."*

Across town that evening, the Raleigh City Council had called an emergency meeting and in a matter of fifteen minutes had passed a new city ordinance curbing sidewalk picketing over segregated lunch counters. The ordinance had been drawn up two months earlier after the first sit-in demonstrations in February, but it wasn't until that evening that the ordinance was quickly voted on and passed with three city council members absent.

The new ordinance, while supposedly enacted to protect picketers from bystanders, also severely limited picketers to only ten people at a time—a city ordinance that incensed students and made us even more determined in our civil disobedience fight.

The next morning on campus after Dr. King's rally, the air was sparked with electricity as two hundred or so students made our way toward Shaw's chapel. No one slept in this Saturday morning. We had important work to do. Ella Baker, at fifty-five, stood before the eighteen- to twenty-seven-year-old workshop participants and prodded her older freedom-fighter colleagues, saying, "The younger generation is challenging you and me, they are asking us to forget our laziness and doubt and fear, and follow our dedication to the truth to the bitter end."

James Lawson, a divinity student from up north who was proudly arrested at a Nashville sit-in protest only the month before, gave one of the keynote addresses. Lawson emphasized both the need for immediate direct action and the power of nonviolent resistance. His speech was so effective that "nonviolent" actually became part of the SNCC organizational name.

The students sitting in those chapel seats that Saturday morning discussed among themselves and our conference leaders the price tag on freedom such as jail sentences or injuries. We sat huddled together talking and singing. Finally at the end of the morning we had established a democratic, non-hierarchical, group-centered culture and structure.

Once the goal had been obtained, Dr. King sent us out on these words, "The greatest progress of the American Negro in the future will not be made in Congress or in the Supreme Court. It will come in the jails." With those words, the Student Nonviolent Coordinating Committee was born.

Later that Saturday evening at the Municipal Auditorium in Raleigh, after an afternoon of protests and arrests, we received the proverbial icing on the cake. Sitting on the floor just under the podium, J.C. Vernon and I listened with a crowd of approximately sixteen hundred students and community supporters as Dr. King set our hearts aflame.

The Negro in the United States is willing to match capacity to inflict suffering with our capacity to endure suffering The student sit-in demonstrations are a refutation of the idea that the Negro is satisfied with segregation. Such an idea is a cliché that insults integrity and intelligence . *Segregation is wrong* because it does something to the soul—it gives segregators a false sense of superiority, while it leaves the segregates with a feeling of inferiority…*Segregation is wrong* because it assumes God made a mistake… These students have made it clear that segregation is a cancer in the body politic…This sit-in movement has transformed jails from places of dishonor to badges of honor…through sacrifice we will be able to arouse the dozing conscience of the South… The eyes of the world are on the United States and the resistance to segregation…. these protests reveal a new sense of respect and dignity for Negroes…."

Walking home that evening, I felt like I had been born again. I felt like I had heard directly from God through Dr. King as he spoke about the beloved community—a community where all races would be treated equally. His message was the most powerful I had ever experienced. I felt myself fill up with conviction from toes to heart like a poured glass of cold, clear water.

After that night, my purpose was clearer than it ever had been. I knew I could not turn back. I lay in bed that night and prayed that God would give me a vision of what I could do personally, for the rest of my life, to help bring to pass the successful result of integration.

That Sunday at the Robertson Chapel Baptist Church, one of the churches that I pastored during my seminary years, my sermon was full of the call to let your voice be heard. I reported all I had experienced over the weekend and challenged my congregation to step up and be a part of the deliverance to freedom. I tried to show my church folk what Dr. King had shown me—our nation not as it was but what it could become with the help of God. I preached hard and long. Afterward, an older lady at my church told me she was "so tired of hearing about that civil rights!"

Maybe I did go a bit overboard that day, but I saw in that good woman something that I no longer felt but understood: fear. She was afraid. She was afraid of what would happen if the students persisted with their protests. Would her world change for the better or the worse? She was of the generation that was persecuted even more than my generation, and she wanted to leave well enough alone.

Her fears were real. Would there be a resurgence of lynchings across the South because of what the students had started? My parishioner was truly afraid to contemplate exactly what would be her own price tag of freedom, and it was a scary thought—one I had to answer for myself a week after Dr. King left campus.

At the Woolworth's counter, soaked in soup, I quickly glanced over at my classmates and saw that three of them had already been dragged off their stools onto the floor and that another one was being pulled through the dime store by his tie—the very tie I had helped him with only thirty minutes before. Another blow with the blackjack, this time a direct hit to my knee, left me reeling as the ranting officer succeeded in pulling me to the floor. My pants leg suddenly became soggy as pain ricocheted from my knee to my brain. As I struggled to stay conscious, I watched my own blood trail behind me as my captor roughly pulled me through the store.

Outside, I was thrown on the police wagon with thirty or forty other protesters. We were ferried across town to the fairgrounds to be held. To our jubilee, the city and county jails were already full of students protesting the inequality of segregation. It was a victory of sorts with the promise of an even greater victory soon.

At the fairgrounds we were shuffled into one of the exhibit buildings and joined more than one hundred others. We were held there for three or four hours as more protesters were arrested and joined us. During that time, we sang and prayed together. I'm assuming Attorney George Greene and other supporters were busy negotiating student releases all day. Once released, we were picked up in cars by community supporters and shuttled back to campus. The plan was to go right back out and do it all over again. It was quite a day.

My knee eventually healed. I still have the scar, my battle scar. Almost every time I touch it or look at it, I remember those early days. I see the young, weary, but hopeful face of Dr. King and the brilliant, encouraging smile of Ella Baker. I remember the youthful defiance of my friend Jeremiah Walker. So many faces come to me—Dr. Grady Davis, one of my religion professors standing on stage with Dr. King. George Greene looking weary but victorious. And then there are the faces of my friends, J.C. Harris, Vernon Malone and many, many others.

Although dime store lunch counters have pretty much disappeared from the American landscape, occasionally I do see a lunch counter-type arrangement in a café and can't help but remember the hard-fought victory of the past. I thank God He allowed me to play a small part—that I was allowed to live during such an exciting and critical time in our nation.

Fortunately or unfortunately, the exciting times were just getting started for me. A month before the formation of SNCC on campus, I got the call to my first full-time church—a small congregation in Fayetteville, North Carolina. In June 1960 I became a full-time minister. My time had come. It was my turn. The dream of Dr. King's "beloved community" was to be in my hands now and with others like me. But as Mount Sinai Missionary Baptist Church awaited the arrival of its new pastor, there was something I had to do first.

Part III: The Little Church on the Hill

TEN

It Begins

*M*id-morning on June 17, 1960, Mattie Miller and I were married by my friend and fellow seminarian, J.C. Harris, at his home in Wadesboro, North Carolina. It was a small, private ceremony without our parents or family in attendance. By mid-afternoon, we drove into the parking lot of Mount Sinai Missionary Baptist Church ready to begin my first full-time church work. When I say I started my ministry right after I got married, I mean right after I got married!

That evening the little church on the hill gave the newlyweds, Reverend and Mrs. Johnson, a reception and welcomed us to Fayetteville. We moved our meager belongings into the little white parsonage behind the church building and began our life together. Mattie found a job teaching in a colored school and began her career in education as I began my routine as pastor of Mount Sinai.

In six months time, at age twenty-five, I was appointed the youngest president of the Black Ministerial Association in Fayetteville. (It didn't take long to consolidate it with our White Ministerial Association.) The older black pastors had grown weary of the position and saw an opportunity to shift leadership to this newcomer who did not have as much at stake as they did. The BMA was charged with peaceful demonstrations and challenging the local political system. Almost immediately, I began leading small student protests into downtown Fayetteville. It didn't seem like I had missed a beat in the civil rights movement, transitioning from seminary student to pastor. Thus my "civil ministry" work began.

With the blessing of my parishioners, I began teaching and preaching about God's design for His own beloved community. I boldly sent out the call for freedom, liberty and salvation for all—black or white. To quote a little bit from the Apostle Paul, *"…whether slave nor free, we were made to drink of one Spirit." (I Cor. 12:13 NASB)*

Pastor Aaron Johnson begins his ministry at Mount Sinai Missionary
Baptist Church in Fayetteville, North Carolina, in June 1960.

Mount Sinai, while a small congregation, quickly became known throughout the region as the "civil rights church." Fayetteville's population at the time was 47,106, with 35 percent of the residents African-American. (Only Wilmington, Winston-Salem and Durham had larger percentages of blacks than Fayetteville.) This meant that one-third of the people in our city were being discriminated against due to their race. That was simply unacceptable.

Located across the street from the all-black Fayetteville State Teachers College (later renamed Fayetteville State University), Mount Sinai was poised to become the center of the movement in Fayetteville. Barred from gathering on campus, students crossed the street to our parking lot to organize. I gave the same instruction to them that I had been given by Dr. Martin Luther King, Jr., only months before on Shaw's campus.

The small church building's brick and stucco walls and modest steeple stood up on a hill looking toward the middle of town. As the handful of students gathered around the building, I was reminded of the way Moses must have stood above the Red Sea with his aching arms outstretched as our mighty God parted the waters toward freedom.

The students who gathered in that tiny parking lot in the fall of 1960 were growing inpatient for the waters of discrimination and segregation to part. I became their spokesman just as sure as the biblical Aaron of long, long ago, did for his people.

The college students mixed well with my parishioners, many of whom also took up the fight. Our protests were small, but the students were fearless as they walked side-by-side in rows with locked arms. Though nervous, they sang hymns of freedom and marched.

In the meantime, Dr. Martin Luther King, Jr., was intensifying his nonviolent integration mantra as the Freedom Riders were arrested, mobbed and beaten in bus terminals and highways in Alabama and Mississippi. As more and more of the students and my parishioners became engaged in the movement, Dr. King's influence continued to fuel my sermons and my community involvement. As crosses were burned on his lawn in Atlanta and his arrest record continued to climb, my determination to do my part continued to grow.

As civil disobedience grew in influence and success, it enraged the likes of Eugene "Bull" Conner, director of public safety of Birmingham, and Alabama Governor George C. Wallace. These two men became the poster children of bigotry and racism. Their hatred and resentment of African-Americans was aired on black-and-white television screens all over the nation. I watched in horror as law enforcement used fire hoses and police dogs on marching protesters, including children.

Yet, Fayetteville stayed the same, despite our efforts or what was happening nationally—segregated hospital floors, theaters, lunch counters and drinking fountains, as well as unequal employment and political opportunities.

Many of Mount Sinai's members were only a little bit older than myself. Our congregation's proximity to the college across the street and to Fort Bragg army base just a few miles down the road helped encourage the direction I felt my ministry and Mount Sinai's mission should take.

My work with the ministerial association had us canvassing the community helping blacks register to vote. We also kept encouraging qualified African-Americans to run for local and state government offices.

During those first couple of years, Mount Sinai grew as our pews began to fill up with those wanting to make a difference.

As soon as we arrived at Mount Sinai, Mattie became involved teaching Sunday School and singing in the choir. She also became a member of the Missionary Society. As First Lady of Mount Sinai Missionary Baptist Church, she was sought after for her wisdom and calm demeanor. As I marched, protested and hammered on the pulpit about activism, my wife began practicing her own brand of community involvement by extending her hand quietly to whoever needed her. We were on our way.

ELEVEN

The Big Little Church

*L*ike most young ministers, I imagine, I had no intention of staying long at my first church. It was a small church in a small town. My sights were set on something bigger. Fayetteville was like a book on a shelf that was being overshadowed by glossy bindings and the gold lettering of the other books. I kept having this vision of me behind the pulpit of the largest church in North Carolina. Dr. King had instilled in me a fiery desire to lead our people toward integration and equality. To do so, I felt God needed me in a bigger arena. While the small demonstrations with the college students were zealous, there simply weren't enough students participating to make a difference.

After two years as pastor of Mount Sinai, I decided it was time to move on. By the end of 1962, our country appeared to be embroiled in a full-fledged gang fight. Young African-Americans would no longer be held back because of their skin color or heritage. America was just as much our country and legacy as anyone with blue or green eyes. I felt I could no longer sit in this out-of-the-way town and work in a small church making only a small contribution to the cause. I was sure God was calling me to something bigger. It was time to go.

As I sat around the table one evening in the church's conference room, my five deacons stared a hole into my soul. They were elderly men and they had not taken my announcement to leave as good news.

When I came to Mount Sinai, the church was almost forty years old and had seen fourteen pastors pass through its doors. Because they were a small membership, Mount Sinai was only able to afford a minister right out of seminary and, like me, none of them planned on staying long—and didn't.

"Why do you want to leave, son?" asked the chairman of the deacon board.

"Well, I have all of my future in front of me, sir," I said. "There are things I want to accomplish for the Lord—things I can't do here." I sat straighter in my wooden folding chair and felt its slatted bottom dig into my thighs like the edge of a rocky cliff.

"What you want is a larger church, is it?" he asked.

"Yes, sir. Well, I think so." Fact is I wasn't sure what I wanted. "All I know is that I have this calling of God on my life," I blurted out, sounding a little like a teenager trying to convince his parents he was old enough to drive.

"I see," answered the chairman.

I had not been this nervous since I'd asked Mattie to marry me. Everyone in the room sat silent as these five sets of brown, deep-set eyes pinned me to my chair like nails.

Then the chairman spoke with a slow, steady voice. His face softened as he leaned toward me just so. "Young man," he said. "It's not how big the church is; it's how big the man is."

My heart was pounding as those words began to do what they were intended to do—dry up any arrogance trying to take root in me.

"Look around you, son. What do you see?" he asked. "Haven't you noticed that not a street in this here section of Fayetteville, the colored section, is paved? We're living on dirt roads in the city. There hasn't been a Negro elected official in this town in decades. Black soldiers just down the road at Fort Bragg, who are being trained to fight for this country's freedoms, are not even allowed to eat in the cafés here in town."

Leaning closer to me he spoke in almost a whisper, "And, in the middle of our city is a historic, hallowed site that sold our people as slaves, yet the mentality of the white folks here hasn't changed much since those days."

The deacon was referring to Fayetteville's historic Market House. It was built in 1832 on the site of the old State House, which was destroyed by fire in 1831. It was within the walls of the State House that the white citizens of North Carolina ratified the Constitution of the United States in 1789—proclaiming their own freedom of sorts. The second floor of the Market House was where the University of North Carolina was first chartered.

The Market House still sits in the center of the intersections of Green, Gillespie, Person and Hay streets. In the 1800s, white farmers and businessmen would gather at the Market House. The famous second-floor meeting room became the town hall, while below, underneath its prominent arches, farmers and businessmen sold meat, produce—and slaves.

Imagine what it must have looked like to shop under the rounded arches of that structure. Polite, Southern women with children underfoot carried baskets as they picked over fresh tomatoes and just-picked summer squash while center-stage, dark human flesh was being auctioned off to the highest bidder.

Today, only the whites in town still call it the Market House. To the rest of us, it is the *Slave* Market House. The clock tower still works and the bell in the cupola still rings at 7:30 a.m. for breakfast, 1 p.m. for dinner, and at sundown at 9 p.m., once the mandated curfew of the city. Whenever I'm downtown and hear those chimes, I silently pray for my brothers and sisters whose flesh was sold as that ancient bell tolled. There but for the grace of God go I.

I looked from man to man as the deacon spoke, and felt the meeting beginning to get away from me. It certainly wasn't going as I had planned.

"In my mind," the chairman continued, "this city is probably one of the most racist, segregated towns in North Carolina. Our people's souls are shriveling up thinking God has abandoned them. Their hurt is so loud that God's voice has been drowned out by their cries. And you think God is calling you somewhere else? Somewhere bigger? You actually think the Almighty needs you urgently elsewhere?"

It was true. Fayetteville was still just as segregated as it had been two years previous. Despite all of the marches and protests, nothing had changed really. Fayetteville schools were second-rate. Employment opportunities for Negroes in the area were pitiful, and housing for blacks was scarce and shamefully substandard.

Did I truly think that I had done all I could to spread the Good News of Jesus Christ to those hurting and aching for His righteousness—after only two years?

The chairman put his hand on my shoulder and repeated, "Pastor, it's not the size of the church that counts most. It's the size of the man."

By the time the meeting was over, my mind, heart and soul had taken a beating, but not by my board of deacons. Mount Sinai Missionary Baptist Church paid me forty dollars a week to be their pastor. For two years, I pocketed that salary and did my job—I thought. The words of Dr. King ran through my veins, but did God's?

The next day or so, I was driving around Fayetteville pondering what the deacons had said when I found myself in a section of the city not too far from our church building. I spotted a tiny house that had all the glass broken out of its windows and cardboard taped in their place. I pulled my car over and got out and walked up to the house. I knocked and was invited in by its occupants. To my horror, I found that the house had no floor or concrete foundation.

Standing on that dirt floor, the scales fell from my eyes and I saw Fayetteville, really saw the city and its people, for the first time. Everywhere I looked was poverty and hardship. Families only a few blocks from Mt. Sinai were lost, both emotionally and spiritually. How could I have missed them? I had been too busy marching, I guess.

A few days later, I met with my deacons again and with my hat in my hand, I asked them if I could stay. The chairman of the deacon board smiled and leaned toward me and said, "This here is a big, little church with the heart of compassion. Cast your net down here as our pastor and you'll also become the pastor to the entire community. There's work to be done, son."

He was right.

When Mattie and I first came to Mount Sinai, the little church building sat on a tiny parcel of land. As the houses around us came up for sale, the church began to buy them and either tear them down or renovate them into facilities we could use in our ministries.

In 1968, we built a new sanctuary on the hill and started Fayetteville's first daycare that was affordable for single parents. In 1971, when Mattie and I moved out of the parsonage behind the church building, we were able to expand the day school into that facility. We built a Family Life Center that year as well. And in the late '70s, we opened a hundred-unit low-to-moderate income housing development.

Mount Sinai and the Ministerial Association became tireless foot soldiers in voter registration. In 1968, only four thousand blacks were registered to vote. By 1972, more than 9,378 African-Americans were registered and ready to be counted among the decision-making citizenry of Fayetteville.

Through the years, Mount Sinai became the home church of state lawmakers, soldiers, educators, students, community leaders, small business owners, single parents, Fort Bragg employees, strong mothers and active fathers. These faithful members became strong voices with compassionate hearts who changed, and are still changing, our community. All of Mount Sinai's children were encouraged to get a college education and to graduate and become servants of God as bright lights in their chosen communities.

I did cast my net at Mount Sinai, for forty-five years. I have memorized every face by heart. We have been partners in our ministries and they have been my primary supporters my entire adult life. Whatever we have done, we did holding hands, holding our breath and taking first steps of faith together. I owe them so much. They gave Mattie and me all that was required and then some for a ministry for which I will never make an excuse.

TWELVE

1963 Protests

By the spring of 1963, our country was on the verge of a civil war. We had drawn lines on the pavement over race, religion and politics. In no era since Lincoln freed the slaves had the citizens of the United States punched and trash talked each other with such venom and hatred.

In April of that year, while in solitary confinement in a Birmingham jail, Martin Luther King, Jr., began feverishly scribbling in the margins of a newspaper and then on toilet paper his famous *Letter from a Birmingham Jail* proclaiming, "Any law that uplifts human personality is just. Any law that degrades human personality is unjust." His words ignited even more fervor for those of us marching and protesting for the cause. We no longer just wanted integration; we wanted desegregation for all schools. Don't close the black schools and bus the black children to white schools. Bus everybody! Upgrade the black schools and bus white students and teachers to them. Mix us up! Bring us together!

That spring, Fayetteville State Teacher's College was winding down its school year. Among the student enrollment of 1,122, many were restless and started meeting together to discuss strategies for protests. This demonstration committee consisted of Willis McLeod, Stanley Johnson, Roosevelt Davis, Sam Dove, Aaron Plymouth, Elijah Williams and James Herring among others. They had demands they wanted met before classes adjourned. The students were encouraged by their education but frustrated by it as well. The more they learned, the more they understood that if things did not change, their education would profit them nothing. They may earn a degree in administration, but they probably would never be hired as an administrator. They could study and work toward a career in business, but very few businesses would hire a black man, much less a black woman.

On May 18, 1963, more than two hundred students picketed on the sidewalks of downtown. Sears, J. C. Penney, The Capitol Department Store, Fleishman's Big Store, Belk-Hensdale Company, The Colony Theater, the Miracle Theater and the Broadway Theater all saw students walking in front of them with signs that read: "Integration Is Inevitable," "Hire Us Now," "Let's Crush Segregation."

The march started at Mount Sinai. Volunteers fed the students, prayed with them and offered security for them at the building once the protests were over. At one o'clock in the afternoon, the students were in front of their assigned stores, singing hymns and chanting. By five o'clock we had them back at the church, feeding them and congratulating them. However, the protest was not over for church members when the students went back to campus. We kept the building open all night as members took turns guarding the sanctuary. We didn't know if the town folk would try and retaliate in any way. But we wanted no burning crosses or burning sanctuary to mar the students' success.

While Mount Sinai embraced the students and their cause, not every black church and pastor did. A lot of our members were maids or yardmen in white households. Their bosses tried to get them to put pressure on their deacon boards to help get rid of their radical pastors. If they didn't, sometimes they would lose their jobs. This type of influence discouraged many ministers and pastors from participating in the protests or being public sympathizers of the students.

Four days later, more than one thousand students protested the closing of the ticket windows of downtown theaters. Fayetteville Police Chief Worrell, in an effort to stop the protests, shut down the stores and theaters so the students couldn't picket these segregated businesses. They picketed them anyway.

The next week, a negotiating committee of a few black ministers and black businessmen presented Mayor Wilbur Clark and the city council with the students' demands for the desegregation of all downtown theaters and restaurants and improved local job opportunities for African-American college students.

I wasn't on this negotiating committee. I was considered too radical, a foot soldier who organized and supported the students. I was even posting bail for them. "We've been waiting forever!" the students cried. "We want desegregation now!" they chanted. And I was right there with them.

By the college's graduation on June 2, the Fayetteville City Council had endorsed the students' major objectives. So, with the interruption of graduation and summer vacation, the students halted their protests with a wait-and-see attitude—hoping the negotiating committee had been successful. The *Fayetteville Observer* reported, "Calm Prevails in Racial Picture in Fayetteville."

A little more than a week later, with local theaters still segregated and restaurants still refusing to serve blacks, the college students who were still in town organized themselves. They added to their ranks vacationing high school and junior high students and the protests resumed.

On June 11, twenty-five local students were arrested, the first large-scale arrests of the protests. Several hundred miles away in Birmingham at about the same time, Governor George Wallace was refusing to allow two black students to register at the University of Alabama. President John Kennedy had to send in the National Guard to force the governor to back down. Unrest abounded.

Of course, those of us at Mount Sinai and other supporting churches were trying to get adults to join in the demonstrations to no avail. The students issued a statement: "The mayor's time has run out…"

The following day, on June 12, the students met at Mount Sinai as I helped them organize a sit-down protest in front of the segregated businesses in Fayetteville. The students sat just to the side of the doors of the businesses in groups of ten to twelve with their arms interlocked. Because they were on public property, the students were not arrested. Unfortunately, on this same day Medgar Evers, an NAACP worker, was brutally killed in Mississippi. Nerves were on edge.

The next day one of our college students, Willis McLeod, was arrested for assault. The charges were eventually dropped. However, McLeod proved to be quite the leader with five arrests under his belt that summer.

Then came the night of June 14. Most of the demonstrations so far had taken place during daylight hours. But there were segregated nightclubs and restaurants open in the evening that the students had not yet impacted.

Meeting at Mount Sinai, I helped the students work out a strategy. In order to get the demonstrators downtown quickly and to their protest posts, Dr. Thomas, pastor of Haymount Presbyterian Church, allowed the students to congregate on the church's property. Because of its close proximity to Hay and other main streets, Haymount's sanctuary would offer a haven if the students were threatened. With soldiers, Klan members and drunks out and about, we wanted to take every precaution to protect the students as much as possible.

At seven that night the demonstrations started as our buses waited behind Haymount Presbyterian. More than one hundred and fifty protesters showed up as sit-ins began. At about 8:30 p.m. the demonstrators headed toward city hall as a crowd of white onlookers followed and congregated around the corner on Green Street. The protesters and onlookers collided on Hay Street and exchanged insults and taunts. By 9:30 p.m. strained and fearful police officers began hurling tear gas canisters and bombs at the feet of blacks and whites as forty State Highway Patrolmen idled on the outskirts of town at the request of Mayor Clark.

In the chaos, those students who were not detained ran back to the buses behind Haymount and were shuttled back to Mount Sinai as quickly as possible. As they filled our small sanctuary, the tear gas from their clothing pushed into the room, replacing fresh air with the thick, gaseous smell of defiance. It was a Saturday night and by worship the next morning, members of Mount Sinai had to let the windows up and turn fans on to chase the smell out. But we had won. Our efforts broke the backbone of the city fathers as we filled up their jails. Forty-seven arrests were made that evening and an additional one hundred and forty arrests were made the next day. Our city leaders were finally ready to talk, for real.

The next evening, a tragic event spurred the city council to make haste in their negotiations with the students. Another NAACP leader was killed in Jackson, Mississippi.

"There will be blood shed on the streets of Fayetteville unless something is done immediately," warned Police Chief Worrell to the twenty prominent members of the community who huddled together on June 17.

On June 18, Governor Terry Sanford got in on the action as he delivered a radio and television address that called for the halt to all mass demonstrations. He called for black leaders to meet with him in Raleigh the following week to discuss racial concerns. I wasn't invited, but C.R. Edwards, our representative on the negotiating committee, was. The students and their adult advisors, me included, called for a moratorium on the demonstrations until we heard from Governor Sanford.

The blacks did not trust Mayor Clark, but they did trust Governor Sanford and President Kennedy. Sanford had open communication with the NAACP and called for goodwill from the whites. This became the early seed for Governor Sanford's Good Neighbor Council.

In response to Sanford's plea for goodwill, Mayor Clark quickly organized a Bi-Racial Committee with five whites and four blacks. However, no student demonstrators were invited to be a part of this committee—a handpicked group. The students thought they had been duped once again.

Enter Councilman J.W. Pate. As a member of the newly formed Bi-Racial Committee, Mr. Pate was a great influence for the good. He did not merely pay lip service to the protesters. Mr. Pate owned an integrated steak house in town and was one of the first to promote desegregation. He legitimately attempted to promote integration and would eventually influence Mayor Clark to take more concrete steps in meeting the students' demands.

J. W. Pate worked tirelessly behind the scenes to negotiate a satisfactory conclusion to the protests. He went from house to house talking to community leaders, urging calmer heads to prevail. He even came to my house to talk. The students trusted him. Most of the blacks in the community trusted him. I trusted him.

By the time Governor Sanford met with the 159 black leaders from around the state on June 25, President John Kennedy had submitted the civil rights bill to Congress. The students waited for word from the governor, but when nothing substantial came out of that meeting except the announcement of the formation of the Good Neighbor Council and a call for students to negotiate instead of demonstrate, student demonstrations resumed on June 28.

By July 9, the demonstrations took on a new urgency as black soldiers and some whites joined the demonstrations. Their commander in chief, President John Kennedy, called them to action by noting that if blacks could serve in the military, they should be able to attend a public institution and be served at a restaurant.

We were cooking now. On July 12, more than two hundred protesters met at the Slave Market House where I gave a brief speech about unity. I prayed for nonviolence, but I knew that the soldiers before me were trained for violence. They had put their careers on the line to join the students. I had a lot of respect for them, but I was concerned that maybe the demonstrations would take on a more aggressive nature with their involvement. Their signs were certainly a little more militant: "First Korea—Now Fayetteville!" they said.

By July 19, the Bi-Racial Committee reached an agreement with the local branch of the NAACP, finally ending the student demonstrations. They initiated a Five-Point Plan that stated:

- The Bi-Racial Committee will become a continuing steering committee.
- The committee will report weekly to the local NAACP, the city council, the mayor and the community.
- Effort will be made for increasing employment of blacks in local department and variety stores.
- Demonstrations will cease provided that none of the businesses return to segregated or discriminatory practices. In such cases, the Bi-Racial Committee and the NAACP negotiating committee will be given a reasonable opportunity to solve the situation prior to demonstrations being renewed.
- No city or county agency will take action against employees who participated in this movement for human rights.

It was a start. By the time the college's fall registration rolled around, all four theaters in town and the majority of Fayetteville's restaurants, hotels and motels had been desegregated. The Cumberland County Health Department removed all segregation signs, and Cape Fear Valley Hospital integrated its dining room.

Celebrations didn't last long. On September 15, 1963, in Birmingham, Alabama, four young black girls were killed when a bomb exploded in a church basement. A little more than two months later, President John F. Kennedy was killed by an assassin's bullet. The world was still going crazy.

Our little victories lightened our load for a short while. But they were victories all the same.

THIRTEEN

The March Ends

One of the tactics the whites used to discredit the local protests was their claim that it was just outside agitators who caused the problem. Get rid of them and everything would be alright. One of the things that gave the Fayetteville protests in the early sixties their success was that we never called in national leaders to help us.

Outside help would have just muddied the water for us in Fayetteville. While we adhered to the nonviolent teachings of Dr. King during our protests, we practiced what Ella Baker would have called a "group-led movement." We had no one leader, especially a national leader. We knew our issues better than anyone and knew how to solve them. All of our agitators were locally grown. The city had to eventually address our demands because we weren't going away—we lived there.

The Monday after the city council and Mayor Clark finally announced there would be integration in our downtown businesses, I received a call from the pastor of St. Luke's African Methodist Episcopal Church, W.T. Holland, Sr. He asked me to go with him to the lunch counter at Woolworth's and be the first blacks who were served.

"Reverend Johnson, it's time for the healing to begin. We must patronize those establishments that dropped their segregation ways."

Pastor Holland was right. We had been part of the agitator movement and now we had to lead our black community to be a part of the healing movement.

"I'm with you," I said. That morning when we walked into Woolworth's together, I felt good. We had won a war as sure as any soldier who invaded the ranks of the enemy. As I sat down and ordered my breakfast, I had flashbacks of another time and another day. The memory of scalding soup running down my face caught my breath. But this time, it was different. No police officers stood over me. The waitress behind the counter smiled and took my order. She was a little nervous, but so was I.

Those were the best scrambled eggs I'd ever eaten. My coffee ran through my veins with pleasure and my stomach was not tied in knots nor my heart filled with fear. It was just breakfast, but I was eating it at the top of Mt. Everest! The climb was hard and deadly, but well worth the moment.

As we sat over our coffee, we chatted like any human beings would. "You know, Pastor, these businesses that desegregate are going to have a falling away of their white customers for a while. We caused the problem; now we must help fix it," I said. I could not live with myself if our actions caused a shopkeeper to lose his livelihood or a business owner his business.

"Dr. King was right; the end of fighting for moral right is redemption—for us and for them. We must forgive. And as Jesus said, our righteousness must exceed that of the Sadducees and Pharisees if heaven is to be our home."

We began immediately encouraging the black community to go in droves to help the lunch counters, restaurants, and theaters to stay open. We wanted no one to lose from this moral victory. Of course, this took some time. Whites were leery of going downtown now. A handful stayed angry at the desegregation efforts and simply refused to patronize any business that allowed blacks. But eventually, most returned when the integration finally stopped being perceived as a "street issue" and became an economic one. The president of the United States and our Capitol Hill lawmakers were finally behind integration. And when Secretary of Defense Robert McNamara issued Department of Defense Directive 5120.36 on July 26, 1963, the coffin was sealed on segregated practices. The directive read: *"Every military commander has the responsibility to oppose discriminatory practices affecting his men and their dependents and to foster equal opportunity for them, not only in areas under his immediate control, but also in nearby communities where they may live or gather in off-duty hours."*

Business owners knew that if their establishments became "off-limits" to military personnel in this heavily military town, they were doomed. They were forced to either accept integration or close their doors.

After the 1963 protests, the local black community leaders formed the Unity Council. We wanted to build a strong organization from the ground up, comprised of low-income people who had no voice, sorority and fraternity organizations from the college, pastors and other church members and citizens. Once the merchants, with our help, were able to get their businesses back on their feet, the Unity Council turned to the next pressing issue—housing.

Federal funds were being made available to tear down old, substandard housing and replace it with new, affordable construction. Fayetteville was late getting into this program. While they formed the Community Redevelopment

Commission, nothing substantial was happening. At least it wasn't happening fast enough. We had families living on dirt floors. We had homes without electricity or running water.

What the redevelopment commission finally did was tear down those old useless houses and move the people out—thus destroying one of the oldest communities in the area. The city council made federal funds available for those folks to buy houses in low-income white neighborhoods, while the whites themselves were then able to move out into the suburbs. Very few of those federal funds went toward new housing for blacks.

Once I figured that out, I was whopping mad. So the Unity Council devised a plan to disrupt the city council's meetings. We wanted new houses built back in the neighborhoods that had lost people. Barren lots now dotted the community around Mount Sinai as a "white flight" relocation pattern emerged. It was segregation all over again.

Our strategy was to allow the Pledge of Allegiance but then not let the council proceed with their agenda until they addressed our issues—issues that were always pushed to the end of the meeting and never given adequate time.

Finally, during one of these disruption tactics, a council member had had enough. Beth Finch, who had always dealt respectfully with the black folks in Fayetteville, looked directly at me and said in a loud voice, "Reverend Johnson, this city has ten acres of land on Murchison Road, just down from Mount Sinai Baptist. I challenge you to get your church to buy that land to put some apartments on it for the poor people in Fayetteville and help build that neighborhood of yours back up."

The group around me settled down a bit. We were taken by surprise. No one had ever seen Mrs. Finch raise her voice like this. "All you know how to do is march, march and scream and holler! I challenge you to find a way for your church people to buy that land and put some apartments on it. Do some real good for a change."

By this time several officers had entered the meeting room and circled the protesters. I tell you what, I got so mad! It looked to me like she was trying to belittle me before my peers. And having the whole police department surround us like this was too much. I could have spit.

Beth Finch went on to tell me that Mount Sinai could form a nonprofit 501(c)(3) organization and apply for federal loans itself. I didn't know this, but I didn't like having it pointed out by this woman.

When I got home that night, I realized that the lady was right. It was time to take matters into our own hands. We could march around and disrupt all we liked, but why not actually educate ourselves on what was available to us? Why should we always be depending on others to get things done? That was when it suddenly hit me: God was trying to get my attention and I wasn't having it. I was being so willful that He had to resort to some old tactics. While God didn't speak to me through the mouth of a donkey like he did in Biblical times, He did decide to use the astuteness of a good but exasperated white woman to shake some sense into me.

My rabble-rousing and marching and protest days came to an abrupt end. A page was being turned for me with Beth Finch's challenge. It was time to switch gears. No longer did I just want our black community to survive; hadn't we already proven we could do that? I wanted us to achieve. We not only should want to ride in the front of the bus; we should want to own the bus. Wasn't it Dr. King who had told us we had to run faster than the man in front?

I became convinced that African Americans in our community had to try harder. We had to achieve for ourselves now. We had to break the inferiority complex that blacks had. Our preaching and teaching had to change. Our children could no longer complain about segregation, so they needed to get into their schoolbooks and achieve, to reach their highest capacity. Liberation theology became my mantra, to build self-worth, self-esteem and encourage achievement.

I never marched again—even when Martin Luther King, Jr., led his march on Washington, D.C. that August. I still wanted to be part of the solution, but it was time for my tactics to change. I stopped magnifying the problems with my unruliness, as Beth Finch had accused me of, and started to dedicate myself to the best solutions for all of the beloved community.

As for Beth Finch's challenge to me that fateful evening—I did apply for nonprofit status. It was our Mount Sinai Day School Foundation that allowed us to offer affordable childcare to parents.

Our second nonprofit organization, Mount Sinai Homes Foundation, charted our course toward offering quality housing to the needy. However, this one was a thirteen-year battle. No one wanted to give us funding.

Finally, one day I called Senator Jesse Helms—what could it hurt—and explained to him our problem. I brazenly asked him if he could help us find a bank that would loan us the money. This was on a Friday. That next Tuesday, I received a call from the chairman of finance of a South Carolina bank. He asked me what I needed. And in no time, we received a U. S. Department of Housing and Urban Development loan for $1.5 million. We were able to purchase that ten-acre parcel from the Fayetteville Redevelopment Commission on Murchison Road just down from the church building. In 1976, Mount Sinai Homes opened one hundred apartments for low- to moderate-income families.

I heard the voice of God through Beth Finch. He brought us together at just the right time, at the right place, at a period in my life when my heart was most open. It was that pinpoint thing again, and it was the beginning point for the next thing God was preparing me for.

Part IV: GNC, KKK, TBPP and The Ten

FOURTEEN

April 4, 1968

*T*ragedy can mark the soul and burrow a permanent jagged rut through your heart that never heals properly. If you live long enough, your life won't be spared this marking. On Thursday, April 4, 1968, such a wound was seared into my heart and into the core of our nation.

Early that evening, I was in my car on the way to a Unity Council meeting at Friendship Baptist Church in Fayetteville. My radio was on but I wasn't really tuned in to it. I was tired from an already long day, and my mind was going over the issues that this civic and church gathering was going to address. A group of us had been meeting regularly to confront issues of the African-American community for months now. And ever since Dr. Martin Luther King's March 18 fiasco in Memphis concerning the rights of black sanitation workers, we in Fayetteville had become engaged in the same controversy.

Earlier in February, more than 1,300 sanitation workers in Memphis had formed a union, which the city refused to acknowledge. The city turned a deaf ear to the union's demand for a 10 percent wage increase and benefits and dismissed their allegations of racial discrimination. Left with no other viable options, the garbage collectors went on strike and encountered several skirmishes with law enforcement, causing the city of Memphis to bring an injunction halting the demonstrations.

Many of us should remember those haunting photographs of sober-faced demonstrators. Walking in rigid straight lines, the protesters carried signs that read, "I AM A MAN." Those photos still haunt me as I remember grown men pleading to be recognized as humans. Could a plantation slave have felt any more humiliated? On one side of the demonstrators were National Guardsmen pointing fixed bayonets at them, and on the other side of them were long rows of armed tanks gating the men in like cattle.

On March 18, 1968, King and his aides organized what was supposed to be a nonviolent march through the streets of Memphis with more than six thousand protesters joining them. Unfortunately, also joining them was a band of black youths carrying signs that read, "BLACK POWER IS HERE." Before the march had even gone three blocks looting, instigated by those young militant protesters, broke out. By the end of the march, a sixteen-year-old boy had been killed, 62 wounded, and more than 280 arrested. Dr. King was devastated and vowed to return to Memphis to try and rectify what had happened. His return date was April 3, 1968.

As I pulled into the parking lot of Friendship Baptist that evening, a voice came on the radio and sliced through my thoughts: *"Dr. Martin Luther King, Jr., has been pronounced dead at St. Joseph's Hospital in Memphis, Tennessee, from a gunshot wound to the head."*

The rip of my heart had me clutching my chest. My mentor. My teacher. My hero was gone.

Our Unity Council meeting lasted only a few minutes as we all mostly wanted to get home to our families. But when I looked at my friend, Rex Harris, and he looked at me, we both understood what we had to do.

Marion "Rex" Harris was a legend in Fayetteville. As the only black businessman in the city to own and operate a million dollar business, he had great influence among African-Americans. His reputation was won by fire—literally. Rex was retired military and had bought a dry cleaners on Bragg Boulevard—a section of town that supported no other black businesses. Securing a contract from Fort Bragg was a huge coup for Rex. However, the day he signed that contract, the Ku Klux Klan burned a cross on his property and burned his business down to the ground. The FBI conducted an investigation, but of course, no arrests were made. Within a matter of months my friend bravely rebuilt his dry cleaners on that same property.

Rex and I decided that we couldn't go home that night—not if there was a chance that our city would join the other cities across our state and nation already starting to implode. Upon hearing the news of Dr. King's death, angry blacks and whites took to the streets and, in a chaotic rage, lashed out with looting, riots and burning buildings.

"Rex, we've got to protect Dr. King's beloved community," I said as we walked out to our cars. "I sat directly in front of him at Shaw and heard him with my own ears. He abhorred violence. We can't let this happen."

"We'll do what it takes to keep Dr. King's life's work from being desecrated by deadly knee-jerk violence, my friend," he answered. "Whatever it takes."

Rex and I agreed to meet at my house behind Mount Sinai within the hour. We were both dressed in suits for the Unity Council meeting, but we knew that most blacks in our community would not respond to us favorably if we wore ties. Our people had no confidence in blacks in suits. So, in jeans and plain shirts we pulled out of my driveway and began looking for those wandering the streets.

"What are we going to do when we see some folks?"

"I guess we'll just stop and try to talk to them. Make them see that violence isn't the answer." I tried to sound more confident than I was truly feeling.

"What about the police? What if they start getting heavy-handed?"

"We'll just have to watch and see what they do and try to reason with calmer heads," I answered.

At that point, the reports coming over the radio were already saying it was believed that only one man was responsible for King's murder. I didn't believe that for one minute. No black man did. To be honest, we felt it highly credible that the police could have been involved. It was a known fact that the FBI had tapped King's phone in recent months.

As Rex and I pulled out from my driveway, we looked at each other like bewildered wide-eyed children. "Who can we trust?" he asked.

"No one," I said as I stepped on the accelerator and pointed the car toward the part of town where we thought the problems would be. "Look for groups gathering," said Rex, "especially if they are standing out *in* the street."

"Right. If we see white folks out walking the sidewalks, we better warn them. The last thing we need is for one of them to get hurt." My throat tightened. "God be with us!"

Our first stop was in a neighborhood where some black teens had gathered on the sidewalk. Pulling the car over to the curb, we both took a deep breath. I don't know about Rex, but I started praying the minute I turned the engine off.

When we got out of the car, the youths turned toward us. "How ya'll boys doing?" asked Rex as we walked toward them.

"Alright," said one, mumbling under his breath.

"What are ya'll doing here?" I asked, looking from one youth to the other.

"Nothin'. Just talkin'," mumbled another.

"Ya'll heard about Dr. King, I suppose?"

"Yessur."

"You know, boys," I said, "Dr. King taught non-violence and we would not be honoring him if we did anything to jeopardize that message here tonight. You know what I'm saying?"

The teens lowered their heads and kicked at the sidewalk.

"Before it gets too late, why don't ya'll get on home? We want no trouble tonight in Fayetteville. It wouldn't be right," said Rex.

The boys didn't look at us but just turned and started walking away. "Anybody need a ride home?" I asked.

They muttered something back that I assumed meant no. Rex and I looked at each other. And so the long night began.

At about midnight, we had just persuaded a gathering of angry black men to go on home when a gang of Negro boys came running toward us as we started to get back into Rex's car. We had driven my car until the gas ran low; then we drove back to my house and got Rex's.

"Hey! Hey! Can we borrow ya'll's car?" one of them shouted. The boys were sweaty and out of breath.

"What do you need it for, young man?" asked Rex.

"We just need it for a while," the boy answered, looking nervously behind him.

Uneasiness crept in around us. The boys had that wild look of desperation. And I knew it wouldn't take much to turn this situation to a whole other level of trouble.

"They's stuff we need to do tonight. Dr. King's been murdered, man!"

"Yes, he has and the best thing we can do for Dr. King and his family is to go home and take care of our own," I replied, quickly assessing how many steps I was away from the car door.

"They killed him, man! Those honkies killed him!"

"But they haven't murdered his mission," I said. "Think about it! Dr. King gave his life calling us to nonviolent ways."

The boys closed in around us, shaking their heads like wild horses while their tennis shoes pawed at the cement.

"We'd darken his memory if we were to do something that he'd given his life preaching against, wouldn't we?"

The boys kept shifting around us. I knew they weren't hearing a word I was saying. Their ears and hearts had been slammed against any kind of reason. I had seen that look before, way back in Willard, where I remembered faces of frustrated Negroes who'd watched as the meager coins were counted out in their hand for a week's labor—short of what was promised. Or on a Negro who had kept walking down the street with spit from some white man still stuck in his hair. I knew that look. It was the sorrowful scowl of injustice and stolen dignity. Once those feelings crept into your blood stream, well, they could turn to poison and darken hearts quicker than spilled ink.

We knew we were in trouble. As the car keys dangled from Rex's fingers, several long minutes passed. The boys kept looking from one to the other waiting for one of them to make a move on us. However, the good Lord was watching over us that night. The boys' bravado and their frenzied anger just hadn't built up enough. Suddenly one grunted out, "Aw, come on! Leave these Uncle Toms alone. We'll find another car!" Spitting at our feet, the boys ran off down a shadowed street.

About two in the morning, we came across a single white man walking down the street in an area that could be trouble. "What is he doing out here?" I said.

"I don't know, but it can't be good," answered Rex, who was already pulling his car over to the side of the road toward the gentleman.

I rolled my window down and leaned my elbow out the opening. "Sir, can we help you?"

The white man looked at me, and then Rex, but kept on walking.

"Sir, I don't think you should be out walking here alone. It's not safe. Could we help you?" I knew full well there wasn't any white man in this area about to ever get in a car with two blacks.

Suddenly he bolted away from us as we tried to follow him with our car. Fortunately, he ran up into a run-down yard not far up the road and went inside a house with closed shades. Rex and I drove on. "We're putting our lives on the line here, you know that," I said, turning to my friend.

"I know. It isn't the first time for either of us, is it?"

Not much else needed to be said. We both knew we'd do whatever it took to keep our city from burning to the ground, even if it meant giving up our own lives.

All night, we drove around Fayetteville dispersing groups of blacks and whites. The police followed us at times, but to our surprise, they basically left us alone. By three or so in the morning there weren't too many people left out. At five a.m. the streets started coming alive again as folks headed out to work.

Not one single building was looted or burned that night and Fayetteville lost no lives.

I wish I could honestly report that we were able to stop all violent acts that dark April night. We found out later those boys who wanted our car did find one. As they drove toward Fayetteville's public library, a homemade bomb detonated in their car. Fortunately for them, they weren't very good at bomb making and the only destruction was to the car.

In another incident, a couple of white Fort Bragg soldiers were walking together on Robeson Street when a station wagon stopped near them and a group of Negro youths jumped out. One of the soldiers got caught and was beaten with a chain and belt buckles. He was treated and released by Womack Army Hospital a short time later.

It had been a long, tense night. By the time Rex dropped me off at my house, the sun was beginning to climb overhead. As I unlocked my front door, I thanked God for the blessing that no smoky clouds hovered over Fayetteville that morning and that the citizens of our city would not be waking up to the charred stench of burnt dreams.

When my head finally hit my pillow, lying next to Mattie, I felt God's hand on my chest. Without warning, I began to weep and thanked Him for the miracle that no Fayetteville mother lost a child that night, nor did any child lose a father to senseless anger. One loss for the day was heartbreaking enough, as my prayers turned to the widow and her four children in Atlanta.

I awoke on Friday in hell. Our state and our country had gone mad. While President Lyndon Johnson had called an emergency meeting at the White House with top Negro and government leaders, a few blocks from the Oval Office, Black Power militant Stokely Carmichael was spouting threatening rhetoric at a news conference.

"Black people know that their way is not by intellectual discussions," Carmichael raged. "They know they have to get guns. Our retaliation won't be in the courtroom but in the streets of America."

While Rex Harris and I, and a few others, had stayed up all night trying to keep the matches and rocks from destroying our city, Mr. Carmichael had roamed the streets of Washington, D.C., leading hundreds of demonstrators on a fifteen-block violent spree.

My heart continued to crumble as reports filtered in about violence and death. From Washington, D.C. to New York City to Detroit, Chicago, Nashville, Memphis, Tallahassee and beyond—riots, looting, arson, shootings, beatings and murder were devouring America's inner cities.

In North Carolina, Governor Dan Moore had his hands full ordering National Guardsmen to various cities. In Raleigh, a state of emergency was called after a window smashing and rock-throwing demonstration by Shaw University students erupted overnight. In Charlotte, firebombs and looting kept law enforcement busy. In Greensboro and Winston-Salem, rock and bottle throwing and a sniper shooting jarred the cities. By Saturday, violence and arrests had been reported in Goldsboro, Greenville and Weldon. By Sunday night, guerrilla warfare had broken out in Wilmington.

The nationwide death toll from street violence that first Friday night after King's death stood at sixteen. By Sunday evening, the death toll rose to twenty-five.

FIFTEEN

Crooked Cross

*T*he Sunday after King's death was Palm Sunday. President Johnson proclaimed it a national day of mourning. On that day in Fayetteville, the Fayetteville-Cumberland Vicinity Ministerial Council, of which I was president, planned a three o'clock memorial service for our fallen leader. We applied and received a permit to march into town and congregate around the Slave Market House. Our permit stipulated that we could walk only on the sidewalks, not in the street; we had to follow a police escort; and we could go no further than the square at the Slave Market House.

Before the service began, a couple of us from the ministerial council drove into town to make sure that the American flag on top of the Cumberland County Courthouse had been properly lowered to half staff. It wouldn't do for us to march downtown only to see that our own community had not acknowledged the sorrow of our nation.

As our car came within sight of the courthouse, my heart sank. Sitting on top of the brick building waved the American flag…*my* flag…and it was defiantly raised to the top of the pole. Our city government had refused to comply. They chose to ignore a fallen hero and the millions of African-Americans who were mourning a great leader—a Nobel Peace Prize recipient no less.

The Evans Metropolitan A.M.E. Zion Church—founded in 1796 by Henry Evans, a black freedman, ordained preacher and former shoemaker— was to host our service. When founded centuries ago, the church was simply named the African Meeting House. The stone steps I climbed that day to enter the sanctuary had been laid in 1893, and the church sat over the grave of Henry Evans.

As I walked through those old doors of that historic church, I looked up and saw the tilted cross centered between the brick bell towers of the entrance.

The intentionally crooked cross was said to be a symbol of Henry Evans's hard-won struggle to establish that church. For me, on that day, that leaning cross became a symbol of my own personal struggle to make a difference. Suddenly I was struck with this powerful sense of failure and anger.

Nothing had changed! The marches, the protests, the civil disobedience, the *beloved community*, the sacrifices, the risks, the petitions…nothing had mattered! An assassin had murdered my inspiration. My people were rioting and innocence was being brutally slaughtered everywhere I turned. In my own community, a community I had served for eight years, not one city official had enough benevolence in his heart to lower our flag out of respect. Their message was clear: The slain hero was black, therefore he deserved no respect.

I was on the brink, teetering on the edge of the abyss of hatred and retaliation. Mama would not have been pleased with me at that moment. What did God want from me? What was the purpose of my calling? Why preach love and sacrifice if in the end it wouldn't make a difference? If sixteen-year-old boys were still getting murdered because of their skin color? If a man was deemed less valuable than another because of a wide nose and full lips? If a black woman who was too tired to walk to the back of a bus could stir such hatred? Then none of it had mattered. I was angry down to my bones.

We had our memorial. About sixteen hundred of us concluded our service by walking properly in single file, as we were told, down the sidewalk up to the intersections of Green, Gillespie, Person and Hay streets—up to but no further than the arches of the Slave Market House. We gave our speeches and prayed our prayers and then we all walked orderly back the way we had come to the parking lot of Evans Metropolitan A.M.E. Zion Church.

I was white hot with rage. Resentment bubbled and frothed through my skin until it soaked my suit coat. My sorrow for a murdered hero cracked my heart like the dry, red clay of parched earth. *"What now, O Lord? What now?"* screamed my soul.

At that moment I lifted my eyes toward that crooked cross again—the one that had been nailed in place almost a hundred years ago. *The cross. The crooked cross.* The answer to my desperate plea came like a flash flood. I did not think or wonder if I heard correctly. I simply raised my arms and shouted, "We're going back! This time we're marching to the courthouse. Anyone wanting to go back with us, get in line!"

Our first march into town had been on the city's terms. This march was on ours. We congregated in the middle of Cool Spring Street. We lined up across the breadth of the street, curb-to-curb by eight or nine persons. The rest of the mourners dropped in behind as we began to march. At times, I walked beside Rex Harris, at others with someone else. Our march was orderly, quiet, nonviolent but determined. As we walked through the streets, careful not to step *on* the sidewalk, others joined us.

And then it happened. A miracle. With each step I took, the rage that had consumed me only moments earlier was wrung out of my heart by a holy hand. Martin Luther King, Jr. was indeed my hero, but he was not my inspiration. My inspiration was Jesus Christ himself. *"Do unto others as you would have them do unto you."* My mama was right: You couldn't harbor both hatred and love at the same time. It just isn't possible.

Violence could never be a part of my own personal code, not because Dr. King said so but because my Lord said so.

On that march, I felt God prodding me and helping me to understand that there were just as many white people who had been victimized and robbed of their own humanity as blacks. Prejudice and hatred had stolen their clarity, compassion and community. If I allowed my own heart to be courted by that same hatred and enticed by that same unholy pride, then I would become no better than the men who refused to lower that beautiful flag—the flag that symbolized *my* freedom…*my* citizenship…*my* value. God intended for us to respect ourselves. When He saved me, He said I was worth something.

By the time we had marched the seven or eight blocks back to the Slave Market House, our number had reached two thousand or more. Our permit required us to stop at the square, but this time we walked through those hallowed arches and didn't stop. As our feet shuffled over the cobbled area of the Slave Market House, ancient cries of victory seemed to ricochet off those sacred walls where our forefathers had been sold.

Our plan was simple. We would not leave the courthouse until our mourning was recognized. We would not leave until *our* American flag was lowered out of respect and honor for one of America's own. We would not leave until someone recognized the value that God placed on all of his people. We weren't budging.

I walked up the steps of the courthouse, turned and looked out toward the crowd that overflowed into the street. Mostly black faces stared back at me, and thankfully, they were not faces filled with hate or anger. The thousands of eyes that looked back at me were bright with tears. The hands that were raised were not clinched but waving in praise.

The flag on top of the courthouse hung limp as if embarrassed by its offense. The police kept their distance as our throng spontaneously broke out in song, hymns and chants.

It didn't take long. We never saw who actually lowered the flag. The police must have sneaked someone in through a back door. At first the flag was dropped down completely. Then it was raised to the top of the pole and then lowered half-mast—the proper ceremonial protocol for a slain leader.

The cheer of the crowd heaved the clouds back. The joyous clapping that erupted was like angelic percussion. And the anger that threatened my soul earlier was totally and completely washed away by a river of tears.

In the ten days after Dr. King's death, racial violence flared in one hundred and twenty-five cities across the country. Between forty-five and fifty persons were killed, more than twenty-six hundred were injured and more than twenty-one thousand were arrested. Our nation was bleeding people through its veins and a long, violent, hot summer lurked just around the corner.

SIXTEEN

The Good Neighbor Council

Guidelines for the Establishment of County-Wide Good Neighbor or Human Relations Councils

Purpose and Objectives of the Council

1. To promote peaceful relations between the races
2. To promote understanding, respect, and goodwill among all citizens
3. To provide channels of communication
4. To promote positive action programs
5. To provide equality of opportunity for all citizens
6. To promote the employment of qualified people without regard to race
7. To encourage youth to become trained and qualified for employment
8. To enlist the assistance and cooperation of all city, town and county officials; in fact, all segments of the population in the attainment of the purpose and objectives of the Council

— D.S. Coltrane, Chairman
North Carolina Good Neighbor Council, 1968

"*I* won't be an Uncle Tom, Preston!"

"Aaron, you won't be. The governor needs you. I need you," said my old college friend.

I had not seen Preston Hill since our graduation from Shaw University eight years earlier. I had lost track of him really. So when he showed up at the Unity meeting in Fayetteville a few weeks after Dr. King's death, employed by Governor Dan Moore, I was more than a little surprised.

Summer was brewing and the heat of racial unrest was already boiling in our streets. Dr. King's death not only rubbed the stinging salt of segregation into the wounds of sympathic whites, it created a greater chasm among African-Americans themselves.

Followers of the likes of Monroe, North Carolina, resident Robert F. Williams, a black expatriate on the run from the FBI hiding out in China, were calling for blacks to arm themselves with guns for protection. The Blank Panthers, under the leadership of Huey P. Newton, were preaching violent retaliation with angry, raised fists. But those of us who still clung to Dr. King's dream of a beloved community became more determined to keep his ways alive. We rolled up our sleeves and continued to fight racial discrimination in the workplace and our schools with restraint and a renewed commitment to nonviolence.

"Governor Moore wants to meet with you and ask you to join his Good Neighbor Council."

"*His* Good Neighbor Council?" I had to laugh. Dan Moore had campaigned for governor of North Carolina a few years earlier, in 1965, with the platform of doing away with the Good Neighbor Council. Two years previous, his predecessor, Governor Terry Sanford, created the council as a tool to help eliminate racial discrimination. On a cold January morning in 1963, Governor Sanford, speaking before the North Carolina Press Institute, boldly proclaimed, "Reluctance to accept the Negro in employment is the greatest single block to his continued progress and to the full use of the human potential of the nation and its states."

He then announced the formation of the twenty-four-member Good Neighbor Council and its two-fold mission: (1) to encourage the employment of qualified people without regard to race, and (2) to encourage youth to become better trained and qualified for employment. "In North Carolina," announced Sanford, "we will attempt to provide the leadership for the kind of understanding America needs today."

Governor Sanford was pouring grant money and other funds into bringing the plight of the Negro to the forefront and to addressing racial discrimination in our state. It was a start.

Two years later, when Governor Dan Moore took office, the most that had been accomplished was a stab at communication between blacks and whites. In a smattering of communities, groups called Human Relations Councils or Bi-Racial Committees were designated to expand educational programs and employment opportunities. Most of what got done was just talk, but that was better than nothing.

Then in 1965 along came newly elected Governor Dan Moore, who thought the Good Neighbor Council was a failure. So, as promised, he gave little attention or funds toward the effort—until 1968, when the backlash of Dr. King's assassination threatened North Carolina and the rest of the country with violent retaliation.

"Is this for real? Dan Moore is resurrecting the Good Neighbor Council?"

"Yes, he is. I'm already a part of it. And, with summer coming he thinks we are going to see a rash of riots erupt all over the state and he wants me and now you to do what we can to appeal to cooler heads."

"Why me?"

"You're a Democrat. You're black. You've demonstrated your leadership abilities right here in Fayetteville and the governor has noticed. He sees you as a level-headed peaceful negotiator," said my friend. "Besides, I've vouched for you."

Preston had always been a smooth talker. I'm not sure how he had won the attention of Dan Moore, but I had seen my friend Preston in action. He could talk a queen bee out a hive. "I won't be used by this man. I will not be his Uncle Tom," I told him.

"Just let me set up a meeting between you two. You'll see."

First, I met with the governor's assistant. Then a couple of days later I met with Governor Moore and Preston at the Capitol in Raleigh.

As I parked my car and walked toward the Capitol, memories flooded through me. I had not been back to Raleigh in some time and was not prepared for the onslaught of visions from my old college protest days. The tense, single-file lines, the protest signs, and the sit-ins all played out in living color before my eyes. I had driven down Fayetteville Street on my way into town and saw, in my mind's eye, myself being dragged from Woolworth's, bloodied and proud. Only a couple of blocks away, I had sat in a classroom where I first met Dr. King. He had passionately preached to us Gandhi's techniques of nonviolence and passionately commissioned Shaw's seminary students "to go do likewise." The sorrow of Dr. King's death once again weighed heavy.

For the past eight years I had been hammered across the anvil of King's dream. The protests, marches and arrests endured by the students I led, and the sacrifices made by the activist members at Mount Sinai during those turbulent first years in Fayetteville, would have made Dr. King proud. Once the marching stopped, we rallied and became zealous in developing programs to help the poor. We canvassed and registered black voters. We organized and began working toward integration in Fayetteville schools and our workplaces—all in response to King's battle cries. Now the dreamer was dead and the dream itself was on the verge of cracking. What was God up to, and what did He want with me now?

Preston met me in the waiting room outside of the governor's office. I was still apprehensive. I didn't trust Governor Moore. I didn't want to be used by this man or be portrayed by the media as his *boy*.

"Good afternoon, gentlemen. Thank you both for coming," said Dan Moore as he greeted us with a handshake.

Sitting side-by-side, Preston and I faced the governor as he returned to his chair behind his desk. His graying hair, broad shoulders and tailored suit didn't impress me much. But, to my surprise, his words did.

"Aaron, we have a dangerous summer ahead of us. North Carolina is poised for violence. Our issues are important, but they shouldn't be used to tear good people apart."

I sat listening to this sixty-two-year-old World War II veteran tell me how much he feared what was going to happen to our state if African-Americans and Caucasians didn't join hands. "We've got to do something, Aaron, before violence rips away everything good that Dr. King has done."

I battled with my conscience as I listened to the governor. Could I trust him? Was he going to make a fool of me?

"Gentlemen, I am a public servant of the State of North Carolina. I've taken up the duties as its governor in a time of great turbulence. White and non-white are going to lose this summer if we don't do something proactive to stop the violence that's boiling just under the surface of our cities."

"What do you want from us? I'm not sure what you're asking?" I shifted in my seat and leaned in closer to Governor Moore's desk.

"I'm asking you two to be my eyes and ears out there. I'm asking you to infiltrate our counties, especially the twelve or so cities and towns that have experienced the worst racial trouble in recent months." Getting up from his leather chair, Governor Moore walked around his desk and leaned against it just a few feet in front of us. "I'm asking you to represent *me* out there. I need you to mediate and establish lines of communication between city councils and local communities; to reduce racial tension, to identify causes of racial problems, to urge local communities to take definite steps toward justice." Dan Moore paused, took a deep breath and folded his hands. "I need you to put yourselves on the line to help educate the general populace about the nature of racial discrimination and how it's killing us."

I don't know what Preston was thinking at that moment, but I was dumbfounded.

Was I hearing right? Did the Governor want to make an honest effort to end racial injustice and inequality? A white man who truly understood that continued racial discrimination was decaying our country? Was he for real?

"Governor Moore, sir, do you know why it's called the Good Neighbor Council?"

Okay, it was a trick question. I figured if the man didn't have a clue about the Jericho Road story from scripture, he really didn't know what he was asking us to do.

"Well, Aaron, Sanford said he stole the name from some program that Teddy Roosevelt started way back when. But I'm thinking The Good Samaritan story. You know—who is your neighbor? Your neighbor is anyone who needs your help," said the governor of North Carolina, looking me straight in the eye.

"Yes, sir. And if I'm being asked to be that Samaritan and put my life on the line for that neighbor, I've got to know I have your support one hundred percent."

Preston was looking from one to the other. I guess he felt like I did. If we were going to go into a community that was fussing and fighting and rioting and looting and killing over race issues, we'd sure as heaven better have the backing and authority of Dan Moore or we'd be dead before the day was over.

"Mr. Johnson, if you do this for me, I promise you on a stack of Bibles that you and Mr. Hill here will have protection from the highway patrol and the National Guard, and they will be at your disposal. You call 'em and they'll be there…on your say-so alone."

"You sincere about this?"

"Yes, sir, Mr. Johnson. I am."

"How do you propose we go about it all?"

"I don't know. Be creative. Smell the smoke. Put out the fire. Rebuild. I'll leave it up to you as to how you do it."

I don't know how long we sat there in silence. I assumed Dan Moore didn't get where he was without calculated risks paying off. I could have walked out. Turned him down. Gone home. But…

I was convinced, much like Queen Esther from long, long ago when she found herself in a unique position to save her people. Who knows that I, too, had not been created "for such a time as this"?

We shook hands. The governor handed me some car keys and a notepad and promised to pay me a thousand dollars a month for six months. "Good luck, gentlemen."

SEVENTEEN

Day One

" **Y**ou niggers come on in here and let's get started." David S. Coltrane was the first chairman of North Carolina's Good Neighbor Council and he was introducing Preston and me on our first day to the GNC staff. When Governor Terry Sanford appointed him in 1963, Coltrane couldn't say the word "Negro" to save his life.

When I met up with him that late spring in 1968, I thought either God or I had made a big mistake. What was I doing in a room with a man so racist he actually thought *that* was the true name of the black race, like God pointed his finger and said, "You're Chinese and you're Indian and you're Nigger."

This is what I meant by whites being victims like blacks. Here was a Christian man who knew that segregation was wrong. Yet he'd been a part of the political structure supporting it for so long that he had no idea how offensive he sounded by using that terminology.

David Coltrane found himself sitting at the table with Negroes whom the governor of North Carolina demanded were to be treated as his equal. Mr. Coltrane fully agreed with the governor, but his mouth had a hard time adjusting.

The twenty-four-member staff of the Good Neighbor Council—half white, half black —was excited about our appointment. I don't remember too much about any of them except for Dr. Andrew Best. Dr. Best had been the only African-American physician in Pitt County, North Carolina, for the last twenty-five years. He was a veteran civil rights activist and worked tirelessly for integration in the medical field and the community. He practiced in Greenville, North Carolina, and had caught the eye of Governor Sanford when he and a white pediatrician, Dr. Marlene Irons, organized the Pitt County Interracial Committee. This committee singlehandedly and successfully fought the fight of integration in Greenville and surrounding areas, eliminating separate waiting rooms in hospitals and inferior care to minorities, among other issues. When Drs. Best and Irons were invited to the Capitol, it was Dr. Best who said, "It is better for us to bring change through orderly evolution than let it come as a disorderly revolution. We can help it to come, or we can permit it through our reluctant attitude to come through violent and disorderly revolution." Thus the Good Neighbor Council was born.

Dr. Best credited David Coltrane as the one who really saved the Good Neighbor Council from getting the axe from Governor Moore. After we were introduced, Andrew Best worked closely with Preston and me to develop the GNC field operations.

The seventy-five-year-old Coltrane motioned that morning for Preston and me to sit down and join the group. "Ya'll, I'd like to introduce you to our new field representative, Aaron Johnson. He's going to be working with our boy, Preston. They're going to be working in more than sixty counties to establish clear lines of communication between the council and local communities."

David Coltrane was considered a moderate by some and a conservative by others. I guess it just depended on where you fell on segregation. Governor Sanford, who was considered the most progressive white liberal politician in the South at the time, and who had made an open stand for the rights of Negroes, hired Coltrane. Then Governor Dan Moore, a conservative who was content to allow the council to die a slow death, kept him on.

In 1963 Coltrane traveled the state putting out political fires and making noises about "good race relations." He was a passable Methodist who preached when asked and expounded on the "race problem" and how it could be solved if the right folks would join the efforts of the statewide Good Neighbor Council.

Coltrane, as an old financier and former state secretary of agriculture, marched to his own beat. However, he sincerely wanted Southern segregated ways abolished. Before I came on the scene, he had earned his stripes working long nights and in the midst of student protests and angry riots with Anne Queen, a Raleigh YMCA employee who organized student protests at the time, and Ralph Scott, the brother of a future North Carolina governor, Bob Scott. Coltrane worked in Raleigh, Durham, Greenville and other cities defusing unrest. Dr. Best often told of the times Mr. Coltrane would pilot his own Cub into the Pitt County airport just to spend the day brainstorming and strategizing with him about how best to attack the issues.

"These *boys* are going to serve in a mediatory role and try to get our communities, especially those twelve cities which have experienced the most violent trouble of late, to take more definite steps toward a just resolution to their conflicts," announced Coltrane.

For years, Pastor Johnson did double duty, leading Mount Sinai and serving under three North Carolina governors as field representative for the Good Neighbor Council, helping to resolve racial unrest.

"Boy." "Nigger." I sincerely doubted if I would ever be able to trust Mr. Coltrane.

That sentiment changed, however, early one morning in Hillsborough, North Carolina. Preston and I had only been on the job a few weeks when we were called to Hillsborough to help ensure the safety of black students who were marching in protest of segregated schools. The school board and community at large were putting up a lot of resistance to having blacks and whites in the same schools, and it was rumored the Ku Klux Klan was very active in Hillsborough.

We had spent long days negotiating with community leaders, teachers and the school board, guiding them through a proposed integration plan as well as listening to the demands of the students. It was about one or so in the morning and Preston and I were still awake in our motel room, working on the next day's strategies.

"Preston, I've worked all I can work tonight. I've got to get to bed," I said.

"I hear you. I think I'm seeing double."

As we prepared to turn in, the phone pierced the quiet of our room, making me nearly jump over into Preston's lap. "Hello."

It was Mr. Coltrane and he was talking fast and loud. "Aaron, don't talk, just listen. Whatever you're doing right now, you and Preston have got to pack at once and get out of that motel as fast as you can."

"What? I don't understa…"

"Aaron! Go look out your window. You should see three highway patrol cars outside your room. Get out of your room now! Run get into one of those cars. Do not…I repeat, do not get in your car. Just leave it."

I motioned for Preston to peek out the curtain into the parking lot. "What's going on?" he whispered. "The highway patrol is out there."

"Aaron? Are you there?"

"Yes, sir. The police are out there."

"Do as I say. Leave immediately. They will bring you directly to my office in Raleigh. Good luck." Click.

I slowly replaced the receiver in its cradle and just stood there. My feet were bolted to the floor. What was happening?

"Aaron?" Preston stared at me.

Suddenly, adrenaline shot through me like a slug of stump hole liquor. "Move! We've got to get out of here! Now!"

We flew around our room scooping up papers, socks and toothpaste. I couldn't think what to leave or what to take. I was just grabbing. With briefcases and clothes bags under our arms, we darted out of our room as a police officer in the middle squad car opened his back door for us. We barely got ourselves settled in the backseat when our caravan savagely jetted out of the motel parking lot, spinning tires and slinging pebbles. With a highway patrol escort—one in front and one in back of us—we silently sped down the dark highway toward Raleigh.

At three in the morning Preston and I walked into the Council office. The lights in the outer room were off, but Mr. Coltrane's office lights were burning bright as he ran to greet us. His white hair was disheveled and his shirttail hung out over his belt. "I am so happy to see ya'll!" He wrapped his arms around us as a father embracing sons. It was obvious that he had been crying as he shook our shoulders and patted our backs once, and then did it again.

As he paced and ran his hands through his hair he told us, "I got an anonymous phone call that scared the hound out of me, boys. Whoever it was told me that the Klan was watching your room and were plotting to kill ya'll in your sleep." Tears started running down his ample cheeks again. "I'm so proud to see ya'll tonight."

Mr. Coltrane saved our lives that early morning and sealed a bond between us that no amount of ridicule, threats or racial slurs would ever crack. For six months he had our backs. Because of it, he lost friends, damaged his reputation and had his own life threatened many times. When he died in October, six months after I joined the GNC, the old activist had been practicing the word "Negro" and was just waiting to spring it on me when I least expected it.

I can honestly say that David Coltrane was one of the noblest men I ever knew, and he was my friend.

EIGHTEEN

The Fiery Furnace

"I see four men loose, walking in the midst of the fire; and they are not hurt, and the form of the fourth is like the Son of God." Daniel 3:25

*O*ur first month on the road with the GNC brought many challenges. No one wanted to learn how to negotiate through the issues from black men, even if the governor handpicked them. If it had not been for the promise of Dan Moore that his office would stand by us, I think Preston and I would have quit after the first week. Since our harrowing experience in Hillsborough, the dangers of what we were trying to do were more than clear.

One crisis after another pulled us from community to community. We stayed busy putting out fires, literally. People were mad, frustrated and without Dr. King's calming sense of reason. The African-American community was rapidly dividing into three camps. There were the ones (mostly the elderly) who were afraid and were shutting their windows, locking their doors and begging the rest of us to stop making waves before we got us all killed. There were those who were more angry than afraid (mostly the young). All bets were off as they began to take things into their own hands—starting fires, tossing bottles, and/or shooting guns—whatever got the most attention. And then there were folks like me who continued to organize, protest, get arrested and sometimes, if we were lucky, infiltrate the system through any door that cracked open.

Unfortunately, black militants were getting more and more press and beginning to make it very difficult for those of us who still believed that nonviolence was the way to bring about lasting change. The most urgent crisis claimed our energies first. Demonstrators needed protection and violence-bent antagonists needed the air let out of their anger. It was our job to help them both. Finding the time to help opinion leaders devise an integration plan for schools, or lobbying for equal job opportunities or fair housing, was constantly overshadowed by fear and chaos.

Just a month or so into our mission, one of the most volatile and chaotic cities in North Carolina at the time gifted me with my first glimpse of the good that could be accomplished—that is, if a willing and cooperative heart could be found. I found one in the most unlikely place.

Wilmington, North Carolina, had a long history of racial unrest. They were still debating the 1898 race riots, where local black leaders were killed or run out of town by angry, white anti-reconstructionists. In 1968, Wilmington school children were still being taught to view those white mob leaders as heroes. The town was still naming public parks, buildings and streets after them. Yet not one single monument had been built to commemorate the innocent African-Americans killed by their brutality. When Dr. King was murdered, the resentment and hatred from long ago injustices boiled up once again.

That fateful summer when Preston and I were sent out, black and white citizens of Wilmington were drawing jagged lines through the city and daring the other to cross it.

School segregation, inadequate housing, unemployment, and segregated everything from waiting rooms to water fountains, theaters and lunch counters all moved from mere protest issues to dangerous battlegrounds. White supremacists and the black militant fringe were heading for a clash. We feared innocent demonstrators and law enforcement were going to get caught in the bloody middle.

This unstable climate greeted me when I arrived, alone on this particular trip. My objective was to get acquainted with the police department and the community powers that be. It was vital that the GNC could count on Wilmington's law enforcement for protection and security. It was my assignment to train them how to deal with demonstrators without incurring fatalities.

It didn't take me long to realize that the chief of police wasn't going to be as cooperative as I had hoped. Within a few days of butting heads with him, it became obvious that he was more than a little friendly with a certain part of the Wilmington citizenship—the part that had sworn an allegiance to an ideology that believed the white man was superior to all others. In fact, if truth be told, he was probably a bona fide, card-carrying member of that group; at the very least, he was a sympathetic supporter. Of course, all of that went unspoken as his cantankerous, disrespectful language threw up roadblocks at every turn.

While I stood talking with the chief one morning, my inner voice shot through me from out of nowhere. It was one of those moments when you look around to see if anyone else in the room saw the lightning or heard the booming voice. *"Bring all of them together!"* Once that thought was planted, I couldn't shake it.

One of the GNC's main objectives was to try to organize a Good Neighbor Council within each city where we worked. These Human Relations Councils, as we called them, were to be made up of stakeholders of all ages and professions, black and white, men and women who could best represent their groups' needs. Once an HRC had its members in place, our first task was to encourage the city to hire a full-time director to keep the commission actively working toward a nonviolent solution to the community's human relations needs. If I was ever called back to that community, I would then work directly with the local Human Relations Council on whatever they needed from me.

"Bring them all together!" That voice was relentless and kept needling me and messing with me. One day, I just blurted it out.

"Chief, I want to meet with members of the Klan. Can you help me with that?"

"Boy, what are you talking about? I don't know nothing about a Klan here in Wilmington."

We sat in the chief's office after a tense day of student demonstrations and white extremists' threats. "Let's assume that isn't true. Let's assume that you do know someone from that group who would be willing to talk to me. How would you go about it?"

The chief just looked at me and shook his head.

"You know and I know that if we don't do something soon, somebody's going to get killed. My job is to try and get people talking to one another before that happens. Can you help me?"

"Are you crazy? There ain't no Klan member going to want to talk to you about being a member of some council. You're a fool!"

"So you *do* know some people that you could set up a meeting with?"

"I didn't say that. I just said, from what I've been told, the Klan isn't exactly into talking to black folks about their *needs*. You know what I'm saying?"

"What about the *Klan's* needs? Don't you think they'd like someone to listen to what they want? They have rights too, you know. And, what better way to make those wants known than to get one of them on the Human Relations Council?"

I looked the chief straight on while in my own mind I thought that what I had just said was the most preposterous thing that had ever crossed my lips.

What in the world was I talking about? Who in their right mind would even admit to me that he was actually a member of the Klan? More importantly, how was I ever going to get one of them to talk to me without first stringing me up from a tree branch in the middle of the night?

The chief got up, walked over to the window and turned his back to me. "Let me get this straight. You want me to set you up with a meeting with the Klan so you can ask one of them to become a member of your little council—a group that's trying to find a way to allow a little black boy to sit in the same classroom in a desk right next to a pink, frilly-dressed little white girl?"

"Yes, sir. I guess I am."

"Are you suicidal, boy?"

"Chief, it's going to happen. Those little Negro children are going to be admitted into that school. It's already happening elsewhere. And I know that you are a good man in your heart. You know that it's your job to make sure that, when integration happens in Wilmington, no one gets killed…black or white."

I went back to my motel. I was dog-tired. And I still couldn't shake the sensation of being *tapped*. Did I actually hear a voice, or was it more like a nudging or a prompting? Whatever it was, it had caused me to ask for the ridiculous.

The next morning, as soon as I walked into the chief's office, he told me, "It's done. Be here tonight at midnight."

"What?"

"I've got someone who wants to meet with you."

"Okay."

"You can call him Sam. It's not his real name, but that doesn't matter."

"Alright."

"Tell him what you want, but don't be surprised if he laughs in your face…or worse."

"Alright."

At midnight, I parked my car in front of the police department and sat there. The light from lampposts glinted off of windshields and wet pavement. Police departments never really closed, but at this hour the building before me seemed to be resting and gathering strength for the next day. To my surprise, I was calm. I didn't know what to expect, but I had a sturdiness that had set up in me that convinced me that God did.

As I walked into the chief's office, two men turned toward me.

Chief spoke first. "Mr. Johnson, this here is Sam. Sam, Mr. Johnson." Sam and I nodded to each other. I don't know what I was expecting—a man in a white hood maybe, or possibly a face that hate had distorted into an ugly, twisted snarl. But the man facing me was ordinary looking enough and dressed in khakis.

"I'm going to leave you two alone to say your piece. I'll be back in a while." Chief quickly disappeared out the door of his own office.

There we stood, black and white. Centuries of hatred, hardship, slavery, prejudice, misunderstanding and fear piled between us like smelly carcasses. Yet I felt called to this moment, to this man I knew as Sam. I was meant to be nowhere else. I found myself on that pinpoint again, brought to this town, this building, this office, this hour, this man. He was no Henry Tupper or David Coltrane, yet here he stood as bewildered as I by what brought us together.

For the next two hours, I reached deep within my bones to convince Sam of my sincerity. Someone from the Klan needed to be on Wilmington's Good Neighbor Council. God had convinced me of that. It was now my job to convince Sam. I told my new friend that if the Klan members cared for their community as their fighting words claimed, then shouldn't they have a say in the inevitable? Schools in Wilmington were going to integrate, like it or not, so didn't his buddies want a voice in the plan?

Sam listened. Nodded. Paced. Argued. In the end, he told me he'd see what he could do. At two in the morning, as the chief walked me out to my car, he put his arm around my shoulders, "I knew you could do it, boy," he said.

Twenty-four hours later I was awakened in the middle of the night by the shrill ring of my phone. I shot straight up in bed. Where was I?

"Mr. Johnson, Sam is going to be waiting for you in the back of your motel in five minutes. Good luck." Chief hung up without another word.

I scrambled around the room hunting for my shoes and praying. As I scurried around to the back of my motel, I could hardly see three feet in front of me. I was staying in a run-down motel on the colored side of town. No lampposts lit the way. No paved parking lot reflected the moon's glow. Only a menacing darkness greeted me while Sam held open the back door of his car. When he spoke, his voice was as prickly as barbed wire. "Quick, get in! Lay down on the backseat and don't sit up until I tell you to."

I did what I was told. Obviously, Sam didn't want me to see where he was taking me. I lay on my side balled up on the seat and listened to the rhythm of the car bouncing toward its destination. Thump-Thump. Thump-Thump. Shadows rolled over me as an occasional stoplight or blinking neon sign found its way through the window of the car. Sam didn't speak. Neither did I.

But I did pray as the Twenty-Third Psalm raced through me and filled me up, "...*surely goodness and mercy would follow me...*"

"Lord, it doesn't matter what happens to me, as long as it brings glory and honor to You."

Mercifully, God kept my mind narrowed and focused. No thoughts of my family were allowed to enter. I fear that would have been unbearable. If I didn't leave from wherever Sam was taking me, it would be God's will. I trusted that He would take care of my Mattie, Dezette and Jamale. As David's Psalm flushed out my fear, my muscles relaxed. The car rumbled down the road, turning left and right, slowing and then speeding up.

I scrunched up on that backseat, wondering if this was what the prophet Daniel felt as he was led to the lion's den. Did he feel this letting go and this peace flooding through him? Was he convinced, as he was lowered into that pit of death, that God would use him for His purposes no matter the outcome?

At one point, as the car began to slow and weave through a driveway or path, the fiery furnace of Shadrach, Meshach and Abednego flashed before me as well. I suddenly remembered *the fourth man!* When King Nebuchadnezzar looked down into the blazing furnace, he expected to see the flesh being burned off of the three men. Instead, what he saw were the three walking about and talking with a fourth man. *The Fourth Man.*

I became convinced that same Fourth Man was in the car with me at that very moment. Jesus refused to let me ride alone in the dark. His presence was as real as my own. His breath was on my face. His arms cradled me as I hunkered in that back seat. *"Not my will but thine…"*

"Close your eyes and sit up." Sam opened the back door and, when I got up, he tied a rag of some sort over my eyes. "Come on," he barked.

As I was led from the car, I stumbled my way down a path trying my best not to fall on my face. With Sam's obliging pull and push, I staggered up some stairs and entered a building of some sort.

I heard feet shuffling and throats being cleared and felt movement all around me. *"Surely goodness and mercy will follow me…"*

"I've brought this nigger here to meet with us. They's bad niggers and they's some good niggers, and this one is one of the good niggers." Sam's words caused some mumbling to start around the room. I felt the space where I stood get swallowed up with contempt.

With my sight diminished, my other senses took over. Floorboards creaked and the room had that unused smell of dust and hollowness about it. As my arms dangled at my sides, I felt the slickness of my pant legs as my sweaty palms gripped the seams. The air around me was humid and clung to my skin like a slimy leech. And then there was the unmistakable stench of loathing as the sour putrid waft of human disdain bore down upon my shoulders and back.

"He's a good nigger and he's on our side," said Sam. And then nothing. I waited several seconds for him to continue, but all I heard was the vile inhaling and exhaling of a mob on the verge of lost civility. I figured that was my cue to speak.

I cleared my throat and straightened myself as tall as I could. "I want to thank Sam here for bringing me to meet ya'll."

Sharp, staccato-like laughter and profanity could be heard ricocheting around the room.

I took a deep breath. "Sam used the term 'good nigger.' I don't care what he calls me. But it's true, I am here to try and bring about some good."

More profanity was spit at me.

I knew I'd only get one chance to say my piece. After that only God knew what would come next. "We are trying to get together this Human Relations Council in Wilmington. I believe in equality and I would like for ya'll to have a representative on the committee so that your concerns can be addressed as well."

No profanity. No spit. I'd gotten their attention.

"The rights of white people need to be heard, too," I said.

The crowd around me hissed their agreement. The floor shifted underneath me as several bodies shuffled as one.

"Choose someone you have confidence in and I will get him on the committee."

An icy silence proceeded and then suddenly a lightning storm surrounded me as shouting and cursing men wrangled to get their say. They griped about "the Jews taking over America" and the "niggers destroying their town." Their words attacked me like killer bees—harsh, biting, stinging words that buzzed nonstop for what seemed like hours.

Yet, in all that time, *not one person touched me.* Not one thump or slap or punch. Fiery, hate-filled words licked at me but none of them burned a single square inch of my soul.

The Fourth Man! He, indeed, was there hovering among the flames. At times He swirled around that room warring with the hatred that oozed from every slurred word. At other times, He tenderly wiped the sweat that leaked from my brow. In the end, He wrapped His divine arms around my drenched shirt and held me up as I stood there for what seemed like hours.

Then, as quickly as the storm of words had begun, they stopped. Thunder, once booming, now floated off into the distance, while silent rain began to drench the flames. Still blindfolded, with my legs aching to give way, I heard Sam's voice from my left. "I'll do it. I'll be on the committee."

Sam led me back to the car with the same instructions. I lay in the backseat with my crude blindfold still in place. By now it felt more like a shield than anything else, a comforting blanket that wanted to call me to sleep. But not just yet. In a low voice, I spoke from my huddled position. "Sam, you called me 'nigger' back there, and that's okay. One day, it is my prayer that you will call me 'friend' instead."

Sam didn't answer for a few seconds. I heard the familiar sounds of driving—foot on the accelerator, a stepping on the brakes, sweaty hands pulling on the steering wheel. When he did speak it came in harsh clips. "I'll... *never...* call you 'friend.' Never!"

We rode in silence the rest of the way. Behind the motel, I climbed out of the car and pulled the blindfold off. Sam sat behind the driver's seat looking straight ahead.

"Thank you. I'll look forward to working with you on the committee." Without looking up at me, he drove off just as daylight was breaking over the horizon.

Several months later, Wilmington was still slowly trudging its way toward integration, but the local Human Relations Council had made some important headway and were working together even better than I had hoped—with no fatalities.

On my last day in Wilmington after long weeks of training and negotiating, I was walking out to my car after a fairly intensive HRC meeting when I felt a tap on my shoulder. It was Sam. Of course, I knew his real name by then. We had spent hours together. We'd worked side-by-side hammering out ordinances and integration timelines. We'd even stood on street corners together and watched as demonstrators protested safely and white agitators threw out profanities but nothing worse. He'd bartered, cajoled, and argued with his folks, as I did with mine. Eventually, we came to an understanding of each other as we began to fear each other less.

"Aaron, you told me once that one day you hoped I'd call you 'friend.' "

"Yes. I remember."

He smiled as he slowly held his hand out to me. "I just want to thank you for all you've done here. You take care, friend."

We clasped hands. Out of the darkest of places, I found hope. Unfortunately, there were even darker places awaiting me.

NINETEEN

In the Heat of the Night

I signed up to work for Governor Dan Moore for six months. Two governors later, I was still a part of the Good Neighbor Council. However, those first few years were the hardest and most dangerous. While I preached and worshipped with my family every Sunday at Mount Sinai, most of my weekdays I could be found in some city or another preaching civil righteousness. My church deacons had stayed true to their word. They meant for me to see God's church in broader terms and His glory in the face of anyone I could serve. My work with the Good Neighbor Council was a calling. I saw my role as a servant and felt God talking through me as I trained, negotiated or lobbied for a better life for all—the *beloved community* was breaking ground.

By the early 1970s, Preston and I were joined by a few other field representatives. We were now sent out in teams consisting of one black and one white ambassador. Occasionally Preston and I still got to travel around together.

Things were changing, slowly. Schools were being integrated, one school district at a time. African-Americans were starting to be considered for a few job openings in upper management. In North Carolina, Cannon Mills was one of the first larger companies to hire African-Americans as professionals and on its executive staff. State and city governments were seeing a few more blacks being elected to offices. Still, one of the hardest nuts to crack was getting the whites in authority to listen to the African-American demands—especially if they had to actually talk to an African-American to know what those demands were.

One day Preston and I were summoned to a little place called Sanford. During the day, students were protesting and marching against school segregation as whites heckled, spit on them and threw rocks. In the evening, black militants were setting fires to everything as nighttime became a cover for rampant violence.

Sanford's county commissioner had put a call out to Governor Robert Scott, who had followed Dan Moore into office. He pleaded for the governor to send the highway patrol. Governor Scott sent us instead.

As Preston and I drove into town that afternoon, it looked like some bully had punched the teeth right out of the mouth of the downtown. Battered storefronts with broken and burned-out entrances lined the streets.

We went directly to the city hall and walked into an office, unannounced, where the county commissioner, the whole city council and what officers comprised the minuscule sheriff's department were sitting around a table—about twenty-five or thirty people in all. The friction in the room practically sparked every time a chair creaked.

"We've just got to control those black folks or this town is going to go up in smoke," someone said, while the others angrily shook their heads and puffed on their cigarettes.

Everyone looked up when we walked in. "You *boys* sit down in those chairs over by the wall there. Ya'll just sit down there and be quiet," commanded the guy we took to be in charge. We'd soon find out he was the county commissioner.

Preston and I did what we were told. We sat down and didn't say a word. As we sat there, I felt this odd sense of pride and civic righteousness start to thump in my chest. You would have thought I would have felt indignant or belittled, being made to sit in the corner like a naughty schoolboy. But God continued to protect my heart. While those in the room didn't quite yet know who we were or what we could do for them, I recognized the power of what I then called "benevolent authority" yearning to be unleashed and proven.

Pity also flashed through me for the white folks huddled together around that table. I believed they truly wanted to understand the needs of African-Americans, but they were completely ignorant as to how to include them in the process.

Ignoring Preston and me, their meeting continued. "We're having all kinds of chaos here. If the governor doesn't send the highway patrol soon, my men are going to have to start fighting back," said the man I took to be the sheriff.

The group nervously traded ideas back and forth about what to do. I can only assume that the county commissioner thought Preston and I were some of the local black leaders coming to talk to him and he just couldn't be bothered. Which illustrated exactly what the problem was. People weren't talking to each other. Wouldn't it have made sense that, with their town being broken into shards by discord, the white leadership would have wanted to talk to the black leadership? But since that wasn't happening, the situation had escalated and was hot-wired for a violent confrontation.

"Now, let's not do anything hasty, sheriff. We're waiting for the governor's representatives to get here and help us out."

"Shouldn't they be here already with the cavalry?" asked another jittery person.

Preston and I continued to sit there. We had called into the governor's office at a pay phone right before we got into town and told the governor's assistant that we had arrived. So Governor Scott knew we were there.

"Okay, ya'll sit tight and I'll go back and call the governor's office again." The county commissioner disappeared behind some doors as Preston and I continued to wait. In a couple of minutes the commissioner came back into the room with a puzzled look on his face. "The Governor says his men are already here." Everyone stopped talking. The only two people in that room that those folks didn't know were the black guys who had been put in the corner.

If racing minds could make noise, that room would have filled up with the sound of clanging cogs and screeching brakes. The commissioner timidly looked over at us. "Is there anybody here by the name of Preston Hill or Aaron Johnson?"

All eyes turned as we rose from our chairs. "Yes, here we are," answered Preston.

I swear, the expressions on all those people's faces! You would have thought that all of them were big old furry tomcats that had just been caught with half-eaten canaries hanging out of their mouths.

"Ya'll here to represent the governor?" asked the commissioner in a high-pitched, pre-pubescent squeak.

"Yes, sir, that's right; we're here from the governor's office," I said.

"You boys come on up to the table," said the commissioner. Now he was the one looking like a schoolboy. "Which one of you boys is Preston Hill?" Preston raised his hand. "Well, ah, the governor's assistant would like to talk to you."

"That's fine. If you'll just lead the way," said Preston. The two men disappeared behind the doors the commissioner had re-entered a moment before. I stood there alone in a silent room with gaping mouths and a lot of folks studying their shoes.

When Preston got on the phone, the governor's assistant told him, "Preston, I don't know what's going on down there, but do those folks want the highway patrol or not?" Without waiting for Preston's reply he continued, "Sergeant Bell should be there any minute. He's your contact man. When he comes, he isn't going to deal with any of those sitting around that table, you hear me? He's only going to deal with you all."

Moments later, Preston and the commissioner entered the room as all eyes and ears zeroed in on my friend. At the exact same time, in walked Sergeant Bell, grinning and looking official with his gun belt, shiny boots and badge. Forgetting about Preston and me once again, everyone jumped up from the table and rushed to shake the law enforcement officer's hand like he was Jesus. "Thank God, ya'll are finally here!" "Where are your men?" "How many units did you bring?"

Ignoring the group of babbling councilmen, the sergeant asked, "Excuse me gentlemen, I'm here to speak with Mr. Hill and Mr. Johnson in private." Again, all eyes turned back toward the two black guys.

"Come with me. We can meet in this room," said Preston, as he pointed back through the doors. The three of us left the room together as the tight huddle of city officials stared after us like rejected beauty contestants.

Talk about on-the-job training! Sergeant Bell didn't know us and we didn't know him. But we had to learn from each other and establish a confidence between ourselves—fast. Lives depended on it. When the officer asked for Preston and me first, he instantly gave us a credibility that no one else in that room would. Without that credibility and authority, we would fail and this crisis would worsen.

The sergeant had no more experience working with a black man in authority than we had being the authority. Once we were alone, the officer reported his situation and asked how he could help. "Gentlemen, the call is yours," he said.

We all looked at each other, and in that pivotal moment something shifted in all of us. Suddenly, there was no black or white, only a collective effort of three men trying to save a town from destroying itself.

We quickly re-entered the room and Sergeant Bell spoke first, "These two men have the plan from the governor's office and they'll have to tell you and me how to proceed."

Preston quickly took charge. "We have twenty-five officers outside the city limits and they can be here in three minutes. Do ya'll want them or not?"

"Yes!"

Later that day, the students once again organized and marched—this time with a permit and with the protection of the highway patrol. That evening, all was quiet. The antagonists and fringe groups had either left town or were arrested. In the following days, hearings were held in the municipal court for students who had been arrested for marching. With our help, most charges were dropped as black student leaders and community leaders began talking to one another around the table.

On our say so, the streets of Sanford had filled up with squad cars and order was restored. The cavalry did indeed arrive, but for the first time, the general on the horse was a black man.

TWENTY

The Radicals

The Good Neighbor Council wasn't always about bringing folks together. During those first few years things were happening so fast, and some folks were jumping on the bandwagon with agendas that were counter to what we were trying to accomplish.

One of the radical fringe groups that organized during this time was the Black Panther Party. It was originally called the Black Panther Party for Self-Defense. This African-American organization was established to promote black power and self-defense through acts of social agitation. Founded by Huey P. Newton and Bobby Seale in Oakland, California, in 1966, this group started out calling for protection of African-American neighborhoods from police brutality. Newton and Seale were heavily influenced by the philosophies of radical activist Robert Williams, who formed a Black Armed Guard with the blessings of the National Rifle Association. Members were trained in using firearms to protect themselves.

In 1961, Williams fled to Cuba to avoid a kidnapping charge and became a persuasive voice over the airwaves, calling for African-Americans to take up arms and protect their families.

By 1968, the Black Panthers' objectives had changed radically several times. They had splinter groups going from town to town assisting and inciting riots.

Another counter movement of radicals poking a stick in the fire of violence was blacks who had joined the Communist Party and found the Marxist ideology an appealing and effective way to be heard. It was rumored that some of them were even being funded through Russian connections. I don't know if that was true or not, but those groups seemed to have way more resources than any of the rest of us.

These radical, militant groups, while loosely organized, were not helping the GNC bring people together. If two or three of them got together, a hundred others with all kinds of agendas would jump on the bandwagon and try their best to cause disorder and mayhem. Their influx into whatever city demonstrations were taking place presented dangerous roadblocks to negotiating peaceful and productive resolutions of the issues.

Hence, I became a so-called infiltrator on more than one occasion. By the early 1970s my role as ambassador for the GNC had me acting as law enforcement, negotiator, trainer, activist, antagonist, organizer and spy.

When the Good Neighbor Council was renamed the Human Relations Council in the early 1970s, it was given legal status and power just like any other governmental commission. What began as an executive order with no real teeth evolved into a bona fide authorized entity with the power of the law behind it. Our undercover activities became classified and protected. Our lives depended on that protection. So, as I tell this part of my story, I'm creating a composite of events and locations to tell a single story. I'm also changing some names.

"Are you sure you want to do this, Aaron?" asked Lynn Martin, my white counter-part who accompanied me to the coast. Lynn was tall, slender and had a heart of gold. We became very close during our five years together. Our families became friends, and on more than one occasion he'd introduce me to a white mayor or city council member with, "This here is my brother, Aaron."

Lynn and I saw ourselves as pioneers in human relations. We were trying to bring a new society to the South, from segregation to integration, from black and white agendas to community empowerment. Lynn Martin worked tirelessly for integration and a better way of life for the African-American family. I absolutely loved this man.

"If we don't get in there and find out what's going on with these folks and what they're planning and what they want, we're never going to get any good done here."

"If they find out who we are, we're dead. You know that, right?" asked Lynn.

"What I know is that when the militants or Marxists see any black man cooperating with the white establishment, they label him an 'Uncle Tom.' And if I were to go and try to talk to them as myself, I'd be a goner for sure. But if I go in as one of them, I can listen and learn and hopefully defuse the hostility."

Lynn worried not only for my safety but also for his. While I was about to don a black leather jacket and become a cigar-smoking thug, Lynn was about to go over to the other side and portray himself as a white supremacist "hell-bent on running those niggers out of town."

We both understood the risks. However, we both believed that if we were able to find a way to get the interlopers out of town, we'd be able to identify the local leaders of these groups as potential HRC members. We felt the risks were worth it. After all, it had worked in Wilmington with my friend, Sam.

No one knew we were in the area. We'd arrived unannounced and were staying in an out-of-the way location. The local Human Relations Council was being held hostage to the horrific violence and disturbances of the radicals on both sides. If Lynn and I failed in our mission, we'd both probably end up dead, and this city would experience a racial clash that would more than likely destroy any efforts it had made toward desegregation—resulting in probable deaths and a ravaged city.

Before we left our motel room that night, we prayed together. Clasping hands as brothers, we were extremely aware of and uncomfortable with how we looked. I wore clothes that undermined everything I believed in. My black jacket was the banner of angry fists and indignation. The bandana on my head called for a violent means to an end. The cigar in my pocket spoke of ignorance and a Godless sense of justice. My friend's clothing reeked of hatred, fear, misunderstanding, and a haughty entitlement that gave the wearer false superiority—all that from dungarees and a denim vest.

I was heading out to a nightclub, a favored black hangout for agitators and out-of-town radicals. Lynn was going to the other side of the tracks to drift among the good ol' boys at a whites-only watering hole. Both establishments were known for their hatred of the other.

The North Carolina State Bureau of Investigation had no African-American agents at the time. They had no one to infiltrate and make contact with the people I was trying to reach. I was totally alone, yet I walked into that club with a firm hand on my shoulder. The Fourth Man had made a return and simply refused to abandon me.

Robert Farmer was black, young, college-educated and a recent communist convert. He was tired of poor African-Americans becoming more and more invisible in this country. Black schools were a farce, job choices limited, housing intolerable. When Martin Luther King, Jr., was murdered, Farmer's heart hardened and he adopted a new mantra full of tight-fisted anger and a burning in his belly to force change with a match to a building, or a fist to a face, or a gun raised in the air. He and others like him traveled from town to town wherever there was a fight to be had. They would bluster their way into leadership. Farmer was charismatic, charming and dangerous. He had come to this town and had taken leadership over from calmer heads.

"These white fools are not moving fast enough to integrate our schools. They figure if they drag their feet we'll quit and go home. They think we'll pull our slave clothing back over our heads, lower our eyes and thank the good Lord for the blessing of picking their tobacco. No more! We got to demand they either get out of our way or die trying to stop us!" Farmer was sitting on top of a table in the nightclub, smoking a cigar and firing up his troops.

African-American high school students had been marching all month to draw attention to the poor condition of their schools and demanding integration in their district. Tempers were bubbling and impending catastrophe hung low in the air like a poisonous gas.

It was into this atmosphere that Farmer and those like him were drawn. They were slowly getting into the students' heads and convincing them that chest thumping and threats were the only way to get the job done. And if their actions were not heeded, it was then their duty to make the city pay for its sins.

I slowly worked my way around the nightclub nodding my head, crossing my arms, going through the motions of agreement—all the while listening and trying to identify who in this group would bring the most to the table as a member of the Human Relations Council in this city. What man in this smoky cavern could best represent the group's views, yet be able to respond to God's prompting when the chips were down? Did that man even exist here? I felt like the Biblical Lot frantically trying to find that one righteous man in Gomorrah.

"If they don't listen, we've got to make them listen. We've got to wipe those smirks off their faces by any means we can." Farmer was good. He knew what buttons to push and how to churn the smoldering pot of humiliation and frustration into anger and action.

The high school students were not in attendance at the nightclub rallies. But they were organized and had their own radical leaders, and thus far they had managed to keep their protests violence-free. Their persistence was infused with their youthful idealism. They were proud to be making their voices heard. A quality education that would afford them careers so they could one day support families and live in decent homes was what they were crying out for. They wanted summer jobs that would help them pay for college and buy clothes. They wanted nothing more than what white children took for granted.

I was deeply touched by their civil righteous fervor and their innocent desire to make America better. I couldn't help but compare my childhood to theirs. What would have happened to me in Willard had I protested more—gone beyond my childish sit-in at Mrs. Chrub's strawberry field? What if I had walked into Mr. Chrub's country store and demanded he pay my daddy what he owed him? What if I had stood my ground until a fair wage was given? In that climate and in that day, I'd probably have been strung up from a tree, or my daddy would have had my hide for sure.

Times were changing. African-Americans were making a difference. It wasn't happening fast enough for some, but in a few short years, our country had gone from lynching black children for the sheer fun of it to walking the gritty road to freedom. That freedom was being won by marching for better schools, jobs, housing and our right to be standing on America soil. Our voices were being heard. Guns weren't necessary. Matches were uncalled for. Thrown rocks and broken windows solved nothing. It was the voice, the heart that was gaining us our freedom. I was convinced that violence would only stop the progress. I was convinced that Christ-likeness at this crucial time in our history would speak louder than a raised black fist. I staked my life on it.

For three weeks, Lynn and I worked to gain the confidence of our "peers." On several occasions we were each able to squelch a destructive plan or convince cooler heads that throwing bottles and looting would get us nowhere. Our covers seemed to be working and protecting us. But something frightening was happening. Farmer and his feverish rhetoric were gaining momentum; my challenges to his calls for aggression were starting to lose their appeal.

One bright spot was that, after three weeks of cloak and dagger angst, both Lynn and I had been able to identify leaders from our separate groups whom we thought would make good HRC members. While those chosen were filled with rage toward the opposite race, we felt the men we singled out were still open to reason. Unfortunately, a threat loomed that could have destroyed all we had done.

TWENTY-ONE

A Beginning

"A demonstration in the dark? Oh, this is trouble," exclaimed the sheriff.

For the most part, the student marches had taken place during the day after school, allowing for better protection of the teens by law enforcement. But I had uncovered a new strategy devised by the more extreme students with Farmer's urging. I had a bad feeling about this.

The students were going to gather at their school after dark and march from the student parking lot to the heart of the business district. Their signs and mantras were calling for the integration of schools in their district. Farmer was manipulating the students toward a face-off downtown.

Once I knew when and where the protest march was to take place, Lynn and I had a secret meeting with the local sheriff, the state highway patrol, the National Guard and a new Human Relations Council team who had joined us from Raleigh.

"It's tonight. I'm not sure how many protesters there will be, but a few hundred at least," I reported.

"What about your folks, Mr. Martin? Are they going to give us trouble?" asked the sheriff.

"As far as I know, none of them know about it yet, but to be safe maybe the highway patrol could position themselves to block the four main streets that come into the square."

"Sheriff, your men need to protect the students. Their constitutional rights need to be upheld. They have every right to march and be protected. Why don't you concentrate on the town square and escorting the students into the square." At all costs, I wanted the students protected. They were just children, really, some not even old enough to drive.

"Fine. Where will you be?" asked the sheriff.

"I'm going to be with the demonstrators. I'm meeting up with Farmer and the others at the school. I'll try my best to keep them from getting out of hand," I said. Directing my next thoughts to the captain of the National Guard, I continued, "Also, I want your troops to be posted on top of the buildings—but make sure they stay out of sight."

Profanities and racial slurs were about as bad as the white radicals had dished out to the students thus far. But this time, a foreboding hung in the air like the sighting of a shark near a crowded beach, or that feeling one gets just before he opens a closet door after hearing a strange noise. It was dark outside. Older agitators had infiltrated the students' ranks, and anything could happen.

I arrived at the school among chants and cheers. You would have thought a pep rally was taking place before a big game. I wished it were as innocent as that. The moment I joined the throng of protesters, I could feel the electricity in the air as Farmer pumped them up with warrior talk. My heart started pounding as the students around me raised their fists and jumped up and down. I started praying with an urgency that didn't stop until I fell into an exhausted sleep much, much later that night.

More than four hundred marchers left the school parking lot chanting and carrying signs. At the head of the pack marched twenty-eight-year-old Robert Farmer and his Marxist comrades.

The march was rowdy and loud. My hope of walking into the heart of the city in an orderly fashion died pretty quickly. Word of the march spread as every radical, white or black, tried to make his way to the town square. Thankfully, the highway patrol was able to keep parked cars from the middle of town, and anyone on foot was stopped behind the line of squad cars blocking the streets.

As the students marched into the square, the sheriff's department kept their distance while keeping a wary eye out for bottles, guns or any kind of weapons.

Once the sea of agitators flooded the square, Farmer began his speech. I have to hand it to this young man. Only a few years younger than myself, he had a gift to motivate. He was sincere. He thought he was right. And on this night, he was determined to get satisfaction, one way or the other.

"What has this town done for you?"

"Nothing!" roared the crowd.

"Have they listened to your cries?"

"No!" answered the students.

"Have they listened to your mothers' cries?"

"No!"

On and on the speechmaking went until the students were in such a frenzy that one more contempt-filled moment longer and I was convinced they would burn the place down—apparently so was the National Guard. As one, the troops silently appeared and pointed their rifles down at the students.

From across the square, Lynn and I made eye contact as both of us bolted into action. He ran toward a patrol car and I ran up on the platform to Farmer. Students were shouting and chanting and poised for action.

"Man, you've got to stop this! We've got to get you out of here or they are going to kill you and slaughter these kids!" I cried. I'm not sure he heard everything I said. The noise level was deafening. But as I pushed him from his perch, the student leaders took his place, as if on cue, and began listing the demands of the students as each proclamation brought on more cheers.

"What are you doing?" shrieked Farmer as I propelled him through the crowd toward the waiting highway patrol car.

"I'm saving your life. Now get out of town and let the students take it from here." I pushed him into the car and watched as it pulled away with its bewildered passenger in the backseat.

The students had their say. They made their demands. And with Farmer out of the way, things calmed down. The protesters were none the wiser as the soldiers lowered their rifles and returned to their hiding places. The night ended with no loss of life and constitutional rights preserved. When I finally fell into bed that night, the only prayer I had the strength to mutter was, "Thank you, Jesus," as I drifted into an exhausted sleep.

It took another week to convince the new radical friends whom Lynn and I had invited to the local HRC meeting to actually attend. And when they did come, nobody came without a snarl and a belief that they were wasting their time. In fact, I'm sure that the only thing that got them there was the promise that they would be able to give the sheriff a piece of their minds.

My black jacket and I sat on one side of the room with my cronies, while Lynn sat on the other side of the small room in his jeans and vest with his buddies. Talk about fireworks! The poor folks from the school board and city council and a few pastors who had joined the HRC a year earlier got an earful that evening.

Our first meeting took place late at night in a pastor's living room. While we didn't call it a secret meeting, that's what it was. Those who attended did not want to lose their credibility with their respective groups.

Five recruited radicals—two white and three black—crossed their arms and waited to unload. Also among our mix were a Jew and an Indian. What a motley crew we were. As the sheriff sat and listened calmly to insults and ranting from both sides (I was sure the vein in his forehead would explode at one point), the other HRC members forced shaky smiles and acted like they weren't afraid for their lives.

Lynn and I were convinced we were on holy ground. People who hated each other were finally talking (yes, at times loudly) to each other. The sheriff didn't bat an eye. The other commission members were speechless as they heard years of frustration, hurt and fear boil over into the room. Both sides talked and raged until their lungs seemed to collapse. Then finally, in the wee hours of the morning, as a collective breath was exhaled, they slumped into their corners like spent prizefighters.

God's presence was thick in the room. He seemed to expand Himself into every corner as He wrapped His arms around us all.

Our next secret meeting was a few days later. Yes, we had a second meeting that was followed by a third and so on. By God's incredible grace, from this angry, bewildered, eclectic bunch of people, a Human Relations Council was born. Rules of conduct were drawn up and, to everyone's surprise, they were actually followed. In an amazingly short time, an integration plan was presented to the school board—a plan that succeeded.

The day Lynn and I slipped out of town, I felt I had been privileged to experience God's power in a most unusual way. It was like I stood before the burning bush, or the parted sea, or witnessed a blind man receive his sight. Miracles are not always what you expect them to be, but I discovered that they never fail to take your breath away.

I left town with new heroes to admire. They were to meet that night, huddled in a room with their knees almost touching as they hammered out the next resolution that would continue to help heal their beloved community.

TWENTY-TWO

The Wilmington Ten

The Wilmington newspaper once quoted me as saying, "We must learn to live with each other with justice, equality and liberty, or we are going to die as fools." I said that almost a year to the day after the city of Wilmington, North Carolina nearly annihilated itself, again.

In February 1971 our country was at war. Yes, the rice paddies in Vietnam were still dangerous and lives were unfortunately still being lost there, but that's not the war I'm talking about. It was the combat being played out on our own streets and neighborhoods that had me on my knees at night. And in Wilmington, a battle was about to ensue that personified the fool in us all.

When I first started working with the Good Neighbor Council, I was constantly seeking out local leadership—black and white, radical and conservative. I wanted students, teachers, law enforcement, government officials and regular citizens with a gift of speech and inspiration to help me organize and strategize.

I stumbled upon such an individual in Oxford, North Carolina. Benjamin Franklin Chavis, Jr. was twenty years old when we first met. I was very impressed with him as someone who could get the attention and allegiance of the young folks. I had learned that if students had a list of demands and a strong leader to help them articulate those demands, then we had something to negotiate.

Dr. King had selected Ben, a college student at the time in his freshman year, as a youth coordinator for the Southern Christian Leadership Conference. He had also been recruited by the United Church of Christ's North Carolina-Virginia Commission for Racial Justice and was mentored by Reverend Leon White. He was the perfect motivator. He was young, charismatic, articulate and passionate. With his help, the Good Neighbor Council was able to bring the student protests in Oxford to a successful conclusion. Ben and I crossed paths several times over the next few months. Three years later, we faced our greatest challenge together.

After Dr. King's death, Wilmington was a hotbed of turmoil. The 1969-70 school year brought desegregation to the New Hanover County school district. However, the transition was a dangerous one. And, quite frankly, both sides of the district didn't want it. The whites didn't want the blacks in their schools, and not just because they were racist—although that was certainly part of it. To be honest, the way that we integrated our schools back then was haphazard at best. There was no transition to speak of. No sensitivity training or political correctness instruction. No trying to ease everyone into this huge paradigm shift with teacher training or school psychologists on hand. One day, blacks were not in the white school; the next day they were.

Today if we were going about this, we'd have a six-month in-service for our teachers to teach them about the culture and tradition of the new influx of students. We would go out of our way to make the new students feel welcome and enlist the current students in the plan. Back then, we had the dream, and it was a good one. We were heading in the right direction. But we sure could have done it better.

As for the black end of things, Williston High School in Wilmington had a long, proud history. But suddenly black students were pulled out of school, placed in a hostile environment, and robbed of any opportunity to participate in their own school activities. If you had been a cheerleader at your black school, it was pretty well understood that you would not be one at your new school. About the only thing black high school students would be able to participate in was sports, but not without a lot of posturing and bloody noses. When the schools were integrated in Wilmington, did any white teachers lose their jobs? Probably not. But what happened to the entire school of black teachers and coaches? How many of them were hired into the newly integrated school system? Yes, we could have done it better. And in Wilmington, we could have done it much better.

For a year, sporadic violence pocked the schoolyards of this coastal port. Tensions and frustrations boiled and churned until the slightest bump of the pot was all that was needed to spew chaos into the city. That bump came in the form of seventeen arrests and fifteen expulsions of black students who refused to disperse outside of New Hanover High School. A skirmish between a white girl and a black girl that wintry afternoon set in motion a racial face-off that would end in death and destroyed lives.

The next day at Hoggard High, another local high school, black students were denied a special school assembly to commemorate Dr. Martin Luther King's birthday, so they staged a sit-in and fifteen more protesters were suspended. The stage was set. Police started patrolling at both high schools.

By the end of the week, more than one hundred African-American students had gathered at Gregory Congregational Church with the blessing of Reverend Eugene Templeton and his deacon board and announced a mass student boycott of Wilmington's high schools and the establishment of an all-black alterative school inside Gregory's building. Immediately Gregory Congregational Church became a target for every radical, hate-filled, white antagonist in town. Drive-by rock throwing and random gunfire quickly followed. The local Human Relations Council called for back up.

Preston Hill, now the assistant director of the state Human Relations Commission, Lynn Martin and I met in Wilmington on Wednesday night, February 3, 1971. It was chilly and foggy. I had come from Fayetteville. Preston drove in from Raleigh and Lynn came in from Elizabethtown. Ben Chavis, now a well-seasoned activist, got there two days ahead of us and had already organized the students and had helped formally announce their demands: more black studies included in the curriculum, more black coaches and teachers, fairer discipline practices and fewer blacks suspended or expelled from school. And a special observance of Martin Luther King's birthday.

On the Wednesday before we arrived, four hundred students led by Ben had marched to Hemenway Hall, the county school offices, for a confrontation with Superintendent Heyward Bellamy. Bellamy did not appear before the students, and Chavis refused the superintendent's offer for a private meeting. The protesters congregated back at Templeton's church.

As I got out of my car that evening, my shoulders were hit with a foreboding and my chest felt heavy and burdened. "Almighty God, I need your strength and wisdom. Please use us to dissipate the anguish in this city."

A flurry of activity ensued as contacts had to be made and meetings set up with the school board, the school superintendent, the mayor, the police chief, the students and their leaders, local ministers and the local HRC.

Mayor Luther C. Cromartie and Police Chief H.E. Williamson weren't the easiest gentlemen to work with. To say that mistakes were made by these men, other city officials and even by us would be an understatement. In our defense, by the time we rolled into town, Wilmington had slowly begun to drop blood into turbulent waters. Despite our best efforts, the sharks were already circling and baring teeth. It would take a miracle to run them back into deep water.

Black radicals with their own agendas poured into the city while white supremacists loaded their guns. By 8:30 that Wednesday evening, the L. Schwartz Furniture Company, located in a black north-side neighborhood, had been firebombed and completely destroyed. By midnight four more fires were reported. Reverend White decided it had gotten too dangerous, pulled Ben from the church and took him back to Oxford.

On Thursday, Lynn, Preston and I were kept busy in long, extended, closed meetings with the school board, black student leaders and local ministers. At the same time, my boss, Human Relations Council Director Fred Cooper, conferred with the mayor, the police officials and even members of the Ku Klux Klan and Rights of White People. Any stakeholder in this boiling mess had a say.

As the city began to swell with angry out-of-towners, I could tell the African-American population was dangerously close to rioting. With no levelheaded leader, disaster was ahead.

"Hello? Reverend White?"

"Is that you, Aaron?"

"Yes, sir. I need your help. I need you to get Ben back here."

"Do you think that's wise?"

"I do. We need someone who can control all elements of the black population. Ben is our best hope of keeping the leadership from falling into extremist hands and taking over. It's critical that he come back. He's trusted by the black youth. He can reason with a calm head. He's our best chance of getting through this thing without violence."

Ben Chavis was back in Wilmington by early Thursday afternoon, rallying the troops, so to speak. We still had a faction of troublemakers we couldn't seem to control, but at least with Ben appealing to calmer heads, we were able to get most of the students to concentrate on negotiating the issues at hand.

Chavis and his student followers, radical sympathizers and clergy supporters made Gregory Congregational Church and the manse next door into their official headquarters. They prepared to hunker down for the night.

By late evening, I had to place a frantic call. "Reverend Templeton! Get everyone out of the building. There's been a bomb threat!" I didn't know if the threat was real, but I wasn't going to wait to find out. During the bomb drill, most of the children left the church building and a good many of them went on home. Those who stayed went to the Templetons' house. Ben was among them.

It turned out the bomb threat was a hoax, but it changed something. Students started returning to the church, but this time some of them had their daddies' old shotguns they'd found in closets, and a few other assorted, aging weapons were brought in. The students were determined to protect themselves and the church building. The stakes went up as the students became sitting ducks hunkered in Gregory Congregational. I was getting very concerned.

"It's alright, Reverend Johnson," said Ben calmly over the phone. "We're holding an all-night prayer meeting here. Don't worry. We're okay."

However, before the sun came up, sniper fire from unseen assailants chipped at the bricks of Gregory Congregational Church and the manse. Under the cover of night, elsewhere an arsonist hit the Southside Baptist Church, and by one-thirty Friday morning, Lums Restaurant had been burned to the ground.

It was time for a city curfew to be put into place before someone got killed. The HRC approached Mayor Cromartie and strongly advised him to authorize the curfew. He refused.

Friday afternoon three hundred angry young blacks marched on City Hall demanding better protection for their neighborhoods. Ben led the march from Gregory Congregational Church to the steps of City Hall. He was angry and greatly concerned that neither the mayor nor police chief had called for a curfew. With students scattered across the wide cement steps, Chavis and Reverend Leon White led the students in staccato-like chants, "We want the Mayor! We want action!"

The mayor did not comply. Instead he announced he would give the city of Wilmington one more chance at normal life and would not institute a curfew for Friday night. Reading a statement before the media, Cromartie looked ragged and taut. "This is an appeal to all the fine citizens of Wilmington to exercise the greatest of self-control. We are faced with a real emergency in our city, and unless we can get the cooperation of everyone, we will be faced with resorting to drastic means. We don't want that."

Mayor Cromartie appealed for the citizens of Wilmington to "take a long hard look at the consequences of having to resort to means beyond our local control to control our citizens.... There have been appeals from some segments of the community for a curfew, but such a measure is in itself a drastic thing and is not only inconvenient but expensive."

As I listened to the mayor's statement, my throat felt like there was a wad of cotton clinging to my tonsils. Everything in me told me this was a mistake. I spent almost the entire night on the phone talking to Ben at the church or at the Templetons' home. Fear climbed its way up my bones as two attempts were made to burn down Mike's Grocery, only three hundred yards or so from Gregory Congregational.

Firefighters called to that area had to fall back as sniper fire threatened them. Once police had reinforced the vicinity around Mike's Grocery, the small fires at the store were easily controlled with only minor damage. The wail of sirens, however, seemed to shatter the night continually as fires sprang up all over town. Fifty highway patrol cars were called into Wilmington.

"Ben, what was that?" I asked over the phone.

"We're being fired on, man! We have perimeters set up and brothers watching with binoculars and a code word and signal in play so we can identify ourselves."

"How many are in there with you? Where are Reverend Templeton and his wife? Are they safe?"

"Yeah. They're at the house. Mrs. Templeton has loaned us some bandages."

"Bandages? For what?"

"Chili got hit, but he's okay."

"Lord, have mercy!"

By eleven that Friday night, countless reports of fires and gunshots were reported. Through the night as Ben and I talked on the phone, I'd occasionally hear shots muted in the background.

"What's happening, Ben?"

"They just keep coming."

"Who?"

"Them! They drive their cars through the barricades around the church and just shoot willy-nilly toward us."

"Are you shooting back?"

Silence.

"Ben?"

"Somebody is shooting back out there, but I don't know who it is."

Much to my dismay, armed blacks were hiding in dark corners and returning fire at car windshields. By dawn Saturday, a firebomb by unknown assailants had destroyed the field house at Hanover High School. Wilmington teetered on the brink of hell.

TWENTY-THREE

February 6, 1971

The morning of Saturday, February 6, the school board announced it would meet with the suspended or expelled students involved in the school protests and their parents to review their cases. At least some of the mediation was working.

Part of the breakdown in Wilmington between the local HRC and the protesting students came because the students did not feel they had a voice on the local committee. Honestly, the local members had done a good job trying to address the larger issue of integration—after all, Hanover County's schools had been integrated amidst great opposition and peril. However, the students had their own priorities and, as with most teens, they felt adults just didn't move fast enough. So they bypassed the committee and took things into their own hands. I was proud of them on one level. But on another level I feared there would be a devastating price to pay.

What I wouldn't have given for a cell phone back then. Lynn, Preston, Director Cooper and I ran up the GNC's phone bill to a record high during those four or five days. We were constantly in and out of the city, frantically trying to bring the right resources together to bring this stand-off to a peaceable conclusion. I was continuously cradling a phone between my ear and shoulder, getting updates from Ben or talking to a city or state official. We also kept the governor informed at regular intervals.

This was the era of phone operators, collect calls and credit card calls. During the crisis there was more than one instance when a surly operator, not understanding the urgency of these calls, gave us a hard time, making our connections more difficult.

"Aaron, there's a white man in a house across the way firing at us!" shouted Ben into the mouthpiece.

"Keep everyone away from the windows. I'll make a call to the chief." My hands were sweating when I dialed zero for the operator.

"This is the operator. How may I help you?"

"I need you to ring Chief Williamson of the Wilmington Police Department. This is an emergency."

I heard the operator dialing the number and then I heard a busy signal. "I'm sorry sir, but that number is currently busy. Would you like to try back later?"

"No, ma'am I wouldn't. This is an emergency. Could you please cut in for me?"

"What is the emergency, sir?"

"I need to talk to the Chief immediately. Please cut in for me."

"Sir, I cannot do that without knowing if your emergency fits the pattern of our emergency cut-in policy."

I wanted to reach through the phone line and throttle this woman.

"Ma'am, my name is Aaron Johnson and I work for Governor Bob Scott. There are some people in Wilmington at this very moment who are being shot at with real guns. I need Chief Williamson to do something about that. Does that fit the pattern of Southern Bell's emergency cut-in policy?"

Pause.

"One moment please."

The police went into the house in question. They stayed for a bit and then left, reporting that no gun was found on the premises. The minute the officers left, the shooting began again. Fortunately no one was injured. However, two FBI agents quietly working the area did abort the scheme of a group of thirty or forty white males who planned to rush Gregory Congregational armed to kill. The men had been overheard saying, "What we need are some dead agitators. They should be shot and left out in the street as a reminder for three days, then bury them." The agents and a police officer were able to arrest three white men, armed and trying to invade the black neighborhood of Wilmington.

About thirteen students were still barricaded in the church building while nine or so others positioned themselves outside as "guards." I believe that Ben Chavis divided his time between checking on the students at Gregory and the Templetons at the parsonage—slipping back and forth unnoticed.

At sundown we still had no curfew. My conversations with Ben indicated that tensions were rising. Cars packed with whites were cruising by the church building shouting threats and randomly firing weapons.

By 9 p.m. things started to fall completely apart. A parked car at Eighth and Nun streets was set ablaze and couldn't be saved. Four fire bombings at various locations were reported in succession. At around 10 p.m. a white officer by the name of Sergeant H. F. Genes was wounded in the leg and a black minister sympathizer, Reverend David S. Vaughn, was shot standing on the steps of Gregory Congregational Church. He was unarmed. By 10:30 p.m. Mike's Grocery store finally succumbed to a fiery blaze after two unsuccessful attempts earlier in the week.

Then it happened.

The tragedy that Lynn and I and so many others had been working around the clock trying desperately to avoid slammed down its defying fist. As the rafters of Mike's Grocery Store collapsed, snipers once again shot at firefighters as they fought the blaze. Police officers were called in for protection. Hearing about the reported gunfire, I honestly could not decipher where the shots were coming from. Did blacks or whites fire the bullets? My guess: both.

I had been on the phone all evening with Ben. He and I talked regularly throughout the night as he kept me informed. At times he spoke to me from the second-floor library of the manse. At other times he was in the church office. I know without a doubt that he never left or ventured out into the community that Saturday night, with or without a weapon. I know without a doubt that Ben Chavis was not the sniper who was shooting at the firefighters battling the blaze at Mike's Grocery or the one firing on police officers as they protected those firemen. I know without a doubt he did not order anyone to start that blaze and he did not order those teenagers to shoot at the police.

Ben was on the phone with me every hour on the hour—on a landline. In 1971, a landline is all that we had. There were no cell phones or portable phones or wireless phones. When you talked on the phone, you were stationary, tied to wherever that particular phone was plugged in.

When Steve Gibbs Mitchell, a.k.a Stevenson G. Corbett, age twenty, was shot by a police officer outside of Mike's Grocery, Ben was not there. During the fire at Mike's, two other houses close by also went up in flames. According to witnesses on the church property, Steve had gone outside to help one of the residents remove what furniture she could out of her burning house. And it was during that time that he was shot by police officer Jack M. Shaw.

Tragedy struck again Sunday morning when Harvey Cumber, a white man, drove his red pickup truck past the barricade and got out and started walking toward the church armed with a .38. When he pulled his gun from his holster, one of the guards standing in front of the building fired in self-defense, striking Cumber in the temple and killing him instantly. It was not Ben who shot him. It was not Ben who gave the order to shoot him.

It was only after Cumber's death that Mayor Cromartie finally called for a curfew and for the National Guard.

Sometime around 5:30 that Sunday evening during a torrential rainfall, Ben, the high school students and the other adult activists who had bunkered down in Gregory Congregational Church for the last four days quietly slipped away unnoticed.

At 2 a.m. Monday when the police and flak-jacketed, M16-toting National Guardsmen raided the church, they found it empty except for one lone female employee and a male caretaker. Later that day, Ben Chavis resurfaced in Raleigh and later in his hometown of Oxford to give press conferences and to tell his side of the tragic events.

Conflicting reports about what was found in the church building after the agitators had abandoned it started to emerge in the media. Some officials said bullet casings and folding chairs were found in the church's steeple, indicating the presence of a sniper's nest. A day later it was reported that a National Guardsman found badly deteriorating dynamite caps supposedly hidden in the basement of the church. Police immediately started posturing and claiming that they did not plant the explosives there after the fact.

There were also two conflicting reports from the police about whether there was evidence found that supported Chavis's claim that sniper fire constantly threatened those inside the church building. In a news report dated February 8, Chief Williamson said, "I think I have talked to every officer who was there and others who investigated the church and the reverend's house, and no evidence indicated anyone had been firing at either place from the outside." The chief reported that all the glass windows in the church remained intact. He also said that there was no sign of slugs having struck the door facings to the church building, and that even the brick walls were checked and no evidence of gunfire was found.

Two days later, Chief Williamson refuted his claim and said broken windows and bullet holes on the outside of Gregory Congregational supported the claim of sniper fire.

On Wednesday, February 10, one week after I had arrived, I was called away from Wilmington to my next assignment. Students at Fayetteville State were organizing demonstrations and protests and I was needed to aid in negotiations.

My last hours in Wilmington were filled with debriefing meetings with students, the mayor, city officials, National Guard officials, a district judge, the local HRC executive and the like. My detailed reports of all that had happened had to be written while everything was fresh in my head and heart. It was a surreal day as the city of Wilmington deflated in population and seemed to rewind like an old newsreel.

The day after I left town, the funeral was scheduled for the young Steve G. Corbett at Holy Trinity Church. Trouble was not anticipated, but about one hundred National Guardsmen were assigned to patrol Wilmington until after the funeral service.

Before I left town that day, I drove over to Gregory Congregational Church. I got out of my car and walked up to the building. I searched until I found what I was looking for. It didn't take long. I placed my right hand over one of the ugly chipped holes left shattered by an angry bullet. With my fingers resting in the jagged wound, I bowed my head. God had remained faithful. We had been fools and yet, He graced us with mercy and miraculously left us a sliver of hope that it could be better than this…much, much better.

TWENTY-FOUR

The Trial

*E*ight months after the incident in Wilmington, police charged ten people—Ben Chavis, twenty-four; Connie Tindall, twenty-one; Marvin "Chili" Patrick, nineteen; Wayne Moore, nineteen; Reginald Epps, eighteen; Jerry Jacobs, nineteen; James "Bun" McKoy, nineteen; Willie Earl Vereen, eighteen; William "Joe" Wright, Jr., sixteen; and Ann Shepard, thirty-five—with conspiracy to burn Mike's Grocery and conspiracy to assault emergency personnel. The so-called Wilmington Ten, most of them high school students, had sadly secured for themselves a place in history.

The trial one year later was moved to Burgaw in Pender County because of the notoriety of the case. James Ferguson, a young, black lawyer from out of Charlotte, represented the defendants. With funds from the NAACP, the United Church of Christ Commission for Racial Justice, and Amnesty International, the truth was still difficult to get at.

In June 1972, a jury of ten blacks and two whites was seated. But a mistrial was granted almost immediately on the grounds that Assistant District Attorney Jay Stroud was ill. Stroud claimed stomach pains and left the courthouse after the jury was seated. James Ferguson was livid and claimed Stroud's illness was faked.

When Stroud returned to court, he was able to use all of his dismissals resulting in a total remix of the jury's make up. When the new trial started the following September, ten whites and only two blacks were seated—a complete reversal of the first jury.

Rumors of coached prosecution witnesses who were offered gifts and special deals for perjured testimony were rife. The trial immediately took on a hopeless tone for the defense. To say the trial was a farce and corrupt would be like describing the Atlantic Ocean as merely a pond.

By the last week of the trial, only one lone witness, Ann Shepard, the only female and Caucasian of the Wilmington Ten, had testified for the defense. One of the most notable trials in our state and nation's history to date, yet the defense had only come up with one witness. Mr. Ferguson was later quoted as saying he all but gave up on the trial, and that his only hope was that the two black jurors could cause a deadlock forcing a mistrial. Mr. Ferguson was also reported as saying hundreds of irregularities happened during the proceedings and that he was already looking to win on appeal.

Then one day while working in the central office I was interrupted. "Are you Mr. Aaron J. Johnson?" An officer from the Wake County Sheriff's Department stood in the doorway of my office.

"I am. What can I do for you?"

He walked over to my desk and handed me an envelope. "Have a good day, sir." Without another word he retreated, leaving me staring at a subpoena.

Both Preston Hill and I were subpoenaed to testify on behalf of the defendants. I immediately, with the help of Preston and my secretary, began gathering all of the files and reports we had written and accumulated about the Wilmington incident. A day later, with those reports from our turbulent days and nights in Wilmington neatly organized in my briefcase, reports in my estimation that could have possibly exonerated The Ten, we started our drive to Burgaw.

I drove out of Raleigh first and Preston was to leave a little bit after me. I was only thirty or forty miles down the highway when Preston overtook me in his car and motioned for me to pull over.

"Aaron, we got a call from Ferguson's office telling us not to come."

We were standing on the side of the road as cars whipped past us. I was having a hard time comprehending. "What? Why? What's going on?"

"I'm not sure. I'm not sure what we should do."

"Maybe we should just keep going and get there and see what's going on." It wasn't making sense to me. Our testimony was needed. We got back in our cars and kept driving towards Burgaw. I felt this urgency to get to the courthouse, kind of like you'd feel on the way to the hospital after you'd been told a loved one had been critically injured. You didn't know how or what or why or how serious their injuries were; you just knew you needed to get there fast.

I was trying to organize my thoughts as I drove when suddenly it was announced over the radio that the defense for The Ten had rested. Preston must have had his radio on too because he started flashing his headlights at me. We were coming through the town of Benson at that time and once again, pulled over to the side of the road.

"Did they say what I thought they said?" I asked Preston as I walked up and spoke through his car window.

Preston put his hand up for me to stop talking and turned his radio up. The announcer had come back on and again reported that the Wilmington Ten lawyer had just rested and the case was now in the hands of the jury.

"That can't be right. We're supposed to testify. What's going on?"

"How should I know? I'm ready to forget this all ever happened. Turn around. I want to be done with this."

I didn't understand my friend's attitude, but I knew that Preston was under tremendous pressure. The GNC had resisted having the organization participate in this case and fought the subpoenas as long as they could. The board feared those who opposed the GNC would use our testimony and involvement in this case against us, threatening the Council's mission and existence. They also feared betraying the confidentiality and identities of those who worked behind the scenes in Wilmington, who risked their lives, jobs and stability to feed us information. This vital information helped us stay abreast of what was happening in the most dangerous neighborhoods.

Not knowing what else to do, Preston and I turned around and went back to Raleigh. We had no communication with the Wilmington Ten defense team whatsoever. I truly didn't know if they were even aware that we had received subpoenas or that we were on our way to the trial. It was the weirdest thing.

Bewildered, when we returned to the central office, I reluctantly filed away my reports. In short order, the jury convicted all ten defendants on the testimony of three key but highly suspect prosecution witnesses.

Allen Hall, eighteen, a convicted felon with a history of psychiatric problems, had been serving a prison sentence by the time of the trial. He testified that Ben Chavis had ordered him and several others to burn down Mike's Grocery. Hall also claimed under oath that Ben was one of the snipers firing on the firemen and police the night of the fire.

Another incredulous prosecution witness was sixteen-year-old Jerome Mitchell, who had been convicted of second-degree murder. This teen gave testimony placing Chavis and the others at or near the scene of the firebombing and sniper fire.

Finally, Eric "Motormouse" Junious, only thirteen years old at the time of the trial, said he overheard Ben encouraging his followers to torch buildings and to fire on emergency officers.

It was on this questionable testimony alone that the Wilmington Ten were found guilty. They were sentenced to a combined 282 years in prison—with Ben receiving the harshest sentence of 34 years.

What had happened that last day of the trial? My mind went over and over it, but I simply could not figure it out. However, I knew what I should have done. I should not have turned the car around that day. I should have driven straight to Burgaw and insisted on talking with Mr. Ferguson and showing him my files. I should have frantically banged pots together or honked my car horn incessantly until someone listened to me. I should have, and I wish with all of my heart that I had, made copies of my reports. Because our documentation was confidential, the HRC policy forbade copies to be made. I complied. I should have known better.

I knew something was amiss at the HRC, but I had talked myself out of it. I knew that the powers-that-be were afraid for us to get involved in the case. But I argued that it was our duty to do so. The GNC had played an integral role in the tragic events in Wilmington. We had vital information to the case. Ten lives weighed in the balance. Where was my righteous authority now? What had happened to my civil disobedience that I so believed in? When a wrong is committed, it is our duty as citizens to try and correct it to the best of our abilities.

It isn't good enough now to say that I succumbed to the rhetoric of the "greater good." Yes, I got the message loud and clear that the Good Neighbor Council, the Human Relations Council if you will, wanted to take a "low profile" approach toward the Wilmington Ten trial. Our funds came from the General Assembly, and someone somewhere had injected into the mainstream of thought that if the HRC cooperated with the defense, we could lose our funding, and then the Human Relations Council would be of no use to anyone. That hypodermic of fear infected sound reasoning like a toxin. Who had injected it? Did it come from my friend, Assistant Director Preston Hill, or Director Fred Cooper? Did it come from someone even higher up? I didn't know. But I should have found out. Cassie Newkirk Johnson would have expected no less from her son.

Of course, the consolation of the conviction was that appeals would be filed immediately on the defendants' behalf. To be ready, a few weeks after the trial, I decided to write a summary report of all that had happened in Wilmington. I wanted to be better prepared this next go-around to testify if called. However, when I went to retrieve my files from Region 3 at the central office in Raleigh (which included Wilmington and New Hanover County), they were gone.

My stomach twisted in knots the size of tree roots as I looked at the ravaged files. All that remained were scattered, benign notes and huge blank gaps in the records. I immediately went to Fred Cooper and told him about the missing files. I even filed a written report. After a three-day search by the HRC staff nothing was found. The files had simply vanished.

The Ten were convicted on October 18, 1972, and after only a brief incarceration all were freed on $450,000 bond while appeals were filed. But after four years of exhaustive judicial defeats, Ben Chavis and the other nine had to surrender themselves to the Pender County Court House on February 2, 1976.

Out on the front lawn of the courthouse, The Ten held an informal communion service with brown bread and sips of wine from bottles wrapped in paper bags. They prayed together as Ben asked for the remission of sins, the sins of the prosecutors, the judges, and the police. Speaking to the small crowd of friends and reporters who gathered he said, "We are victims of racism. We have been persecuted for political activity, not for criminal acts." By the end of the day, all ten were locked behind prison gates.

TWENTY-FIVE

The Missing Files

A year before The Wilmington Ten entered prison, I had resigned from the Human Relations Council. I had been proud of my work there and felt God had used me for His purposes. But after seven years, I felt Him pulling me in another direction.

A year after Ben and the others began their prison terms, Hall, Mitchell and Junious recanted their testimonies and accused prosecutor Jay Stroud of coercing them into false statements at the trial. The three men insisted that Stroud had indeed coached them and made promises to reduce sentencing as favors were exchanged. Junious, a mere child at the time, even claimed that Stroud had bought him a mini-bike in exchange for his erroneous testimony against Ben Chavis.

A post-trial hearing was conducted in front of Judge George M. Fountain based on the newly recanted testimony. Public interest in The Ten was once again sparked and hope born anew that the defendants would at last be exonerated.

When the CBS television news program *60 Minutes* did an exposé of the Wilmington incident and the recanted testimony, commentator Morley Safer strongly indicated that the Wilmington Ten were innocent. A flood of news articles followed.

And then God did his thing. He brought Stan Swofford to my door. Mr. Swofford was an investigative reporter for the *Greensboro Daily News* and had a question to ask me.

"Reverend Johnson, why didn't you testify at the trial? After all, according to witnesses, you're the one who asked Ben Chavis to come to Wilmington to help. Isn't that right?"

"Yes, sir. Ben had a way with the students. They trusted him and they needed a leader who'd do anything he could to keep order and keep the students from committing violent acts."

"Why didn't you say that at the trial?" Reporters, like lawyers, do not ask a question they don't know the answer to already. They're just looking for corroboration.

"I was going to. In fact, Preston Hill and I were on our way to the trial to testify with all of our files and reports in the car. But before we could get there that day, the defense rested and the trial was over. It was like nobody knew we were coming."

"Yeah, about those files, Reverend. What was in them?"

"Our documentation on all that went on in Wilmington during that time."

"Would those records have changed the outcome of the trial, do you think?"

"It's hard to say, Mr. Swofford. But I was convinced they would have been highly favorable toward the defendants."

"Why is that?"

"Because I had documented every telephone call Ben Chavis and I had over the course of the uprising. We talked every hour on the hour. I knew where he was at all times, and my records would have proven where he was *not*."

"Where are those files, Reverend Johnson?"

"Mr. Swofford, I wish I knew."

The minute I uttered those words my life got very complicated and dangerous.

Stan Swofford wrote a series of articles within a span of a year that stirred up a hornet's nest of controversy about what really happened in Wilmington and in particular the curious case of the missing files and the Human Relations Council's apparent apathy about the whole thing.

"Recent developments in the case, along with extensive interviews with state officials and persons familiar with the activities of the Wilmington 10 at the time, indicate that information which would have been vital to the defense of the Wilmington 10 has never been revealed," wrote Swofford.

"The Good Neighbor Council members, although they worked hand in hand with Chavis and his group, and although the Good Neighbor Council had requested that Chavis come to Wilmington to help ease tensions, did not wish to testify on behalf of the Wilmington 10 because as one former Good Neighbor Council field worker said, 'We were concerned about maintaining a low profile. We were very aware that our appropriations came from the General Assembly.'"

"...Johnson insisted to the Greensboro Daily News *last November, and he still insists, that they [the records] did exist...those files would have been favorable to the defense of the Wilmington 10..."*

When Stan Swofford's article quoted me about the stolen files, I had no idea of the backlash I was about to endure.

Of course, Swofford didn't blindside me. I gave him permission to quote me. I felt God directed me to go on record and finally let light illuminate the dark corners of this tragic event. My conscience had bothered me for long enough. Had I done anything wrong? No and yes.

No, I had not tried to cover up or hide anything about the events surrounding the Wilmington uprising. In fact, I did my best to record it as accurately as possible in my notes and documentation. I did my job as passionately and God-led as I could.

I remember the first night I spent in Wilmington all those many years ago, sitting in my motel room. I sat in the dark as I pulled back the curtains and looked out over the water and the lights. Right then, I asked God to move in that city. I asked Him to help me make the right decisions and to take me to the right people. I asked Him to replace hatred with love. I prayed for Mayor Cromartie and Chief Williamson by name. I prayed for the schools and the students. I pleaded with God to save this city and to allow me to be an instrument in His hands. By God's grace, I did my job in Wilmington.

Nonetheless, I did do wrong when I let sleeping dogs lie. Those files were stolen for no good purpose, and I let the powers-that-be convince me otherwise. Repentance means nothing if restitution, if it is within your power, doesn't follow. I told Mr. Swofford I'd testify in court anywhere at any time.

Director Ron Ingle, Fred Cooper's successor, corroborated my story of the missing files in an interview with Mr. Swofford. Three days later, Secretary of the Department of Administration Bruce Lentz fired Ingle. Then Lentz himself requested the State Bureau of Investigation look into the matter. It didn't take the SBI long to show up on my doorstep.

Through their interrogation, my story never changed. I had kept meticulous files during those days in Wilmington and now those files were missing.

As for my friend, Preston Hill, he had already denied that the files existed. He had even denied that we had them with us that day on our way to testify. In fact, Preston during the next two years refused repeatedly to comment publically at all on the Good Neighbor Council's role in the Wilmington case. We never talked about it with each other. He went to his grave knowing what he knew, and I can only believe he was at peace with it.

I was called a liar and just about everything else nasty and sorry. For the longest time, Fred Cooper claimed to have no recollection of the files or my report submitted to him about the missing files. No one at the HRC backed me up, even though I felt the entire staff at the time knew about the missing files. We had talked about them during our staff meetings numerous times. The office had conducted an all-out hunt for them. No file cabinet or drawer went unturned. Yet no one would back me up.

One day not long after the SBI interview, as I pulled out of the parking lot at Mt. Sinai Church, a police car pulled in right behind me. At first I didn't think much about it, but when the squad car started riding my bumper and turning corners with me like we were attached at birth, I became suspicious. The officer followed me home and all through the evening a cruiser patrolled in front of the house. The next morning, another police car followed me back to my office—front bumper to back bumper.

That started a long line of incidents where local law enforcement tried to intimidate me or provoke me to react in some way in order to find an excuse to arrest me. I made sure I always went the speed limit, that my signal lights were working and not burned out, that my brake lights were functioning, that I never changed lanes without signaling and on and on. I became the model driver. I couldn't take the chance of ever being placed into police custody. I feared I would have suffered the same fate as my missing files had I ever been forced into a police car. Unmarked cars started parking in front of my house as faceless men watched my house.

Through this period, I clung to my ministry at Mt. Sinai. The congregation circled around us and tried their best to protect my family. Despite their love and encouragement, I found myself sinking into despair. And on top of everything, I felt guilty. I had brought Ben to Wilmington. I blamed myself that ten innocent young people were in prison.

I had hoped that the Greensboro article would help shed light on what really happened. Instead, my reputation as a minister and citizen was called into question. People scoffed at me. Some made no secret of their contempt towards me. Others simply pitied me. But what hurt the most was that my word was no longer perceived as trustworthy.

Over several months, the North Carolina Justice Department interviewed sixteen employees and former employees of the state Human Relations Council and compiled a three-hundred-page report concerning the stolen records. Their conclusion: *There were no missing reports because they never existed to begin with. Aaron Johnson was a liar. Aaron Johnson was just a black man lying to save the skin of another black man.*

I ached and wanted desperately to clear my name. I wanted to be believed. I thought I was helping Ben and the others by coming forward. I feared all I had done was make things worse.

Then one night amidst all my self-pity, I remembered my mother. I recalled the many times she'd been on her knees on that cold kitchen floor by the woodstove as she prayed for God's protection over her children. I remembered the confidence she had that God heard her every time. And I remembered the holy stories she'd tell us about the persecution of Jesus Christ. He was only believed by a small handful of folks, really. He was cursed, beaten and killed for telling the Truth.

I felt Cassie Johnson's reprimand. How dare I think I deserved better than my Lord. We had never been promised from scripture that we'd be free of persecution if we tried to do the right things. In fact, if we believed in Him, chances were pretty good that some kind of strife would follow. If trying to live a Christ-centered life was taken seriously, you could just count on hardship from time to time.

So I did what my mama taught me and I got on my knees and I thanked my God for the opportunities He had given me. I handed over to Him my willful spirit, my trials and my fear.

I was watchful and careful and allowed God free reign. Did anything get better? Did the threats stop? Did the stares subside? Was my reputation restored? Not really, not for a long time. But *I* got better. I climbed out of my despair and held on to the one sure thing in my life: *God Almighty is and was and always will be. And, He will never abandon His own.*

Eventually, God's grace was sufficient. Fred Cooper came clean and admitted that he did recall that it was reported to him that documents were missing from the GNC files. He even said he thought it *might* have been me who told him about the missing records. A few days after Cooper's disclosure, a former secretary for the Human Relations Commission remembered that records were missing from "Region 3." She also said she remembered Preston and me taking the documents with us when we left the office that day to testify at the trial. Apparently, Mr. Swofford was a relentless soul.

When Governor James B. Hunt commuted the sentences of Ben Chavis and the other nine in 1980, I knew I'd done all I could do. Of course, I was no hero. I was barely a blip on the screen. Justice had finally encountered some sanity and The Ten were given back their lives.

I closed that chapter of my life. I never saw the next one coming.

Part V: Mr. Secretary

TWENTY-SIX

Republican Johnson

*M*y daddy was a Democrat. So was his daddy and his daddy before him—not registered ones, mind you, because the law wouldn't allow for that. But they were Democrat in spirit all the same. However, I'm sure that the day Mr. Lincoln freed my great-grandfather from bondage, he might have been a little more partial to the Republican Party than his children's children.

In 1971, when I exchanged my Democrat liberalism for Republican conservatism, folks thought maybe I had gone too far. In those days it was the kiss of death politically for a black man to join the Republican Party.

I discussed the change with Mattie. Even though she wouldn't change with me, she supported me. "I won't do any more in the Republican Party than I've done in the Democratic Party, so there's no need for me to change," she said. She also warned that if I did this, my enemies would be great among blacks.

Our daughter, Dezette, was about five years old and our son, Jamale, had just been born. Mattie was teaching full-time. She had her hands full, but she backed me all the way and even attended some meetings on my behalf.

I announced my party affiliation change from the pulpit one Sunday. "Family, I feel that God is leading me to the Republican Party. Now before you get all in a dither, let me explain.

"First, ever since some of us here helped our community form the Fayetteville Area Poor People's Association, I've seen some of the dark side of welfare—how it can steal away self-respect and pride if we're not careful. We need to be teaching folks to do for themselves, not depend on the government to do for them.

"Welfare should be for lifting blacks out of poverty, not keeping them there. We do not want a class of those who would forever be dependent on it, do we?"

My church knew what I was talking about. They'd seen it. When welfare becomes a way of life, the *family business* so to speak, it can mean death to dignity and self-reliance.

The Democratic Party has always been strong on assistance programs—to a fault, God bless them! But welfare is no magic pill. The government shouldn't do for the people what they should do for themselves. What the government gives, the government can take away. Pride, self-determination and authority over our own destiny should never be sold to the government or to the highest bidder. Didn't our slave forefathers teach us that?

"What the Democrats call Affirmative Action, the Republicans call Equal Opportunity. I like that better," I told my church members. "Welfare should be used as a step up. It should be used for training and education so you can get better employment. Better jobs lead to home ownership and financial security… and dignity.

"It's not a sin not to have, but it is a sin to not take advantage of what you do have. When God saved me, He said I was somebody and worth something!

"God gave us the best he had," I preached that Sunday morning, "who is Jesus Christ, and then sent His best from heaven to keep us close to Him—the Holy Spirit. Finally, He gave us the highest gift of all—His love. We should recognize that and live that way—with a humble pride, not with our arms stretched out for handouts.

"God always seemed to put me in a place where He could use me best. One of the things I've learned being on the Good Neighbor Council is that for the civil rights movement to continue its good work, it has to be represented on both sides of the aisle; and the Republican Party is sorely lacking when it comes to African-American representation. By joining the GOP, we would have a better chance of having a voice and giving a voice to African-Americans from a Christian perspective, in human relations as well as politics.

"Family, the line is shorter and the opportunities are greater in the Republican Party."

Several of the church members followed me into the Republican Party, while others said they'd support me if I ran for something but would remain with the Democrats.

Those who joined me became the core of the African-Americans in the Republican Party in our area; even at that, we made up less than one percent of the Republican Party in the county.

But we were an active one percent. We organized precincts and became delegates to the county convention, the district GOP and state conventions. And a couple of us later became delegates to the national GOP convention.

Our one percent joined with other blacks across North Carolina and formed a black caucus. Nationally, we joined with Hispanics and other minorities and became a full-fledged minority group in the Republican Party. It was from this group that President Ronald Reagan later chose a few to join his administration at the White House.

As for me, encouraged by Dr. Williams, a professor at Fayetteville State Teachers College, and Mr. Fleishman, a Jewish shopkeeper, I decided to run for Fayetteville's city council.

I ran for the Fayetteville City Council once in 1968 as a Democrat and lost. Even after an organized effort from church members and other supporters to get Negroes to register, we couldn't beat the hold that white precincts had in our city. In 1968, there were thirteen thousand Negroes living in Fayetteville. Only four thousand of them were registered.

When President Lyndon Johnson signed The Voting Rights Act in 1965, thanks to the heroic efforts of all those black students and soldiers in 1963, Fayetteville had already turned the corner on some segregation issues. African-Americans had already been registering and voting without much hassle, although the Justice Department did have to send a federal contingent to our county once to scrutinize our registration practices. It seemed the white registrar in Cumberland County had been requiring Negro registrants to pass a reading and knowledge test before they could register. After the Voting Rights Act was passed, it didn't take long for Federal officers to swoop into town like bloodhounds and put a quick end to the registrar's impromptu quizzes.

Mattie did vote for me when I finally ran for city council again in 1973, and she even attended several meetings on my behalf.

Early on the evening of the election, to everyone's surprise, I was leading in the polls and had the most votes of any candidate. It seemed the strategy Dr. Williams, Mr. Fleishmann and I had instituted was actually working.

In Fayetteville you had to vote for five candidates; you couldn't just vote for your favorite. For decades, the five strongest candidates had a stronghold on this election, making it impossible for a black candidate to ever be among the top five.

Our strategy was to get the word out to our people to vote for the four strongest white candidates on the ticket, because they were going to get elected anyway, and then for me. We ran a campaign that once again encouraged African-Americans to register and pay attention to the issues.

As the voter tally started coming in that night, it felt like Christmas Eve. With only two precincts left to report, I was still top dog on the ticket. The holdouts were the two largest white precincts in the city. The polls had been closed for hours, but those precincts, for whatever reasons, were withholding their reports. When they finally sent in their tallies, I slid from first place to sixth. Did something underhanded take place in those precinct counts? I don't know—but I lost by 130 votes. It was an eye-opener. We had come so close! We'd figured it out. The next time, we were determined to win.

My duties with the GNC kept me from running in the next race, but our organization kept intact as we increased efforts with voter registration and informing citizens of the issues. We were a bi-partisan group with about twenty-five members from Mount Sinai, but the whole committee numbered one hundred or so. Our goal was to try to get blacks elected to not only the city council but also the school board and the county board of commissioners. In fact, one of Mount Sinai's own, Mary McAllister, got elected to the county board as a Democrat. We also got C.R. Edwards elected to the board of education. Today, we have African-Americans on every political group in the county—both Republican and Democrat. Like they say, you should never put all your eggs in one basket.

The next year, our group got behind Marion George—a black Democrat, professor and attorney at Fayetteville State—and got him elected. He became the first African-American to be seated on Fayetteville's city council in many, many years.

In 1978, the year I received my honorary doctorate from Shaw University, I ran for the county commissioners board with an unlikely supporter—Republican Senator Jesse Helms. Senator Helms came to Fayetteville and campaigned for me. Jaws were dropping right and left, black and white, when the senator endorsed me publically.

Senator Helms was publically known for his bigotry and opposition to integration. Yet, here he was working to get a black man elected in a local election. Over the years, as our friendship grew, I came to know that Senator Helms had a public persona of racism and a private one of compassion. I can't explain the man; I just know that my experience with him defied his public image.

Our strategy wasn't well suited to a run for the county board because every district voted for their own member. My district had two African-Americans running against each other in that race—my Democrat friend, Arthur Lane, and me. Arthur won. Black Democrat trumped black Republican in most any election in North Carolina when those were your two choices.

In 1978, I made another run for city council and this time, with our strategy and black voter registration in high gear, we had a good feeling. Plus our friend Marion George had decided to vacate his council seat, but he did not make this decision public until I had a chance to announce my own candidacy.

At the time, we had our first Republican mayor in Mr. Jack Lee. Jack got behind my run and helped with the strategizing of the campaign. He was convinced that I could get elected with only a three thousand dollar budget.

One afternoon after a meeting, I was walking out of Jack's office with Mr. Bill Bailey, another campaign supporter and owner of an advertising company. "Jack just told you a lie, Aaron."

"What do you mean?"

"No way in this world can you get elected with only three thousand dollars. It is going to take a miracle to get you elected, the kind of miracle that's right up there with the virgin birth, if you ask me!"

"I thought you supported me in this?"

"I do, but let's not be stupid. First off, you're a Republican, and this is North Carolina. Second, you're black. And third, no one knows you."

"Yes, sir, folks know me! I've been around here for ten years."

"Yeah, but the majority don't know you. You just can't win on black folks. You've got to appeal to white folks and their issues as well. You've got to rise above the racial mentality. And to do that, it's going to cost you twenty-five thousand dollars to even have a chance to win. If you want to win a race, you've got to get a winner horse. You've got to feel winning in your soul, and find out what to do for the people—*all* the people. You think about that for a while—then we'll talk."

I left angry. How dare this white man tell *me* to rise above the racial mentality of it all! It was men like him and his bigotry that had not allowed the black man to cross any kind of political line until just recently. How dare he!

I was hopping mad ... for about a day. And then I started thinking about what Mr. Bailey had said, *"all the people."*

I started thinking about the issues and what I wanted to do for my community and whether I really wanted to win for the people or just to push a black face out in front of them all.

I started to pray. Now let me warn you—don't ask God for his advice if you really don't want it. I asked God to show me what to do. Do I run or not? If I do, then I asked Him to give me a reason to do it.

It only took minutes for God to push His words into my heart—like He'd just been waiting for me to ask the right question.

"Righteousness exalts a nation, but sin is a reproach to any people."

Those words from the book of Proverbs slammed into me like a gut punch, wakening in me, once again, my call to civil righteousness.

It didn't take long for the Lord to point me toward Fayetteville's most pressing issue. The main street in Fayetteville at the time was Hay Street. It was a decaying area of town that was plagued with nightclubs and prostitution. All of the legitimate businesses had been run out and in their wake was rot and immorality.

A few days later, Bill Bailey called. "You thought about what I said?"

"Yes, sir, I have. I'm entering this race and I'm going to win it!" I told him about my intentions of cleaning up Hay Street and revitalizing our downtown. "It's time to bring thriving businesses back to where they belong," I told him. I was on fire with ideas of cleaning up poverty-stricken neighborhoods and paving streets and taking care of our tax dollars and extending services such as police protection—and the list went on.

Finally Mr. Bailey interrupted me. "Now that sounds like a winning horse to me! Let's get started."

He had been playing me, of course. He dared me to look beyond race and see only people with needs—a city that needed compassionate leadership. My campaign cost fifteen thousand dollars, with eight thousand dollars coming from my own pocket.

I loved being one of Fayetteville's policymakers. Almost since the day I arrived in Fayetteville, my deacons at Mt. Sinai had encouraged me to think of God's church outside of walls. They encouraged me to stay in Fayetteville and pastor the community at large.

Finally as a councilman, I began to truly see my role as the conscience of the community. Fayetteville had serious moral problems. Social, economic and sexual problems abounded in our small town. The presence of Fort Bragg and rowdy soldiers did not help us. As minister and councilman, I could not look the other way. As directed by God, I had to help my community deal with these problems on both a spiritual and humanitarian level.

The church has been given the word of redemption from Jesus Christ. The way I see it, our task as Christ's followers is to try to redeem society. The word redemption also is the word for love that reaches out and asks nothing in return. The people in this city and county needed God's love to help counter the evil that had eroded our city's pride, self-esteem and moral judgment.

As I drove around Fayetteville, God once again opened my eyes to see—really see. I spotted hungry folks walking about town whom I had ignored before. On our downtown sidewalks huddled the homeless and aimless, people who had almost grown invisible by their constant presence. We were a city bleeding, and I felt God's prodding to play a part in leading this community into a brighter light—a deeper hope.

Rezoning, neighborhood planning, downtown revitalization, central city neighborhood improvements, police complaints—through all these issues I tried my best to ensure that the poor and impoverished had a voice. I couldn't vote to revitalize our downtown unless we finally paved the dirt streets in the black neighborhoods surrounding the downtown area first. I couldn't get into neighborhood planning without including the neighborhoods that still had outdoor toilets.

I formed an alliance with council members Mylo McBride and J.L. Dawkins. Together, we were able to revitalize our downtown as we expanded the business system. We paved 95 percent of our unpaved streets and added sidewalks. We fought hard not to raise taxes. We were able to bring more employment to blacks by adopting an equal employment policy citywide. As a team, we were also successful in building more housing for low-income residents. We were even able to infiltrate our police department and get minorities hired on the managerial level. For a brief time, Fayetteville had its first African-American chief of police.

I served four terms on the Fayetteville City Council and one term as mayor pro-tem. I'm very proud of this service. You are granted the privilege of serving as mayor pro-tem by getting the most votes of the elected candidates. That year I got one thousand votes more than the next closest candidate.

When I resigned from the city council in 1985, I felt God had used me for His purposes, as I tried my best to meet the challenges He had called me to. However, God wasn't done with me yet. He had only dangled my feet in the political pond and was getting ready to push me in headfirst.

TWENTY-SEVEN

Ronald Reagan

ecause I was one of only a handful of African-American ministers who was a registered and active Republican in our state, I was always being called on to give the scripture and prayer at North Carolina Republican Party gatherings around the state. I had also become a member of the North Carolina Minority Committee to elect Ronald Reagan for President of the United States. It was 1978.

By 1980, the former actor and governor from California was the frontrunner in the Republican Party to unseat President Jimmy Carter. The National GOP convention in Detroit was still months away when Mr. Reagan came to Greensboro, North Carolina, to speak and campaign for his nomination. Being the token black Republican minister, I got the invitation to recite a prayer at a Reagan fundraising banquet.

I always feel humbled that God would use me in such a capacity as public prayer. What an awesome privilege it is to direct open minds and hearts in a conversation with the Almighty. On that evening, I felt no different. Longer and greater speeches may have been on the docket that night, but asking the Good Lord to bless us as a people was certainly the most important—at least it was in my heart.

Sitting at the head table three seats down from Mr. Reagan, I waited for my cue. When given the nod, I headed up to the podium. I'm not sure what happened, but I do believe that I got carried away in talking to God. I prayed for His help over our trials, our country's ills, our plight to do right for His Glory, the protection of unborn children and the like. I might have asked Him to bless our food that evening but I can't swear to it.

When I sat down, Mr. Reagan immediately got out of his seat, came over and tapped me on the shoulder. With tears streaming down his face, he said,

"Reverend Johnson, I've met a lot of pastors, but you're a pastors' pastor! I would be honored if you would give a prayer at the national convention."

Of course, I said I would, but I really didn't expect it to happen. Mr. Reagan didn't take my name down or anything. The convention was still a long way off and I was sure he had about a hundred more banquets to attend and more impressive prayers to hear. I was sure he'd forget all about it.

Three months prior to the convention, I got a call from my friend Jack Lee, who was mayor of Fayetteville but also chairman of the state Republican Party.

"Aaron, do you remember having a conversation with Mr. Reagan about you saying a prayer or something at the National Convention?"

"Yes."

"Well, he just called and asked me if you'd do it? If so, we'll get to work getting you the proper credentials."

That's how I became an alternate delegate for the convention serving under our delegation leader, Senator Jesse Helms. In the meantime, I also continued campaigning briskly as part of the minority committee to elect Ronald Reagan. Our goal was to capture 10 percent of the black vote. We had our work cut out for us.

The thirty-second Republican National Convention was held in July in Detroit, Michigan, at the Joe Louis Arena. That summer, as I walked into that auditorium named after the great boxer and hero of my childhood, I felt like I was entering consecrated ground. When I was growing up, Joe Louis was every black boy's fantasy. Now to be in this great building carrying his name with this great task before me, I felt God standing next to me—cautioning me to watch my step and to hold my head high.

The 1980 Republican National Convention was not without drama. While Ronald Reagan had sewn up the primary handily, the choice for his vice presidential nominee remained a thorny issue.

Two prominent names were being batted around: former Texas congressman George H.W. Bush and former President Gerald Ford. Of course, never in our history had a former president ever turned around and run for vice-president. The buzz about this scenario was white hot as two camps began to form, one for Ford and one against him.

One afternoon while I was on the floor of the convention hall, I got a call from someone who wouldn't give his name. This person asked me if I would be willing to consider making a motion for Gerald Ford to be Ronald Reagan's running mate. My mystery caller kept calling the Reagan/Ford ticket the ultimate dream team.

President Ronald Reagan welcomes Aaron and Mattie
Johnson to the White House, May 1982.

I knew that the North Carolina delegation didn't want to make such a motion. We didn't want to force Mr. Reagan into a choice he didn't want. We refused to oblige. I'm sure other delegates received similar calls.

For a brief time it looked like the Ford pushers were going to win the day, but Ford's demands for certain powers and prerogatives made the Reagan team nervous. Former President Ford was basically asking to be co-president and wanted Henry Kissinger installed back as secretary of state and Alan Greenspan appointed as secretary of the treasury. Reagan and his team thought wiser of it and turned, instead, to George Bush. The rest is history, as they say.

Another piece of drama was that, for the first time, pro-life became a plank of the Republican Party platform. With a motion by Senator Jesse Helms, seconded and championed by the Republican Party and our formidable candidate, Ronald Reagan, the unborn child would finally have a voice. It was exciting stuff.

Monday, July 14, 1980 was a busy first day of the convention. Caucus meetings, luncheons, strategy and policy meetings abounded. If you have never been to a national convention—go! It will take your breath away as you're swept up in the frenzy and pride of participating in our highest privilege as American citizens.

The floor of the Joe Louis Arena was electric. Delegates and alternates scurried about voting and making motions. Press conferences were held just about every hour on the hour.

The Minority Committee was quite a popular group as the media gathered around us to hear our thoughts and recommendations for the new administration. Reagan had made a commitment to minorities from African-Americans to Latinos and Native Americans. He promised that our voices would be heard. As a group empowered by our next president, we expounded on future staff positions and economic policy. How strange it was being listened to as microphones were pointed towards us and notepads filled up with our quotes.

That evening, Mattie and our children, Dezette and Jamale, were escorted to the back of the auditorium, high up in the stands reserved for alternates and family members of those participating in the night's program. My children were young but pinched with excitement. My Democrat wife was proud of me and took in her surroundings with grace.

While my family looked on, I was escorted behind the main stage to labor through the hour and a half security screening, then join the others who were to take part in the convention presentations. We were made up as powder puffs took off our shine. Our clothes were tugged on and adjusted while we were briefed and then made to wait.

177

As music director Manny Harmon conducted the convention orchestra through its classical backdrop of sound, I was backstage meeting one celebrity after another. My favorite was Jed Clampett. The Beverly Hillbilly himself, Buddy Ebsen, was charming and we had a good time talking about our upbringings. We wandered around the backstage lounges together snacking on table after table of hors d'oeuvres and spring water. The Osmonds, Olympic skater Dorothy Hamill, Michael Landon, Jimmy Stewart and Efrem Zimbalist, Jr. were a few high profilers with whom I rubbed shoulders. As a boy from Willard, my head was turned for a moment. I even sought out autographs for my convention program like a teeny-bopper at a rock concert.

But when the call to order came and the gavel fell, the celebrity and commoner status fell with it as we all covered our hearts with our right hands. The presentation of the colors by the American Legion and the Pledge of Allegiance led by a distinguished Vietnam War veteran united everyone in the arena as Americans.

When the Honorable Robert Michel from the 18th District of Illinois sang the National Anthem, a lump climbed up in my throat and stayed lodged through Reverend Billy Graham's invocation. With Dr. Graham's petition, God had been invited to preside over us. I was never prouder to be a citizen of this great country.

Watching from backstage on television monitors located in the lounges, my behind-the-podium compadres and I were all suddenly struck with the magnitude of the event and humbled by the bit but proud parts we were to play that evening. I met the Honorable Donald Rumsfeld as he waited to make his introductory remarks about former President Gerald Ford. And before President Ford walked out on stage, I shook his hand. No matter your politics, you can't help but honor those who put themselves out there for the rest of us. We honor, we ridicule, we agree, we disagree, but we should never forget the courage it takes to step out from the pack and put your convictions on the line.

His fellow countrymen honored Gerald Ford that evening for his service to his country. He stepped into his presidency during a time when we had lost faith in our leaders. President Nixon and his administration had driven us hard through the desert of lies, cover-ups and sleights of hand. Greed and lust for power whipped us into a frenzied mess. Mr. Ford inherited an angry and distrustful nation with a pledge to help us heal. His speech that evening was gracious.

After two more presenters and a star-studded presentation highlighting the convention theme of "Together…A New Beginning," it was time for me to close out the evening of the first day.

I was waiting just out of sight under a large American flag standing by the entryway. All of a sudden, I felt my mother's presence. I had a sense of joy that my mama's prayers were being answered and that her prayers were still following me. An old hymn we used to sing in Willard came to me that went something like, *"I'm so glad that somebody prayed for me… My mama prayed for me. She had me on her mind… ."* Her prayers were still seeing me through.

The time came as my trembling knees helped me step between the two high-rise dignitary platforms that led to the podium. I slowly approached the royal blue stage that looked out upon the throngs of people, flags, posters, hats, buttons and balloons. I knew right where my family was sitting and immediately looked up toward them for courage. The arena quieted down, as much as several thousand folks gathered in one contained area can get quiet.

As I stood there, I felt like I was on a moving ship as nodding heads, shifting seats and the collective breathing of the masses slowly rolled toward me in waves.

I needed to calm myself before I called upon God, so I said the first thing that came to my head, "We Republicans would not think of ending this convention without giving God the praise." A burst of applause followed my words and allowed me time to get my bearings. Some marvelous speeches were made that night, but as I bowed my head and readied myself to pray, everything fell away except for my God and me. I felt like Jesus in the garden when he petitioned God's will to prevail over man's. I asked His favor upon this presidency:

"Almighty God, we stand at this moment to reaffirm our belief in your Holy will as the one in whom we place our full trust. You are the Supreme Ruler of this universe, worthy of our praise. Your government is righteous, your laws are perfect, good and just, your love for your children is unfailing.

"We pray your blessed benediction upon our work today in this session. If we were wrong in any way with the decisions we made—correct us. If we made any mistakes— forgive us.

"Oh, Father of Heaven and Earth, we desire that you would make this convention an instrument of your divine will. Help each delegate and alternate to see clearly our responsibilities to each citizen, rich and poor, of this homeland. Let us not forget the refugee and stranger among us as we perform the awesome task before this convention.

"We thank you for guiding this people in peace and war, bad times and good times.

"Give us the courage to conserve those values that have sustained this beloved country, the liberty and freedom we have in Christ and as citizens, the worth and dignity of the individual made in your image. Help us to be true to the principles of equal opportunity for every man, woman and child of this free soil.

"We sincerely pray for your servant, Ronald Reagan, the person whom this convention is turning to as our standard-bearer for the highest office of this country. Grant him courage, wisdom, knowledge and a compassionate heart that he might fully understand and hear the cries of all his fellow citizens from every walk of life. Be with him all the way.

"Now, we humbly thank you for the gift of life; protect the lives of the born and unborn of this land. Our lives are our most precious thing we have.

"God bless America! America needs you! The greatest nation on earth is facing one of its darkest hours, burdened with many perplexing problems. Give us hope for today and tomorrow.

"Yes tonight, God bless America, the land that we love, stand beside her and guide her through the night, from above. Amen."

When I finished, the whole auditorium rose to its feet applauding. The few faces I could see up front had tears streaming down them.

That night NBC news commentator David Brinkley, an old Watha, North Carolina, son, signed off with, "that was the Reverend Aaron Johnson from Willard, North Carolina."

A couple days later on July 17, Ronald Reagan accepted the Republican nomination for president of the United States with a beautiful, heartfelt speech. Mattie, the children and I were in our reserved seats in the balcony as the great man walked to the podium amidst giant American flags, hundreds of red and white carnations and the adoration of an entire political party.

Mr. Reagan's speech was articulate and forceful and instilled in all of us in that room, and in the nation looking on, a sense of hope and restoration. At the end of his speech he tilted his head, paused and then did something very Reagan-esque.

"I have thought of something that's not a part of my speech and worried over whether I should do it," he said. "Can we doubt that only a Divine Providence placed this land, this island of freedom, here as a refuge for all those people in the world who yearn to breathe free? Jews and Christians enduring persecution behind the Iron Curtain; the boat people of Southeast Asia, of Cuba and of Haiti; the victims of drought and famine in Africa; the freedom fighters in Afghanistan; and our own countrymen held in savage captivity. I'll confess that I've been a little afraid to suggest what I'm going to suggest.

"I'm more afraid not to.

"Can we begin our crusade joined together in a moment of silent prayer?"

Following our leader, the entire coliseum bowed, from the greatest to the least of us. Motion suspended for a brief moment as our country paused. If you were someone comfortable with prayer, the gesture came naturally. If you weren't, you bowed your head anyway. When Mr. Reagan opened his eyes and looked out toward the crowd, he completed his speech.

"God bless America. Thank you."

For the first time in a long time, I felt our country fill up with refreshed hope like ice-cold spring water being poured into a Mason jar.

The eight years President Reagan led this nation, I was invited to the White House numerous times. Right after the election, I had been asked to submit my resume to Reagan's transition team to be considered for a cabinet position in his administration. I prayed about it numerous times and kept coming to the same conclusion: God wanted me to stay in North Carolina.

I sent my resume in along with a note declining any position offered. However, I did ask to be considered in an advisory capacity at the president's pleasure.

Mr. Reagan and his staff took me up on my offer. I found myself walking through the security checks at the White House on many occasions. One of my favorite remembrances had nothing to do with politics but rather relationship. Mattie and I were invited to a steak dinner at the White House with about thirty-five or so other folks. We were gloriously entertained that night by the Harlem Boys Choir. I remember Mr. and Mrs. Reagan being gracious and deeply touched by the voices of those children.

One of my proudest occasions at the White House took place in the Rose Garden on November 2, 1983. I was present along with members of Congress and other guests when President Reagan signed the bill establishing the third Monday in every January as the Martin Luther King, Jr. national holiday.

It was an unusually warm fall day as Coretta Scott King stood looking over President Reagan's shoulder. She had carried this fight for many years, since her husband's death, to convince the country to recognize her Martin's place in our nation's history. Testifying before Congress and the House of Representatives on several occasions, she would not give up until Martin Luther King, Jr. Day became a reality.

Mr. Reagan's Minority Committee would occasionally bring various ones of us to Washington to discuss ideas and options. The most memorable one for me was when President Reagan brought about thirty of us to Washington for a week of intensive discussion and brainstorming. The President was in a quandary about what was going on in South Africa and apartheid. He was in communication with President P.W. Botha and was trying to go the moderate route in his negotiations with this leader. Botha, of course, was not publically known as a friend of the black African.

President Reagan opposed just about everyone on what the United States response should be to South Africa. To sanction or not to sanction was the debate. Reagan was in favor of limited sanctions. One of the ideas he was toying with, and the reason those few of us were called to the White House, was his idea of initiating import/export collaborations between as yet to be created African-American businesses and Africa. This was part of his foreign policy for Africa. He wanted to go to the blacks for help. He wanted African-Americans to back Africa like the Jewish Americans backed Israel.

We had sessions on how to work with the United Nations and the World Bank. We were schooled in how to get loans and given a crash course in diplomacy. We were taught how our harbors worked and how to ship from one country to another. Just as this country had been doing with China, President Reagan wanted us to go to Africa and take our goods and bring theirs home. Mr. Reagan saw this as a win-win endeavor for the African nation and for black entrepreneurship and small businesses in America.

Of course, politics being politics, the majority at the conference were full of debate and many present were more concerned about the effects this proposed endeavor would have on the Small Business Administration, a federal agency instituted by President Lyndon Johnson back in the 1960s. I remember a discussion within our group as we sat around tables in the West Wing. Most conference attendees wanted nothing to do with Africa and simply wanted more support for the small businesses African-Americans were already struggling to build.

Commerce Secretary Malcolm Baldridge was getting impatient with the group's reluctance when he abruptly barked, "Here we are talking about billions of new dollars being poured into the African-American economy, and for some strange reason, most of you are concerned about peanuts!"

Of course, what didn't help this idea gel was the fact that Archbishop Desmond Tutu of South Africa was visiting Washington, DC at about the same time and was publically accusing Reagan of racism. Apartheid had rubbed us all raw, and many in our conference were in agreement with the Archbishop. Several conference attendees even accused Secretary Baldridge to his face of being a racist. His comeback to that accusation was startling and direct. "I accept my racism if you accept yours. We're all racist, but we're trying to overcome it here. Let's work it out and move on and accomplish the goal."

After a long, intense week, the delegation went home to our separate states and basically forgot about the president's proposal. Most didn't believe he was sincere. And when Congress voted overwhelmingly to invoke economic sanctions on South Africa, the proposal died a quick death. However, I thought President Reagan's idea was innovative and revolutionary and that African-Americans in this country were being given a chance to do something positive about our own economic development.

Hindsight can be cruel. I wish I had taken more initiative. I see it as a missed opportunity. I had a chance to be a leader in a groundbreaking initiative for my people and I regret I didn't step forth.

From where I was sitting, President Ronald Reagan was not a racist. According to a national report, from the end of 1982 to 1989 black unemployment dropped 9 percentage points (from 20.4 percent to 11.4 percent), while white unemployment dropped by only 4 percentage points. Black household income went up 84 percent from 1980 to 1990 versus a white household income increase of 68 percent. The number of black-owned businesses increased from 308,000 in 1982 to 424,000 in 1987, a 38 percent rise versus a 14 percent increase in the total number of firms in the United States. Receipts by black-owned firms more than doubled, from $9.6 billion to $19.8 billion.

Once, seventy-five of us African-American pastors were invited to a lunch at the White House. President Reagan wanted to hear from us about how to help the black community in this country. He invited some straight grassroots talk from us. Only four of us were Republicans.

One of my great moments was sitting at the table with the president that day and simply talking one-on-one. It was shortly after the assassination attempt by John Hinckley, Jr., when a bullet had punctured the president's lung. We talked about the shooting some. Then we started talking about our families, our fathers, our upbringings, and our childhoods. We were two men having a man-to-man talk—a store clerk's son and a sharecropper's boy remembering our roots.

At a White House dinner one evening, I was touched when our fortieth president remarked, "Abraham Lincoln freed the black man. In many ways, Dr. King freed the white man."

And I believed Mr. Reagan on September 15, 1982, at a National Black Republican Council dinner when he said, "For too long now, black Americans seem to have been written off by one party and taken for granted by the other. And for the vast majority of black Americans, that's been a strictly no-win situation. Changing it will require a commitment from all of us. So, tonight I want you to know that the Republican Party stands ready and willing to reach out to black Americans."

And I think he did. I was proud to have known him.

TWENTY-EIGHT

Secretary of Corrections

"I, Aaron J. Johnson, do solemnly swear that I will well and truly execute the duties of my office as Secretary of the North Carolina Department of Corrections according to the best of my skills and abilities, so help me, God." January 1985

When Governor James Grubbs Martin took his oath of office on January 5, 1985, he placed his right hand on the Bible that his wife, Dottie, had given him on their first Christmas together almost twenty-nine years before. The son of a Presbyterian minister, Martin became only the second Republican governor of the state of North Carolina in more than one hundred years. A few days later, he stood beside me as I took my oath to serve him as the first African-American to be appointed as secretary of corrections for North Carolina. Had I known this opportunity was coming, I might have taken Ronald Reagan up on his offer. God was up to something.

Governor Martin had made a pledge that qualified minorities would be given roles in his administration, and not just positions as clerks or assistants but rather positions with authority. I heard Governor Martin say once, "I had a particular objective—my predecessor had established a pattern of having each department appoint an assistant secretary who was black. But in each case, it was always assistant secretary of minority affairs. I wanted to go the next step, that is to have a high-ranking officer in each department who was not limited to minority affairs."

Never had a cabinet position been given to an African-American that had nothing to do with his race. Jim Martin changed that. With Mattie and our children looking on, I took my oath of office as I found myself balancing at the end of yet another pinpoint and heeding yet another call.

In 1983 Senator Jim Martin was looking for a palatable way to retire from his congressional seat. After six consecutive terms he wasn't looking for another costly race. So, to bow out gracefully, Congressman Martin and Dottie decided he should run for governor of North Carolina and, if he lost, they would take it as a sign that it was time to re-enter private life.

I met Jim on the campaign trail. I was impressed with this preacher's son and former chemistry professor and county commissioner. He was soft spoken and had a handshake you could trust. I could tell he was a man I could pray with.

By this time, I was serving as mayor pro-tem in Fayetteville and continuing as pastor at Mt. Sinai. Mt. Sinai Homes and our church's daycare center were doing much to help those in need. We were still a church called to a congregation-at-large, to serve our people where needed.

As a black Republican, I began to run across more and more African-Americans who were disenchanted with what they saw in the Democratic Party. About ten of us, some Republicans but most unhappy Democrats, began meeting together regularly at a local motel. My friend, Lonnie Horton, organized us and several from Mount Sinai joined us. My good friend, Richard Bishop, and his wife, Joann; my secretary, Claudia Simpson, and Bernice Evans helped form the core of this group. We spent our time discussing our city and state's ills and what we collectively could do about them by pooling our resources and influence.

We set up a meeting with Jim Martin at his campaign headquarters in Raleigh. Mr. Martin's soft-spoken ways and his confident manner impressed us all at that meeting. He had a master's degree in chemistry from Davidson and a doctorate from Princeton, but he spoke to us black men sitting around the table that evening like we were his peers. He looked us each in the eye and made us believe that our voices would be heard. By the end of the meeting that night, each of us laid a thousand dollars on the table toward his campaign. We used that money to campaign for Jim in the black community. We hired a consulting firm to help us organize, and in the end we were able to secure 18 percent of the black vote for our candidate. Surprisingly, Jim Martin won his bid for governor and made this predominately Democratic state hold its breath. But I wasn't surprised. Jim Martin was a Christian, and God had plans for him.

"Aaron, I want you to fill one of my ten cabinet positions," said Governor-Elect Martin. He had called me up to his office in Raleigh in late November after the election. I thought he just wanted to thank me for helping with the black vote. But after a few minutes of chitchat, Governor Martin got right to the point, "What cabinet position would you like?"

Aaron and Mattie Johnson greet Jim and Dottie Martin at Martin's inauguration as North Carolina governor in January 1985. Soon after, Martin named Johnson the state secretary of corrections.

Normally, with an offer this potentially life-changing, I would have asked for time to pray about it and talk with my family. I did neither. I accepted right on the spot. Have you ever felt you were exactly at the right place at the right time, with the right person being asked the right thing? It was like I was this push pin on God's map and He had stuck me between some squiggly lines with a jab and said, "There! That's where you're to be."

"I don't know, Governor. I'll serve wherever you need me."

"Well, then, I want you to be my secretary of corrections. I want a man of compassion in there. I want you to breathe a breath of fresh air into this position."

Now I was no fool. I knew that North Carolina's prison system was a mess: overcrowding, a failed parole system, extremely outdated prison facilities and a threat hanging over the state's head by the federal government to take over the prisons if state legislators didn't get their act together.

At that moment, I should have seen a whole parade of red-flag bearers jumping up and down just behind the governor's chair shouting, "Run for your life, man!"

I did see the red flags, but God was standing in front of them smiling and nodding His head, so it didn't matter. But I did have one concern. "I don't have any large operation management experience," I told the governor. "You know that."

"I know. Don't worry. I'll surround you with people who can help you with that. Aaron, what you'll bring to this cabinet position is a special kind of leadership that is so desperately needed."

"I'm a Baptist minister. The press is going to kill you on this. I'm afraid they'll see me as a joke."

"Maybe at first, but you'll make a believer out of them. Be you, Aaron. Use your compassionate spirit, your decency and your integrity as you lead, and the rest will fall into place."

I gulped, agreed and took my oath of office, becoming the first African-American in North Carolina's history to be appointed secretary of corrections. The good folks at Mount Sinai Missionary Baptist Church revved up their prayers, told me they'd see me on Sundays and bid me God-speed.

TWENTY-NINE

The Church on Life Row

"BAPTIST PREACHER TO HEAD PRISONS"
"GOVERNOR PUTS MINISTER OUT IN THE FIRING LINE"

he Democrats were licking their chops, the Republicans were shaking their heads and the press couldn't wait to crucify me. I don't know which aggravated the media most—the fact that I was lacking a political pedigree, that I was a Baptist pastor or that I was African-American. My political mongrel status was simply too hard for any of them to resist. The political hound dogs and media watchdogs started sniffing my pants leg and growling the minute I uttered, "So help me, God."

"We have never understood why the governor chose a Fayetteville preacher with no significant business or administrative experience to head up one of the most complex, troublesome and potentially explosive departments in state government."—Raleigh Times

"Put him in charge of the chaplains—that's what he's good at."— Rep. James Craven, R-Moore, in the *News & Observer*

To say I was naïve was a slight understatement. To say that I became paranoid the minute I took office was an understatement of gigantic proportions. I did not know how to play the political game. I said what I thought. I was loyal to the governor and to my staff to a fault. And I never hesitated to give God credit in my speech or actions. Those were all political *faux pas* that got me misquoted in just about every state newspaper before the month was out.

But it didn't matter. My first day on the job, the tone and direction of my administration was set in motion by a knock on my door. I had barely hung my coat up and straightened the pencils on my new desk when I looked up to find this short, white man rapping on my door frame like a Fuller Brush salesman behind on his quota.

"Secretary Johnson, I'm Richard Payne, regional field director at Prison Fellowship. I called 'cha yester'de, 'member?"

Barely. After my swearing in, I went home with my family. During the evening, I received one phone call after another from well-wishers. I did seem to remember this Richard calling, though, and asking to meet with me sometime. We hadn't set a time or date—after all, I didn't even have the keys to my new office yet. "Mr. Payne?"

"Yeah, I just thought I'd come on out here and meet 'cha and welcome ya to your new position." With that, Richard Payne barged into my life and administration like a Tasmanian devil. "Mr. Secretary, you and I are going to be a great team. I'm here to pray with you cuz you're gonna need it."

Two hours later, Richard and I were family. We had experienced something that only happens a few times in one's life—instant friendship. After talking about our lives, families and ministries, we knelt together on the floor by my desk as Richard asked God to bless my calling to North Carolina's prisons. During that prayer, I found myself smiling at God's definition of a blessing. Apparently it can come in the form of a wiry, Southern, fast-talking farmer-cowboy.

It didn't take me long to know that Richard was right. I needed his prayers and a whole lot more. I had taken a job fraught with disaster. Severe overcrowding was threatening the state's control over our own prisons. Prisoner lawsuits were being filed every seven seconds it seemed. Inmate healthcare was practically non-existent. Inside the walls, AIDS was fast becoming a threat and drug and alcohol addictions were running rampant. And all of a sudden, after only being on the job three months or so, I was the cause of it all—at least according to my detractors, who were legion.

It was this environment of heavy scrutiny that caused me to pass up the invitation I received from the inmates on death row via Chaplain Skip Pike at Central Prison. They wanted me to come to their Bible study group. I was only one month into my administration, but even I knew that invitation had disaster written all over it. I could imagine the headlines all ready: "Corrections Secretary crosses the lines between church and state!" or, "Prison Chief caught praying with death row murderers!"

Also, because the prison chaplain was the one making the invitation, I feared the press would make this death row visit a huge issue.

A couple of weeks later I got another invitation through Chaplain Pike. I declined a second time. To be honest, I wasn't just afraid of what the media would do to me. I was afraid to meet with the inmates on death row because of my image of them. I was afraid they might take me hostage and make demands, and then the news media would consider themselves justified in their skepticism of my appointment.

A week later, however, the warden at Central Prison called me. He told me that I would probably be surprised at what I'd find on death row and encouraged me to accept the invitation. With grave misgivings, I called Chaplain Pike and set up the meeting.

It was a cold March morning and the wind whipped through the prison yard with a stinging snap. An hour earlier, I had signed myself out from my office and considered myself on personal or civilian time. I had accrued just enough vacation time from my three months on the job that I could make this meeting on my own time. I was determined to do everything I could to make it clear that this visit was not official. I even asked Richard Payne to make the visit with me, hoping that would make the meeting look even less official.

Accompanied by Richard, Michael Smith, a young assistant chaplain and a former corrections officer, and Head Chaplain Skip Pike, the four of us made our way toward Unit III.

At the time I was appointed secretary, I had never been to a prison. I knew nothing about corrections. The only correction I knew, I learned from my mama. We had a "correction board" in our home and she was never shy of using it. But as the steel doors clanked and scraped across the concrete floor at Central, I was about to learn first-hand why my mother was so determined to make her children law-abiding citizens.

The locked door slammed behind me like a steel trap. My heart balked and tried to retreat deeper into my body. My tongue betrayed me and lay across my teeth like a lead spike. Walking down that long, stark, corridor toward death row, the silver hairs on the back of my neck lifted straight out like one of those experiments in seventh grade science class. Closing and locking. Closing and locking. As we were escorted through each cellblock, the sound of those gates scraping the floor and closing with a clang brought with it a deepening sense of doom. As we got deeper inside the prison, it was all I could do not to throw my arms up in the air and beg to be led out of this cement tomb. The fact that I didn't know my way out on my own almost paralyzed me.

When the last steel door slammed shut with an ominous hollow buzzer announcing our arrival, we found ourselves standing in the darkest place in North Carolina—the bowels of death row.

At Central Prison, the cellblocks of Unit III weren't pretty. Cellblock D wasn't any different from the others on death row. The cinderblock walls were painted beige and the gray paint on the concrete floor had long lost its luster. The stainless steel tables and surrounding benches, covered with smudgy fingerprints and a dull shine, were screwed into the floor. The cast-iron columns holding up the two-tiered cellblocks were as nondescript as trees barren of their leaves. Each cellblock was divided into eight pods with twenty-four single cells—twelve cells on each level. Nothing was movable. Nothing was comfortable. Nothing was inviting.

That is, except the broad smile and extended hand of death row inmate Andrew "Sonny" Craig. Sonny was African-American and a murderer. He had been on death row since 1982. He was also known as "The Preacher."

Inmates were milling around. Some were standing outside their cells. Some were leaning over the railing to see what was going on. And then there was this pocket of men sitting around the steel tables waiting for their guests. Of the sixty-three inmates on death row at the time, about twenty-five of them worshipped together regularly. It was they, these worshipers, who had offered the invitation to me. As they later explained, they thought it was time to meet the man God had sent them.

When I walked into the common area where the men were waiting, one by one they stood up. Then the beaming Sonny Craig grabbed my hand and said, "Welcome, Mr. Secretary, to the Church on Life Row."

Once Sonny had become a believer in Jesus Christ, his spirit was on fire. He wanted nothing more than to tell others about the forgiving grace of Jesus. When he shook my hand that day, he had no way of knowing the power his words would have on me.

Usually when this motley crew of Christians gathered together, the bolted tables became their pews and an overturned trashcan their pulpit. But that day was special. Because I was the honored guest, chairs were brought in and an actual podium was in place.

Once the introductions were made, the inmates quickly assumed control of the service. A chorus of three men stood and sang a couple of hymns together, with each singing a solo. An inmate led us in prayer and another death row member read scripture.

The panic, anxiety and fear that had earlier threatened to disarm me fell away as the songs of praise and the prayer of thanksgiving started to take hold. I had never experienced anything like it. Other inmates joined us and sat on the bolted tables. A few others gathered and leaned across the railings on the second tier of cells to listen. The men of the church began telling me how they had started praying together, about a year before, that God would give them a Christian man to be the secretary of corrections.

I was speechless. Could I actually be someone's answered prayer? Dawning on me like a sunrise heralding a new day, I finally understood God's purpose for putting me into this most unlikely position. It was true I knew nothing about corrections. It didn't make sense that Governor Martin had appointed me from his cabinet to head this department. Yet here I was. I was placed in this most dubious cabinet post, without a doubt, because these inmates—this Church on Life Row—had prayed that God would send them a prison chief who knew Him. I didn't feel worthy to be sitting among these believers.

One by one, the men told their stories, how God's grace and forgiveness was the only thing that gave their lives any value. It was all they had left.

Somewhere between my entry into Unit III and their gripping testimonies, I stopped seeing these men as inmates and began a kinship with them as brothers in Jesus Christ.

When all had spoken and finally drained their hearts of every ounce of sorrow and confessed sin, we stood together, arm-in-arm, as the body of Christ. A voice somewhere among us began leading the song which for centuries has cleansed so many: *"Amazing grace, how sweet the sound that saved a wretch like me. I once was lost, but now I'm found, was blind but now I see."* For the first time in my life, I knew what it felt like to stand on sacred ground.

I had preached for years but never experienced worship like I did that day. Although sorrow and remorse still flittered about them like heavy dust, these men had embraced the forgiveness only offered by the grace of God. They clung to it as if it were their only source of air and food. The peace that reflected from their relaxed countenances came from somewhere unearthly— it transcended those thick, haunting walls and immovable steel bars like prayer itself.

The men of Life Row talked of salvation and sorrow in the same breath. They confessed their sins with an honesty I had never experienced before. As they spoke, I kept hearing the words of the Apostle Paul, "…if we but confess our sins then God will graciously forgive us."

I've been in a lot of churches, but never was the Spirit of God hovering and moving like it was among the Church on Life Row.

As the confessions, testimonies and singing wound down, Sonny Craig spoke up and said, "We have one request to make of you, Mr. Secretary."

My heart sank. I had lulled myself into thinking that this gathering would be different. It would be free of requests for special favors. I braced myself for a request for better food, more visitation rights, or more television sets on the cellblock and the like.

Sonny smiled and lowered his head and then a second or two later said, "Mr. Secretary, they's never been a revival in Central Prison. Would you let us have a revival—a week-end revival?"

Suddenly, the floodgates opened and the Church on Life Row began to zealously explain that, although they were on death row, their church was very much alive. They wanted my help to spread the Good News of Jesus to others in their prison.

I was ashamed. Why had I allowed my fear and my reluctance to stir up the media keep me from these men? I felt God nudge me with a strong shoulder and was humbled by this sincere request by these odd-duck believers. I also had been secretary of corrections just long enough to know that their request might get me in trouble—big trouble.

Despite the problems I knew would loom ahead, I promised the Church on Life Row I would do everything within my power to bring a revival to their prison.

Our time together lasted just over an hour. I was honored when asked by Sonny to end our worship with a prayer. As I petitioned our Father, I had a hard time keeping my voice even. The powerful heart of this holy church overwhelmed me.

As we left the block, none of the four of us spoke—quite the deed for my friend, Richard. Something momentous had just happened, and none of us were sure of the words we could use. As Richard and I were escorted back through the yard by chaplains Pike and Smith, I still hadn't found my voice.

When I drove out the gates of Central Prison that day, I felt, for the lack of a better term, anointed. I had taken my oath as secretary of corrections in January. But I had been *anointed* by the Church on Life Row to a greater calling. This small church had embraced God as few men have, as their broken hearts had been heard. Once again, I was reminded why my mother had named me Aaron—a reluctant spokesman for an imperfect but forgiven people.

Driving home, I had a flashback to when I first came to Fayetteville as a young pastor. I had a young man's dream that I was going to have the largest church in the state of North Carolina. Alone in my car, I heard the whisper of God. "This is your church, Aaron. I don't want you to be a secretary. I called you to be a pastor."

I balked and answered, "God, be a pastor to inmates?"

I know I can't ever prove it, but I'm sure God nodded His wise, old divine head and nudged me along.

In 1985, almost 18,000 inmates lived in the 94 state prisons, with 62,000 on probation and parole and 8,000 corrections employees. And God told me that day, in no uncertain terms, that this was my church. I guess in a sense I did become pastor to the largest church in the state.

A month later, I visited a field prison in Durham County. I arrived unannounced and uninvited. Since my visit to death row, I had started doing drop-in visits at various prisons. What better way to learn my way around than to see first-hand what was going on behind the walls.

When I arrived, I gave the officer my name and told him I'd like to see the superintendent. He didn't recognize my name and told me that I'd have to make an appointment and come back later. I insisted that he call the warden and give him my name and tell him I'd like to see him. Reluctantly, the officer made the call—still not knowing who I was.

The superintendent appeared in a matter of minutes, out of breath and looking like a scared rabbit. He knew exactly who I was and he was afraid I was there to fire him. That's what happened a lot when a new administration took over. They'd clean house and put their own folks in. Governor Martin did not do that, so neither did I. I told him I was just there for a tour.

I had heard of the triple bunks in tiny cells. But when I actually saw them for myself, I was reminded of what you'd find in the sleeping quarters of a submarine—minus the luxury of oxygen. Squeezed into an eight-by-fifteen-foot cell, alongside a sink and a toilet, were these stacked beds three high. There must have been quite the lottery by inmates vying for the top bunk, because the other two bunks only had a slit between them where a full-size man was supposed to lie. Forget sleeping on your side. And if you had any girth to you, squishing yourself in between your mattress and the mattress only inches above your nose was a feat for Houdini himself. The cramped cell was infested air space ripe for an epidemic of violence. A spark of agitation could turn deadly. A simple elbow bump had the potential to turn into a fistfight or worse. Something had to be done—quickly.

As I was leaving the prison from my impromptu visit, it was raining and icy cold. An inmate was working out in the yard. I forget what he was doing—trimming a hedge, digging a hole—something. What struck me was what he was wearing, or I should say *not* wearing. No long sleeves. No coat. No hat. He wore just a thin, short-sleeved prison shirt, pants and worn shoes. The officer supervising him wasn't wearing any better. Both of the men were soaked to their skin. I called the officer over. "Man, where are your coats?" I'm sure neither man knew who I was.

"They don't have any, Mr. Secretary?" replied the superintendent.

"What do you mean? You should have a regulation-issued jacket for your officer and this inmate should be dressed properly to work out in the elements like this."

"This is all we got, sir."

I immediately asked to be taken to the Clothes House—the warehouse that stored all employee uniforms and prisoner clothing.

"Won't do no good," replied the warden.

"Take me there," I ordered. I followed him through a couple of buildings until we eventually stopped in front of a huge room—a huge *empty* room. "What's this?"

"It's the Clothes House," answered the warden.

"Where are the clothes, jackets, shoes, shirts? Where's the stuff?"

"We don't got any! That's what I'm trying to tell you, Mr. Secretary."

By law, all prison employees were to be issued proper uniforms with the seasonally appropriate jackets, coats, long sleeves, whatever. Prisoners were to be issued clothing appropriate for their work assignments. Apparently, that hadn't happened in a long time.

I looked at those two shivering men and saw no difference in them. God had had high hopes for both of them. He loved them both. He expected me to treat both with compassion. I vowed that day that I would somehow fix this. If it was cold outside, both prison staff and inmates would be properly dressed to do their jobs. This vow would eventually be my demise.

THIRTY

Executive Order

*M*y first year as secretary became consumed with addressing the problems Governor Martin had inherited from previous administrations, some dating back to 1969. Craggy Prison was sixty-two years old, being compared to an eighteenth-century dungeon and an embarrassment to the state. It had been slated to be closed ten years previous, but it was still housing inmates when the governor and I were sworn in. Antiquated facilities like this one and overcrowding at other sites became the fat elephant in the living room.

After a yearlong learning curve trying to get my bearings, Governor Martin asked me and my team to draw up a comprehensive, ten-year plan to tackle the prison system's most urgent needs.

In March 1986, Governor Martin and I introduced an aggressive, innovative plan we called *Corrections at the Crossroads: Plan for the Future*. This plan would reduce triple bunking, re-invent our parole system, introduce creative, alternative options to the incarceration of lesser offenders and offer a construction plan that would add approximately five thousand new beds into the system. It also sported a $52 million price tag.

Meanwhile at Mount Sinai Missionary Baptist Church, I tried my best to get back to Fayetteville on Wednesdays for prayer meeting and to attend to business. If a member was in the hospital, I'd try and visit him if possible. If a family were in need, I'd do what I could or delegate to someone else who could.

Once again, my church family stepped to the plate and filled in the blank spots. Each week, a new deacon or two was designated Deacon of the Week. This servant attended to the everyday needs of service and ministry of the church. And no matter what my week was like in Raleigh, each Sunday found me behind the pulpit.

Not long after my appointment as secretary, our church began to experience an unexpected influx of visitors—with job applications in hand. Many figured that if they attended Mount Sinai and sat politely through one of my sermons, they'd be more likely to get my attention to ask for a job—either with the prison system or in some other state position. It didn't take church leaders long to figure out that we had a problem.

Our solution was to turn no one away. Anyone who walked through the church doors was welcome—whatever his or her reason for visiting. We designated a special deacon to greet these folks and take their applications with the promise that I would receive them. That seemed to satisfy folks. Of course, all I could do was pass those job applications along to the right folks in the system. Our reputation as a church that cared continued to grow and our ministries to the community became even more effective. During that period of time, we became a church of more than five hundred.

The first year of my prison duties was full of long days and agendas. Once we revealed our ten-year plan, I spent months stumping for it around the state, trying to sell it to the public and lawmakers.

Before I took the corrections post, various inmates serving time in the South Piedmont area had filed a lawsuit on the grounds of inhumane treatment caused by prison overcrowding.

In September of 1985, the court ruled in the prisoners' favor. This lawsuit was filed before I took office, yet I became the one responsible for constructing or renovating fourteen prisons in the South Piedmont area—accommodating the inmate demands. Triple bunking had to be eliminated and fifty square feet per inmate was to be the new standard. Plus, I had to increase staff in those locations in order to provide more adequate supervision of inmates for their safety.

The General Assembly quickly allotted $12.5 million for this massive construction and renovation project. We built those prisons faster than any ever constructed in North Carolina history—but not without major delays or criticism. The cumbersome state bidding laws plus the small, inadequate engineering division of the Department of Corrections hampered compliance. My little engineering division was equipped to do maintenance, not full-blown construction.

Traditionally, the Department of Administration maintained responsibility for overseeing all state construction. But because the state insisted on using inmate labor to save money, this massive project landed in my lap. The prisoners didn't have the skills nor would they receive the training in which to hone the needed skills. Added to that, the General Assembly would not provide the funds for the needed equipment to do the job. It was just like the Biblical story where the children of Israel were not given straw to make bricks, but they were expected to make those bricks all the same—and in record time.

Then disaster struck. A state of emergency was called as our prison population rose to more than 18,000. If we did not reduce our population significantly within a matter of weeks, all of the state's prisons would be taken over by the federal government. At the time, several other states also were threatened with a federal take-over.

Wardens began combing their populations looking for candidates for early release. Before the federal axe could fall, we had released 1,875 inmates back to the public. Forty-six of those released had only served half of their sentences; more then 250 had served 20 percent or less of their sentences; 11 of those released had served 10 percent or less of their original sentences. Almost all who were released were felons.

Twenty-four murderers, twelve rapists, twenty child molesters, fourteen armed robbers and thirty prisoners serving time for manslaughter were among the mix of those given early parole. It was a nightmare.

By March of 1987, we scrambled to have in place the Emergency Prison Population Stabilization Act. This state-induced prison cap was a preventative check that would alert the Department of Corrections when it was dangerously near the federal regulatory cap. The alert would allow us time to reduce the population without federal interference.

The emergency measure dictated that once the prisons system housed more than 17,460 inmates, 97 percent of the 18,000 cap, for fifteen consecutive days, the state parole commission had sixty days to find enough prisoners to release in order to reduce the inmate population below 17,280.

During my tenure, we had to declare a state of emergency for over-population four times. If Governor Martin and the Department of Corrections were going to be able to bring any kind of future stability to North Carolina's prison system, our ten-year plan desperately needed to be passed by the General Assembly.

In the meantime, reporters continued to dissect my every move. One day it dawned on me—people expected me to be different. Because of my faith, they *wanted* me to be different. Of course, the media and my detractors yearned for me to "step in it," as they say, so they could have fodder for their columns and witty sound bites for their news shows. It was during this scrutiny that God made something very clear to me. He too wanted me to be different.

I could hardly wait to summon my chief legal advisor, Ben Irons, into my office.

"Ben, how much power as secretary of corrections do I have?"

"As much as you want."

Governor Martin (center) and Secretary Johnson (front right)
celebrate the March 14, 1989 dedication of a dormitory and
recreation center at Randolph Correctional Center.

"I mean how much authority do I really have?"

"Sir," he said, "You can do anything you want in your own prisons."

"Great! Then I want my first executive order to outlaw cursing. I want my staff to act honorably and professionally."

Ben looked at me like I'd just asked him to quote the twenty-third Psalm— backwards and in pig Latin.

"Are you serious?"

"I'm just as serious as a heart attack."

"You can't be."

"Ben, I am. I want you to go back to your office. Do some research on every statute you can find on the books that relates to prisons and cursing and humane treatment."

Three hours later, my beleaguered legal advisor entered my office with a big grin on his face. "Mr. Secretary, I found a statute written in the 1800s where it is against the law to curse in public. It's still on the books."

That's how my first executive order came to be. And, boy, did they laugh. I'd given my critics just what they wanted. But in my heart, I think I was just starting to find my way.

The memo read in part:

Rules Regarding Human Relations in The Work Place

Employees of this department will not direct profanity toward other employees, inmates, probationers, parolees and members of the public.

Employees will not utter obscenities in the presence of others. Employees will not sexually harass others. Employees will not direct racial epithets toward others, or use racial epithets in the presence of others.

I have been told that in the past it has been accepted practice in some areas for employees to curse each other and to curse others. It has been said that employees have cursed prisoners in the past "to get their attention." Department rules clearly prohibit such conduct, and those rules will be enforced.

I wasn't trying to impose any personal moral standards on my employees, but I did want to set the tone for better human relationships. I wanted the memo to remind my staff that they were to maintain professional standards in the workplace and that my administration would be a humane one. And that humane treatment would begin with what came out of our mouths.

While there was snickering behind my back from employees, I surprisingly started getting letters from inmates and their families thanking me for my conviction on this matter. Other Christians in the department began to write me letters telling me how the memo had given them hope and courage to just be Christians. Those letters lifted my spirits. Church groups began to call and encourage me. Different groups started dropping by my office to pray. Before long, Richard Payne and I weren't the only ones kneeling in prayer on my office floor.

Judges who were Christians called me. Christian legislators dropped me notes or called and invited me to join their prayer groups. Because of the memo, I found that there were lots of Christians in government and that my one little act had given them courage to live their faith out loud.

My second executive order followed close behind. I learned that the state was paying for pornography for inmates. Magazines like *Playboy* and *Hustler* were being brought into my prisons compliments of the state of North Carolina.

"Ben, how much authority do I have?"

"Go for it, Mr. Secretary."

THIRTY-ONE

Order of Execution

I never believed in angels. I mean not the kind that appear to people at the grocery store or in their bedrooms and give them important revelations. I was on board with Michael and Gabriel. Over the centuries, God has put great trust in those two heavenly creatures and their friends. But in our present world, I wasn't convinced that God used these winged warriors in that way—until I had to order my first execution.

John William Rook kidnapped his female victim, beat her with a tire iron, raped her and then ran her over with his car. On September 19, 1986, he was scheduled to die by lethal injection at 2 a.m. in the death chamber at Central Prison.

The day of the execution, more than one hundred people came in and out of my office throughout the day to offer support. At any given time, twenty or so could be found standing outside my door. Church folks brought food for my staff and me while others stayed and prayed together.

I had had several death threats from opponents of the death penalty (that's never made any sense to me), so Governor Martin sent over some patrol officers for my protection. All the comings and goings made their job difficult.

Outside the prison walls, protesters on both sides shouted at each other and waved their signs with gritted teeth and balled up fists while others lit candles and held vigil.

The day of the execution, I prayed with John William's mother in a visitor's room near the execution chamber. Thinking I was going to comfort her, she hugged me instead and assured me that her son had been forgiven for his sins.

When I accepted the secretary position, I had already wrestled with my own convictions about the death penalty. In reality, I was naïvely hoping that no one would have to die on my watch. I had not allowed myself to think the scenario through far enough that I would actually be the one that had to call the warden with the green light to execute. The burden compressing my heart that day felt like a jagged, steel beam that had been placed over my chest and threatened to crush it with each struggling beat.

Seven days before, I stood in Governor Martin's office as the Governor's General Council, Jim Trotter, finally put John William's case to rest. Jim had organized witnesses, evidence, and documents and had listened to the pleas of several appointees advocating for the families of both the victim and John William. By Governor Martin's decree, only two standards would be considered to validate a stay of execution: 1) the evidence in the case was lacking and faulty, and/or 2) the punishment did not fit the crime. No other issues were allowed to enter into the determination. John William Rook's prosecution was solid. Governor Martin and General Council Jim Trotter determined the evidence was foolproof and the horrendous crime warranted the harsh sentence.

Governor Martin refused to play into the circus atmosphere that was building around this execution. He did not believe in letting the victim's family or the inmate's family suffer in the "not knowing." Unless something extremely unusual and unforeseen happened, there would be no stay of execution. The case had been reviewed and a decision had been made. In the governor's office the day of the decision, Jim Martin and I prayed together for ourselves and for the families involved.

Richard Payne had been with me for those seven days prior to the execution date. He rarely left my side. If he felt the stress was getting unbearable, he'd stop me and take me off to pray.

About ten o'clock the evening of the execution, I decided it was time to be alone. The waiting area outside my office was crowded. I tried my best to comfort my staff and the warden. It was just as hard on them as it was on me. I had prayed with those who asked and encouraged others as best I could. Now, it was time for me to hold the hand of God and wait.

Inside my office was a phone with a direct line from the governor. No one knew that number except for Governor Martin himself. I didn't even know it. As I knelt in prayer, or sat in my chair waiting, I couldn't keep from willing that phone to ring. If it did, the news would be good—at least for Mr. Rook.

I closed my eyes and finally gave my mind permission to remember. I first met John William Rook at the Church on Life Row. Standing beside Sonny Craig, he welcomed me to their worship with a grin almost as big as Sonny's. I remembered his voice blending with the others as we sang praises together. We held hands in a circle when I ended our worship in prayer. As I recalled our conversation, his haunting words settled in on me and twisted my heart up like a wet towel. His execution date was at that time a year out.

"Mr. Secretary, if you have to make that call, don't worry about me," he said.

Of course, I knew what *call* he meant. I looked him in the eye, wanting desperately to show him the respect of not blinking or turning away.

"Don't worry about me. If you have to make that call ten minutes before two in the morning, just know that five minutes after two, I'll be in heaven."

My eyes were closed and my head bowed when a ring blared out like a megaphone. It was after midnight. For an instant, I couldn't determine if it was the normal phone on my desk ringing or the hotline behind my desk.

It was the hotline. "Hello, Governor," I answered.

I heard movement on the line, but no one spoke. "Governor Martin?"

To my complete surprise, it was a female voice on the other line. "Mr. Secretary, I want you to know that there are a lot of us praying for you."

"What? Who is this? How did you get this number?"

"I can't tell you that, but we wanted you to know that everything is going to be alright. John is going to be alright."

"Who are you?"

"It doesn't matter. We know that you have been sitting in your office agonizing over your role in this, but please, just know it's okay. You go do what you need to do. John is okay." Click.

As I hung up the governor's line, the burden of the last seven days suddenly fell away from me. The stress was like a zippered suit of dead skin that I had finally been able to unzip and step out of.

At 1:45 a.m. my office phone rang. The warden told me everything was ready. His words were brief. We hung up. I picked up the hotline that I had only moments ago held in my hand—it was still warm.

"Governor Martin. It's time."

The Governor's words were brief as well. Nothing had changed. I was instructed to tell the warden to proceed.

Those two phones in my office seemed as heavy as dumbbells. As I answered them and hung them up in succession, my grip was sweaty. I dropped each into its cradle with a loud thud.

One more call to make. *The* call. I pushed the button.

"Mr. Secretary?"

"It's ten till two. Proceed."

John William Rook was led from the deathwatch cell into the small, sterile execution chamber. Through three observation windows, a handful of witnesses watched as he was strapped onto a gurney. Just moments later, John

William was injected with three plungers, but only one of them carried the lethal drug. He was pronounced dead at 2:05 a.m.

I never knew who called me on the governor's hotline. I'll never be convinced that it was anyone less than a heavenly winged warrior. As for John William, only heaven knows.

THIRTY-TWO

The Doctor Is In

"Are those maggots?"

"Yes, Mr. Secretary, I believe they are."

"What color is the paint smeared on those walls?"

"It's hard to say, sir."

"When was the infirmary last painted?"

"I don't know. I've been here twenty-five years and it's always been like this since I've been here."

"Where are all the medical supplies and equipment?"

"We don't really have any to speak of. Just what you see here."

I was on a tour of the inmate hospital at Central Prison a few months after my appointment as secretary. The puke green walls were dirty and stained. It seemed like they'd stick to you if you touched them. The bedding was soiled and infested with insects. The only piece of medical equipment I found on my little tour that actually worked was a thirty-five-year-old X-ray machine.

"If an inmate gets sick, what goes on here?"

"We give him some aspirin."

"Aspirin?"

The director of health care fidgeted like a schoolboy sent to the principal's office, but looked me straight in the eye like a bully unashamed of his actions.

"Mr. Secretary, these are criminals sent to us for punishment. We do what we can with what we've got. We're not a spa."

A few weeks later, my phone rang. "Mr. Secretary, my name is Henry Parker Eales. I'm a nurse at Central Prison and I hear you're a Christian. Is that right, sir?"

Mr. Eales wanted a meeting to discuss the possibility of accrediting that rat hole of a hospital at Central. I almost laughed out loud.

A few days later, I sat and looked across my desk at Parker Eales, director of nursing at Central. Dark hair and thick, horn-rimmed glasses framed the face of this determined young man. He had brought with him his assistant, Richard Jeffreys, who looked even younger than Parker.

"We can do it, Mr. Secretary, if you back us. If you run interference and help us through the red tape, I promise you we can bring that facility up to code."

Central Prison was North Carolina's oldest prison facility. Construction started on the gothic building in 1884. It took inmates fourteen years to complete as they quarried the granite just outside the prison's east wall for the construction. By the time it was finished, it looked like the foreboding castle of some brooding dark knight. All that was missing from the towering turrets was a surrounding moat and starving crocodiles. One hundred years later, a massive renovation project had brought the prison into the twentieth century—except for its medical facility.

"When was the last time any piece of medical equipment was purchased?" I asked.

"Well, sir, we're still using thermometers from the 1950s."

"And tongue depressors from the twenties," chimed in Jeffreys.

"I don't even want to ask how old the magazines are in your waiting room."

We laughed that nervous laugh of folks sizing each other up.

"Mr. Secretary, we have elderly inmates who need geriatric care and we can't give it to them. We have men incarcerated with heart conditions that need to be monitored. We can't, so we don't. Central Prison hospital is not equipped to set a broken finger much less handle a strep infection or stitches. We have prisoners with cancer, AIDS, kidney disease and the list goes on—just like in any other community."

"I've seen the place. It needs a huge bug bomb set off in the middle of it. What has gone on there, Mr. Eales?"

"Nothing, sir. Absolutely nothing. The thinking of those in charge is that they're just prisoners. Who cares? But I was hoping, Mr. Secretary, with you being a Christian, that you'd see it differently."

I was Cassie Newkirk Johnson's son—of course I saw it differently. "You can get that nasty, foul place brought up to code to meet the American Medical Association standards?"

"I believe we can, but it's going to take going over some people's heads."

"What do you mean?"

"If we're going to have a chance at doing this, I am going to have to report to you alone and nobody else. We've got to cut through all red tape. I can't go through the warden, or anyone else; I have to work directly with you."

This was unheard of. You just don't bypass the chain of command. It makes people mad and uncooperative down the line. But those maggots and that rancid smell still haunted me. "I'll take care of the red tape if you can take care of getting us accredited," I promised.

As I ran interference, Parker went out and made contacts with pharmaceutical companies and doctors. The donations of medications and supplies he arranged were incredible.

For the first time, the North Carolina prison system had a shot at an accredited hospital. If I was in charge of the health care of about 18,000 inmates, I would settle for nothing less. Yes, they were criminals, but they were also human beings. I could not look the other way. And besides, the class action suit that Governor Martin and I had inherited also demanded adequate health care for inmates—in short order.

The two young men hit the ground running. I'm not sure they or any of those helping them slept for weeks. But in April 1986, six months after Parker and his assistant galloped from my office, the Central Prison Health Facility was awarded its AMA accreditation after a grueling, three-day audit by the National Commission on Correctional Health Care. And they did it without any state funds. Parker Eales walked on water as far as I was concerned.

Freshly painted white and yellow walls adorned every nook and cranny of the hospital. Cheery, huge wall murals hung in each infirmary. Clean curtains and bedspreads now covered those bare windows and stark beds. Privacy curtains hung between examination cubicles. Plants were placed throughout the facility, and even Gideons got into the act and placed Bibles in every bedside table drawer.

A new X-ray lab and physical therapy room was added to the first floor. Administrative offices, medical records, clinics and an emergency room were outfitted on the second floor; the third-floor infirmary was now up to code, and the maximum care unit, acute care unit, and operating room on the fourth floor boasted adequate and proper medical equipment and supplies for the first time since Moses parted the Red Sea.

The space was always there, we just hadn't maximized its use. After all, they were just prisoners, right?

One of the most crucial problems we had to address for accreditation was the addition of twelve nursing positions. My budget was stretched, but after all, I was the secretary and my legal council had assured me that I could do anything I wanted. For the first time, the longstanding tradition of "men only" working in the prison hospital was done away with as the arrival of eleven female nurses brought the health care staff at Central up to code. The nurses were transfers from Wayne Correctional Center. I took a lot of heat for that one.

After the main hospital was brought up to code, Parker set to work getting the Mental Health Program at Central accredited as well. For his exemplary work, I promoted Parker Eales to the health director position, bypassing several medical physicians who were vying for the job. Again, it wasn't a popular move, but the right one.

During those six months, red tape was sliced through and tossed aside like day-old bread. I had never had so much fun.

THIRTY-THREE

Beds and Programs

$\mathcal{B}$uilding and improving prisons is not a sexy political move, and it can be a nasty political hill to die on. But I must hand it to my friend Jim Martin. He planted his flag on that ugly hill and committed himself to humane treatment coupled with tough sentencing—a dangerous tightrope to walk.

In the end, the budget for our comprehensive, ten-year plan got cut in half by the lawmakers at the state capitol. But even at that, prying the allotted funds out of their hands took an act of Congress, literally. A second class-action lawsuit, *Small vs. Martin,* charged that prison overcrowding was now so severe that it violated inmates' constitutional rights. This lawsuit forced the General Assembly's hand and did not allow them to push our prison woes under the rug. *Small vs. Martin* dictated that the state improve living conditions, health care, educational programming and drug rehabilitation programs in forty-nine more prisons throughout the state.

From the get-go, I was overwhelmed with construction and renovation woes. Because of the September 1985 ruling, I was given a year to build fourteen prisons, but I wasn't given the manpower or equipment to do so. Stringent and cumbersome regulations were making rapid construction of state buildings nearly impossible. Yet the Democratic House majority refused to do anything about those regulations. In 1986, lawmakers added nearly $14 million to the budget to begin expanding the rest of the prison system — $14 million dollars that I had no time to spend. I was still trying to create a major construction crew out of a meager maintenance and engineering staff.

Then the state was once again threatened with a federal take-over if the required prisons and dorms weren't built posthaste. Finally in an emergency meeting between Governor Martin, Lt. Governor Bob Jordan and House Speaker Liston Ramsey, a plan was devised. This summit touched off a series of private negotiations between the administration and legislative leadership and a compromise was finally reached. As a result, my closest aide, C.C. Cameron, was given responsibility for the emergency construction program.

I was relieved. I gladly gave up my duties as construction site boss and the day-to-day oversight of prison renovations. Finally, help had arrived. Of course, the media interpreted this appointment of Cameron as Governor Martin's lack of trust in me, but he and I knew what was going on. The lawmakers needed a scapegoat for North Carolina's embarrassing prison overcrowding fiasco—a nightmare that years of legislative neglect had brought about. I was going to be that scapegoat.

I'm proud of the many successes my staff and I had during my seven-year tenure in corrections. Contrary to the claims of my critics, my administration was the first to get our hands dirty over the real issues destroying North Carolina's prisons and parole system.

By the end of 1987, the South Piedmont area had several new minimum-security dormitories. Proudly, all were built in record time. By 1989, the new Craggy Correctional Center added 314 beds, while the new Buncombe Correctional Center helped us add 104 beds. All in all, Governor Jim Martin and my administration added more than three thousand new beds to the system.

North Carolina became the first state to use an electronic ankle surveillance system. We implemented its use with inmates relegated to house arrest for nonviolent offences and for young, nonviolent offenders still in school.

The BRIDGES program—Building, Rehabilitating, Instructing, Developing, Growing, Employing—began in 1989. It was a cooperative effort between the North Carolina Division of Prisons and the Division of Forest Resources. BRIDGES trained young, nonviolent inmates to help manage the state's natural resources. This innovative idea was conceived as a result of the serious mountain fires North Carolina was experiencing. The program enabled the state to assemble a fire-fighting force at a moment's notice, all the while developing a strong work ethic and marketable skills in inmates.

The Department of Corrections could pull this program off without biased criticism because it was implemented at a facility far off the media's beaten path. Inmates built the entire camp almost totally on donations. On a few occasions, the inventive staff would even get a cow donated to the program to help feed the inmates. Participants were expected to do their own cooking. There was no fence around the camp. In the program's history, only two men ever tried to escape. Within a few hours they came hobbling back full of thistles and thorns and begging to sleep in their own cot. The remote, stark terrain just wasn't conducive to any kind of "prison break." The embarrassed inmates lost their right to participate in the program and were sent to another facility in the city.

I traveled to Avery County to check things out. The inmates loved the several-acre pond on the property. Whenever I visited, they encouraged me to do a little fishing. My first fishing experience was astonishing as I snagged a trout about three seconds after casting my line. Applause and laughter surrounded me as inmates and staff congratulated me. Come to find out, one of the youths had been standing behind me tossing in breadcrumbs luring the fish directly toward my hook.

I'm very proud of the BRIDGES program. It became an excellent alternative for youthful offenders who were determined to make a change in their lives.

Programs like Motheread, a literacy program that taught female inmates to read or improve their reading skills, began on my watch. The program was designed to encourage incarcerated mothers to read to their children during visits. To walk through visitation rooms and see a child sitting on his mother's lap as she read him a story was a highlight for me.

Our Drug Testing and Rehabilitation program for inmates began in 1990. Inmates who were arrested under the influence and addicted to alcohol or other drugs came into the system but were not treated. Neglect only made the problem worse. We also had inmates who had not kicked their drug habits going out on probation and parole, making the recidivism rate skyrocket. This drug program became a successful component of rehabilitation, so much so that we dedicated an entire prison facility as a rehab center. Along the same lines, we began a wellness program for the employees.

Our first-ever Family Service Program Center for families of inmates opened during my tenure. This program helped inmate families maneuver through the system. Once someone was sentenced, his parents or spouse had no communication with him for quite a period of time. Inmates were transported from the local jail to a particular prison as a holding tank. They could be kept there for months before receiving their permanent assignment. All the while, the family had no clue where the inmate was. I saw this program as humane and designed for families in crisis.

We began a volunteer program at various sites with a goal to recruit six thousand volunteers. Governor Martin's wife, Dottie, was a huge supporter of this program and helped plan services such as cookouts, Christmas programs and worship programs for inmates.

IMPACT was a boot camp for inmates ages eighteen to twenty-two. This program provided much needed structure and skills training for young men motivated to get their lives back on track. If they went through the program successfully, many times their sentence was cut short. IMPACT helped to responsibly reduce overcrowding and it had to be maintained as part of the *Small vs. Martin* agreement.

I may have been a scapegoat and a laughing stock to some of my contemporaries, but I knew God was using me for good. While the ridicule stung, it did not break my spirit or determination to do the right thing for inmates, personnel or the community at large.

In the late 1980s and early '90s, when AIDS threatened to overwhelm the state's prison health care system, the Department of Corrections instituted the first-ever screening and treatment plan for AIDS patients. But not before I was personally challenged and brought face-to-face with the disease itself.

THIRTY-FOUR

The Woman

"*I* want to go home to die," she pleaded. Her words rattled like bones. They had a haunting echo about them as if each word lined up and stepped off a jagged cliff one at a time.

The female inmate had asked for a meeting with me to discuss the possibility of an emergency parole in order to spend Christmas with her young children—if she lived that long. It was November 1990 and the woman was in the end stages of HIV/AIDS.

Before I made the trek to her cellblock, I met with Parker Eales to learn all I could about this devastating disease. During those years, panic, rumor and misinformation ruled how AIDS patients were treated. In the prison system, an inmate with full-blown AIDS was a leper. The halls and cells in North Carolina prisons might as well have been Jerusalem, 33 AD where leper colonies housed the diseased. Sentenced to live alone without human contact, the woman was unwanted, not only in the system but in the outside world as well. She was living a hellish life in her own private leper colony, compliments of the state of North Carolina.

"So, you're telling me, Parker, that AIDS cannot be transmitted by simple touch?"

"That's right, Mr. Secretary. As long as those around her are cautious and careful, I think this woman could go home to die without the fear of passing anything on to her children or the community."

I trusted Parker. After praying together in my office in Raleigh, I decided to do the unprecedented—visit a female prisoner in her own cell. I had to. No one wanted to bring her to me. The officers and other staff members were afraid to have any contact with her. Even the infirmary nurses had banished her from the clinic, admitting their fear of spreading the disease to themselves or other inmates.

As I drove to the Women's Prison in Raleigh, I wondered what condition this woman was in. I had seen footage in the media of people ravaged by AIDS. The sores, the emaciated bodies and the empty eyes had been broadcast like the old 1950s polio public service announcements.

The dorm where the woman was housed didn't look different from the others surrounding it on the prison grounds. Yet it felt very different. The minute I led my entourage through the doors, heaviness fell over us. The air around me instantly grew stale. My lungs struggled to inflate as if I were climbing the summit of Mt. Everest instead of the few steps to a dark cubicle.

"Here's the cell you want, Mr. Secretary," said the sergeant, pointing toward the first cell on my right.

"Why does it look like this?" I asked. Spread over the front of the enclosure were several heavy wool blankets. As I peered inside, all I could make out was the slight movement of a shadow.

"Because no one wants to go in there, and we don't want what's in there coming out," replied the officer.

I took a step toward the opening and ducked my head as I looked inside. As my eyes adjusted to the rank darkness, the frail body of a human being began to materialize before me like a milky apparition.

Sitting on a thin mattress over a small cot was what remained of a woman who had once been more. Gone was anything that distinguished delicate features or womanly curves. In its place was a pile of fleshy sticks with sunken eyes. She smiled at me with lips that were parched and teeth that looked like the slightest ting of a fork would knock them out.

I moved further into the room and told her who I was. She told me who she was. I told her I wanted to talk about her request for early release but that I needed to get to know her first—that I wanted to hear her story.

Turning slightly, she reached over in front of her and picked up two tattered photographs that had been lying on the cot on another one of those awful wool blankets. Reaching out toward me with those photos in hand, she said, "These are my children."

As I went to take the photographs from her hand, I realized to my horror that I couldn't move. It was as if my arm was glued to my side. When I looked at the pictures of those two smiling babies, all I saw was AIDS, contamination and a horrible death. I could not make myself handle those little school pictures.

Shame flooded through me like dirty water. Did God want to hide His eyes from me at that moment?

The woman withdrew her hand. Sadly, my reaction did not appear to surprise her. She simply took my shunning in stride and began talking. "I want to tell my children, don't take the road I took. I want to be a mother to these kids at least the three months I've got left. If you can find any way in your heart, Mr. Secretary, to send me home, I'd really appreciate it."

This Winston-Salem mother had served half of her eight-year sentence. She wouldn't live to finish it out. "I did wrong. I did so very wrong, and now I'm paying for it. But I've got to think I can still do some good for my children. They can't do like me. I've got to tell them that."

As I listened to her plead for mercy, I felt my arm finally unlock and my legs move. Without further hesitation, I sat on her cot and put my arm around her. The woman sighed and leaned into my embrace like I had offered her a down-stuffed comforter around her shoulders instead of my measly, uncomfortable arm.

"I sit day in, day out. Nobody talks to me. I'm in constant pain. They'd take me to the infirmary, but nobody wants me there."

I continued to embrace her as she cried on my shoulder. All along I knew I was breaking my own rule. This was totally against the code of behavior of a secretary of corrections—a man hugging a female inmate. But the law of God's love was holding her, not me. I had no choice. As I looked around, the other people with me had started to cry. At the end of our visit, I told her that I'd do everything I could to get her home for Christmas.

I went back and had Parker write up her medical history so I could present it to Governor Martin. In the meantime, the press had picked up that I had visited this inmate and that I had embraced her. They told a negative story of how I had violated my own rules.

At the same time, Winston-Salem, her hometown, got wind of her request and started a very public campaign protesting her coming home. Unreasonable fear clouded compassion—just as sure as it had mine those first few minutes in her cell. Unfortunately, the venom of fear and panic enabled some folks to scribble signs and posters of hate that made lively footage for the media.

By the time Parker and I could pull our report and recommendation together, time had run out for the governor to commute her sentence—at least in time for Christmas. I was devastated. I had to go back and tell her I had failed.

The day of our second meeting brought a nasty winter chill. The wind swirled relentlessly outside as my insides matched the cold temperatures— bitter degree for bitter degree.

I couldn't bear to meet the woman in that life-depleting cell again, so I had the officers prepare a special visitor room where we could sit and talk. As the officers brought her out of her dorm, her tiny body somehow mustered enough strength to actually stomp. "I'm not speaking to this man. He lied to me!"

I had built her hopes up so high, yet I had not produced. I was her last hope and I had let her down. My failure turned this woman into a tiny, fierce bee who wanted nothing more than to jab her stinger into me and then die. The fact that Richard Payne and his boss, Charles Colson, had personally visited her on Christmas day on the approval of the warden did not temper her anger toward me.

To get her to the administration building, the officers had to walk her across the yard. By this time, rain had mixed in with the wind and cold. As the sergeant tried to hand her the raincoat and umbrella I had ordered for her, she refused them.

"I want pneumonia and want to die. I want him to feel in his heart what he did to me."

"Now you listen here, ma'am," said the sergeant. "You ought to be ashamed of yourself. The secretary has taken a lot of misery because of you, yet he's still taking time out to come over here to talk to you."

No amount of coaxing would get her to wear the raincoat, but the sergeant did manage to keep the umbrella over her head on the walk over. As she entered the room where I was waiting, she brushed past me scowling like an angry vagrant made to evacuate her dilapidated refrigerator box under a bridge.

Suddenly, as the woman turned toward me, her demeanor changed. Her thin shoulders started shaking up and down as her tears mingled with raspy giggles. I expected her anger, but this reaction caught me off guard. "What?" I asked. Slowly hobbling over to a chair, she dropped down into it like her body suddenly sprang a flat tire. "Where's your billfold?" she asked just above a whisper.

"What?"

"I said, where's your billfold?"

I instinctively put my hand in my suit coat pocket and felt. My billfold was gone.

With a sly grin that made her bones a little more bearable to look at, she waved my wallet in front of her. "That's how naïve you are. I may not have been much, but I was good at this."

She didn't have enough time to stay angry with me. And I surely didn't want to waste any of what she had left. "I didn't lie to you. I just wasn't able to get all the required paperwork done before Christmas. I'm sorry."

Governor Jim Martin was more than my boss. He was a brother—a compassionate brother. With his help, that January we were able to send this woman back home on house arrest, despite community protests. For a few weeks she got to be a mother to her children. She was dead before spring.

Because of this woman, the inhumane treatment of North Carolina inmates diagnosed with HIV/AIDS stopped. The AIDS initiative that my administration began in 1990 promised compassionate care to any inmate suffering from this horrific disease. Fear, panic and ignorance could not be allowed to win on this one. I knew their stranglehold first-hand, and I was certain God expected better of us.

THIRTY-FIVE

The $65,000 Hit and Miss Men

In June 1990, Mattie and I celebrated our thirtieth year at Mount Sinai Missionary Baptist Church. The Sunday morning of the anniversary, we woke to sunshine and a knock at the door. Mattie had gotten used to unexpected callers at the house—even on Sunday mornings. Unannounced visitors went with both jobs. As Mount Sinai became known more and more as a church with a compassionate heart, people in need found their way to our front steps. The line of folks who showed up at church or at my house with resumes in hand was continuous.

Mattie was getting the children dressed when she heard the knock at our back door. I was in our bedroom. "May I help you?" she asked, opening to door to a face she didn't recognize.

Staring back at her was a gentleman roughly dressed with dirty jeans, wrinkled shirt and a black windbreaker. Standing behind him on our carport was another man almost his exact twin. "Yeah, we're here to see Secretary Johnson."

Mattie stared at the men for a second and then told them to wait in the carport and that I'd be with them shortly. "Aaron! There're two men in our carport wanting to see you."

I came through the back hall and peeked through a window, but the men had their backs turned toward me. "Why don't you and the children go on over to the church and I'll be there in a minute."

"Come on, Dezette. Get your Bible. Jamale, get in the car." My family walked out through the back door in front of the men. Mattie smiled. "We're going on to church, gentlemen. My husband will be out to see you directly."

The men backed away from Mattie's car and watched her and the children get in and then back out of the driveway.

219

I tried once again to see the faces of my visitors from inside the house but couldn't. But the moment I stepped out onto the porch, I knew that something wasn't right. I recognized one of the men as a former inmate. He was nervous, and his sidekick kept looking around as if riding shotgun.

"Good morning, gentlemen, how can I help you?" I saw the guns tucked into their belts a half a second before they pulled them out and pointed them at my head.

"Do what we say and you won't get hurt!"

I raised my hands and started to back slowly toward my back door. "Now, take it easy. Just tell me what you want. Let's see if I can help."

Sidekick walked closer and pulled me away from the back door. "Don't move!"

Ringleader pulled a crumpled piece of paper from his shirt pocket and shoved it into my chest. "Read this. If you don't do what it says, we'll kill you."

I put my hands down and took the piece of paper. On it was written an inmate's name with instructions to call Central Prison and ask for the warden.

"So, what am I supposed to tell the warden?"

"Tell him to get a van ready and some clothes and to pull it outside the gates. That prisoner there," he said, pointing to the name on the paper, "is to be allowed to drive the van away. If they follow him, you'll die."

To my surprise, by walking out onto my carport, I became the victim of a kidnapping, a murder threat and a poorly planned prison break.

"Gentlemen, I'm not sure you know how much trouble this is going to get you into."

"Shut up! Just do what you're told!" shouted the ringleader.

"Tell me, how much are you being paid to throw away your freedom?"

"I said shut-up!"

"I hope it's worth it."

"For sixty-five thousand dollars, I'd shoot you right here if I had to," piped in Sidekick, waving his gun in front of my face.

"Make the call!" shouted Ringleader.

My kidnappers were starting to get too jumpy for my liking. With every car that drove past the house, either on the way to church or a Sunday outing, they pushed me further into the confines of the carport. I knew I was a good talker—most preachers are. This gift of words and reason had saved my life more than once, but I also knew that a loaded gun, a nervous trigger finger, and a scared assailant were as unpredictable as a skittish skunk walking up your front sidewalk. I needed to end this before someone got hurt.

"Okay. Okay. If that money means so much to you, I'll help you. What I'll have to do is go and call my assistant, who will call the warden, and we'll arrange to have the prisoner released."

"Just like we said… with a van and clothes."

"Yes, with a van and clothes."

Ringleader pushed me through the back door and into my den. But for some strange reason, he didn't come into the house himself. Sidekick stood behind him, still on the carport.

"I don't have a phone in this room. It's over there in the kitchen. Okay? That's where I'm going."

Standing in the doorway, Ringleader said, "Fine. Hurry up!"

I walked into the kitchen and picked up the phone from the wall and started dialing. As I talked to the person on the line, my kidnappers talked among themselves and kept an eye on me. I hung up and walked back onto the porch.

"It's done. But it's going to take a little while to get the van and clothes."

"I'll have you call them back in a few minutes to see what's happening."

And then we waited. Me with my hands up, Ringleader with his gun pointing at me, Sidekick with his arm and gun down to his side. When the police and SWAT team silently surrounded the house and my hostage-takers realized that twelve or so rifles were aimed at their heads and hearts, there wasn't much fight in them. They surrendered without incident. Stuffed in their pockets, the police found large bills that totaled sixty-five thousand dollars.

Obviously, I hadn't called my assistant.

The inmate who had planned the escape and my demise was housed at a medium-security field prison, so I had him immediately moved to Central. When the officers came in to move him, he pretended to be sick. They moved him anyway.

On Monday, I had the inmate brought to a holding area at Central. As he shuffled into the room in steel ankle bracelets with shackles on his wrists, he hung his head and wouldn't look at me.

"Officers, please wait outside," I said.

The inmate's head snapped up like on a spring. I'm sure he didn't know who he trusted the least—the officers or me.

"Mr. Secretary, we can't do that. This man tried to kill you."

"We'll be fine in here. Now, please wait outside." The officers still didn't move. "I'll take full responsibility. You'll be just outside the door. It'll be okay," I assured them again.

Reluctantly, the officers shoved the inmate into a chair and as they turned and started to walk from they room they ordered him not to move. I followed them and closed the door behind them.

Walking back over to the warden's desk, I leaned on it in front of the inmate. Sitting before me was this angry, broken and lost man. He had more fingers missing than were still attached. Scars defined his features. And his eyes, once they finally looked at me, were as hard as overcooked egg yolks. Suddenly, he did the unexpected. He started weeping. An eerie, howl-like sound began leaking out of him like ooze. In between sobs he choked, "Mr. Secretary… forgive me… didn't mean it… so desperate…."

The man went on to tell me that his mother had cancer and that he had only wanted to leave prison to go see her. She could no longer visit him because Central Prison was too far away from his hometown. His mother was now too sick to travel that far.

My family was unharmed. I wasn't too much the worse for wear. But *this* man had forfeited everything because of his actions. He was now never going to leave his barred and locked existence. I watched his crippled hands clumsily wipe the tears streaming down his face. He expected nothing from me, except maybe the worst.

As a child, when my mother truly wanted to get my attention, when she desperately wanted me to *get it*, to understand that God truly does hate the sin but died for the sinner, she made me get on my knees and kneel beside her. Then in a gentle, calm voice she asked God to shoo away the bad and fill me up with good.

When I got down on my knees next to the inmate, his eyes got as big as boulders. He didn't know what to expect, but I'm sure he didn't see a prayer coming his way. With my own hands covered over by this man's few stubby fingers, the sin was forgotten and the sinner was forgiven as Cassie's boy did his best to shoo away the bad.

After the man's trial, the inmate was moved to a prison closer to his mother.

Part VI: Man from Macedonia

THIRTY-SIX

Man from Macedonia

"During the night Paul had a vision of a man of Macedonia standing and begging him, 'Come over to Macedonia and help us.'" Acts 16:9

The year was 1990.

"Let's do it!" Richard Payne held the door to the airplane open as he motioned to me to climb in. I'd never been in this small a plane and I wasn't sure I wanted to be.

"Do they even know we're coming?"

"Naw! But it'll be okay. You'll see."

Trying to fit my girth into the back seat of this tiny plane was like squeezing biscuits into a too-small pan. "Who's going to be there?"

"I'm not sure exactly, but I'm thinking this here's the day that the executive leadership team meets." Richard had talked me into traveling to Reston, Virginia, unannounced, to the headquarters of Prison Fellowship Ministries.

The promise I made six years before to the Church on Life Row for a revival was weighing heavy on both of us. So much had happened during my administration from the get-go that bringing a spiritual revival to Central Prison kept falling further down the list. But it was not a forgotten promise. Richard and I had been praying about how to go about it for years. With my permission, Richard had been in touch with those death row brothers regularly and had started prayer meetings with them and others with volunteers from local churches.

Two people in particular stand out to me during that time. One was a wealthy businessman who participated in a three-day Prison Fellowship seminar on Central's death row. The crisp, white-shirted volunteer had never done anything like this before, but with Richard Payne on your tail, you can be convinced to try anything once.

John S. Gardner Jr. was an inmate as rough as they come. He had a disturbing tattoo on his neck and a tongue tattoo on his cheek. In August 1979, he shot and killed two people in what was dubbed "the Steak and Ale murders." Gardner, in his written confession, revealed that he had spent the earlier part of the night of the robbery and murders drinking and shooting up crystal meth.

As only God can orchestrate, this Ivy-League volunteer and John Gardner found themselves sitting next to each other the first day of the Prison Fellowship seminar. For the next three days, the businessman and the murderer became partners. By the last day of the event, a friendship had formed. The event ended but not the relationship. The volunteer kept going back to the prison regularly to visit John. Over time, John Gardner's countenance started to change as he began to look somehow softer. Together, the men held a Bible between them while they read and prayed over each other. Eventually, John became a member of the Church on Life Row.

A year and a half later, John's execution date arrived. On that dark October morning in the wee hours, the volunteer sat behind those daunting glass windows and witnessed the lethal injection of his friend and brother. After John's body was released, the man had him buried in his own family plot. I'll never be convinced that God is not alive behind those bars.

With the frantic building of new prisons, addressing overcrowding and prison population emergency caps, developing new programs, creating a parole system that worked and steering clear as best I could from the bias of the media, I hadn't found the time to focus on a true revival. Until one morning when Richard announced that God had nudged him and declared the time was at hand. Because I trusted Richard, I found myself stuffed into an airplane that weighed less than me, flying off to a meeting to which we weren't invited.

Once we arrived at the Prison Fellowship facility, I wasn't sure what to do next. The executive leadership team was indeed having their monthly meeting and all were present.

"Why don't ya sit here for a second, and let me see what's happening," said Richard. So I sat down in the lobby and thanked God, for the hundredth time, for our safe flight, while Richard took off for parts unknown.

What I didn't know at the time was that the leadership team was on a short break and that Richard had cornered Tom Pratt, then president of Prison Fellowship, in the men's bathroom. "I've got the director of corrections of North Carolina out in the front lobby. Why don't I bring him on by and let him talk to you guys?"

Tom Pratt was not amused and was more than a little resistant to Richard's suggestion. "Richard, you can't do this. You're only going to embarrass yourself.

Secretary of Corrections Aaron Johnson and Prison Fellowship's Richard
Payne work together during a 1991 community service project.

You can't march in here and demand a meeting. We're in the middle of some serious conversation. You know that Prison Fellowship is having some financial woes and we're looking at cutting some positions. Now is not the time. You should have called."

"Well, if I'd done that, ya'll probably wouldn't have seen us."

"We're not seeing you now, my friend." Richard and Tom had a shared admiration for each other, but Tom thought Richard had overstepped his bounds.

"Now come on! This here is a guy with power and he wants to ask Prison Fellowship to come to North Carolina. How can we not at least listen to him?"

One very seldom tells Richard "no." I was given five minutes to come before the leadership team as they ate their boxed lunches. "Five minutes and not a second more," warned Tom.

Richard just smiled.

I entered the room as seven or eight men were rummaging through their lunch boxes; they smiled cordially at their intruder. Richard quickly introduced me and left me standing before the group. As I stood in front of these men and opened my mouth to speak, God struck me mute. It was as if my tongue had disappeared and my voice erased. To my dismay, tears came. They streamed down my face like a gushing Niagara waterfall. I put my hand to my heart and pressed, hoping that would help pump the words out of me.

I looked over at Tom and Richard through blurred vision and was surprised to see that they, too, had started to cry. In fact, everyone in the room had tears washing down their cheeks, and I hadn't even been able to utter a word yet.

As I wept, I kept thinking of the faces of those behind bars—how hopelessness and guilt had stolen their expressions, leaving eyes as hollow as any black hole you'd find in space. Broken lives, homes and families lay in their wake like clutter in an alley. I knew that their only hope of salvation and true rehabilitation was the power of the blood-stained cross and the empty tomb.

Suddenly, I felt my voice enter back into my body, like it had just been on loan somewhere else for a time. I slowly opened my mouth and spoke from a place only God knows, recalling the vision of Paul from Acts 16. *"I am the man from Macedonia, and I've come to ask for your help."*

No one breathed or blinked or twitched as a holy stillness encircled the room. With my face sticky and wet I continued. "It has been my dream for a long time now that someone would come help me share the word of God with every man and woman in my prisons. I have the authority to open every dormitory, every cell, and every room where inmates sleep, study, eat and get health care. And with God's help, I am willing to use that authority to open up these prisons so that every inmate can hear the Gospel of Jesus."

The more I talked, the less they ate. I wasn't sure if those staring at me thought I'd sprouted a halo or dollar signs over my head, but I kept talking and sharing the promise I had made to the members of the Church on Life Row.

Two hours later, Richard, Tom and every other man in the room had our arms around each other's shoulders as we bowed our heads and petitioned God for his guidance. I was invited back the next day to speak at the Prison Fellowship staff devotional and make my plea before them.

That morning at chapel, Tom Pratt introduced me. "You will sense the Spirit of God in this man. And what he is going to ask of us is gigantic and quite outside our way of working and our ministry."

As I walked up to the podium and turned and looked out over those two hundred or so folks, I again gave the Macedonian call, asking everyone in that room to help me fulfill the promise I had made to Sonny Craig and his brothers on death row.

As I spoke, tears once again spilled down my face and it wasn't long before the whole room had joined me in this watershed of uncontrollable tears. We were a collective mess.

Somewhere running through my mind was the thought that if I was successful with my plea, a spiritual revival implemented and encouraged by me would probably be my last official act as secretary of corrections. The outcry would be tremendous, and I'd probably get fired. But none of that mattered. I was convinced that this was what the Lord wanted, so the tears continued.

Between the sobs and praise, I preached. "The Lord has laid it on me to evangelize each one of my prisons before I leave office. Now I know that what I'm asking would require colossal commitments of time, money, staff and volunteers—not to mention some pretty inventive strategies to attract religion-skittish inmates."

In the back of my mind, I kept hearing one of the team members caution the day before: "Step into those waters and we could be swept under by the riptide." Which was true. What I was asking was fraught with political suicide. More importantly, there would be the choppy water of resistance from the prison chaplains themselves over theology and methodology; both had proven to have the potential to kill any good idea.

I couldn't let fear or skepticism stop me. I was convinced now more than ever as I stood before this crowd of good folks that this moment was a God appointment and I must fear not.

When I finished my invitation, you could have heard a baby sleep. "Prison can only confine prisoners; it can't change their hearts. Please, will you come?"

I was asking Prison Fellowship Ministries to do something on a scale that they had never attempted—ninety-four prisons canvassed with the Gospel of Christ in a week. Before this time, Prison Fellowship had taught weekly

Bible studies, run a three-day seminar here and there, and administered the annual Christmas Angel Tree, a program that helped give presents to children of inmates. But what I was talking about had not been attempted inside the walls of a prison anywhere.

I was also coming to them during a time of economic recession. Just the day before, hadn't the leadership team been discussing layoffs? And now I was asking staff members to embrace a huge project that would probably cost a couple million dollars at least.

Tom Pratt was the first to jump to his feet. The standing ovation of the crowd was an affirmation in itself, but Tom's arms around my neck held me up as I realized that Prison Fellowship, from staff to executive leaders, would answer the Macedonian call—full hearted and undaunted. No roundtable of men voted, no papers were signed, but everyone in that room already knew we were going to do this.

Richard and I flew back to Raleigh after the devotional. I was still a little stunned by our reception, but my friend wasn't. He told me he knew that if I could just get to speak, I'd win them over.

I love my friend, but I don't think I won them over to anything. God has His own ways and His own timing. We can plan and strategize and make lists, but we do so with limited knowledge and wisdom, and the inability to see around corners and beyond a day. God, however, sees all from His throne and has a Gods-eye view of schedules, budgets, mission statements and hearts. We can ask, but we must allow Him to decide when and if to push the start button.

The Holy Spirit was given His freedom to fill me up that day with the Macedonian message. Then the Holy One scattered from Reston like an electrical current. Within two weeks, Prison Fellowship had been awarded a $1.5 million grant from the Maclellan Foundation for Project Macedonia—the name the revival was given almost immediately. Only $1.5 million to go!

Mr. Charles Colson, the founder of Prison Fellowship, wasn't at the executive leadership team meeting that Tuesday or the staff devotional the following day. But as is God's way, He was preparing me for yet another pinpoint meeting.

THIRTY-SEVEN

Lots of Big Shorts

"The reports of my death are greatly exaggerated." In February 1992, I was feeling Mark Twain's pain. While my premature obituary had not appeared in the local newspapers, the papers were predicting my political death.

Seven months before Project Macedonia was to kick off, the press was calling for my resignation—and surprisingly not for planning a Christian revival inside the walls of North Carolina state prisons. That wasn't public knowledge yet.

At about the same time in 1990 when I was appealing to Tom Pratt and his folks for help, something was brewing in the Department of Corrections that I had unwittingly started back in 1985. The day I spotted that poor inmate and corrections officer working out in the freezing rain without the proper clothing, I made a promise to fill the prison Clothes House back up with proper attire. And with the teeth of *Small vs. Martin* chomping at the department's tail, adequate clothing was one of the prisoners' demands that had to be recognized and addressed.

I delegated the ordering of clothing to my department controller, C.R. Creech, and purchasing service officer, Rick Hursey. The class action suit specified that inmates were to have four sets of clothing at all times. For those working in the kitchen, they had to have whites as well, so they had to have five sets of clothing at the ready. Those that worked on the highways or in the health center also had to have five sets of clothing.

The problem to solve was how to buy enough clothes for twenty thousand inmates to have four changes of clothes at all times. We came up with a formula where inmates would have four sets in their lockers, four sets in the Clothes House at the prison, four sets in the laundry and four sets at the warehouse. That added up to sixteen sets of clothes for each inmate, which we had to keep ready at all times. That was a lot of clothes.

Once *Small vs. Martin* was settled, we began to, I thought, systematically order proper apparel. I signed the orders, but Hursey and Creech were in charge of all the ordering. Warehouse Manager Terry Thompson took on the task of warehousing the orders. My failure was in trusting them all too much.

In 1990, unbeknownst to me, Mr. Hursey had begun some questionable ordering practices. He unwisely began ordering from several companies to which he or a family member had ties. He also found a way to circumvent the department's ordering practice of obtaining sealed competitive bids. By state law, purchases over five thousand dollars had to be bid out. Hursey was splitting orders in half or more so that he did not have to receive bids but could simply order from the companies he wanted to use. Hursey ordered tear gas, rifles and ammunition this way.

In October 1991, Julie Carpenter, a department budget officer, reported to her boss, C.R. Creech, that she had discovered that Hursey had entered into a $1.2 million contract with a newly incorporated company. Coin Tel, Inc. was headed by M. Winston "Twig" Wiggins, a former college basketball player who had been introduced to Hursey by his supervisor, B.J. Mooneyham. The red flag that caught Julie Carpenter's attention was that Hursey's wife, Ellen, had just been given a new job at another company owned by Mr. Wiggins the same month. Creech didn't seem concerned and dismissed Ms. Carpenter's warning.

The following month, in November, an audit completed by Julie Carpenter, Rex A. Whaley and Jeff McCauley, all financial accountants in Creech's office and certified public accountants, again made Creech aware of Hursey's illegal ordering practices. Their 1990-91 audit reported thirty-three instances in which department purchasers obtained only one quote before making purchases. The audit also showed that some companies were paid even before the goods were received or the work that was promised was done. Creech decided to ignore the audit, as did B. J. Mooneyham, assistant secretary of management.

Unfortunately, the audit was never reported to me. In fact, the day after this audit was in the hands of Creech and Mooneyham, the Coin Tel contract was brought to me by my attorney, Lorrie Dollar, for my signature. I did not know when I signed it that day that it was a $1.2 million contract nor that it had never been bid out. Had I read the contract thoroughly, I would have known the size of the contract. I didn't. That fault lies with me. I trusted the people around me to do the right things, another fault of mine.

In the meantime, Hursey was ordering prison clothing to beat the band. He mistakenly thought that one complete pair of clothes came in a box, when in fact four complete sets of clothes came in a box. He accidently quadruple ordered.

Again unbeknownst to me, beginning in the summer of 1990 truckload after truckload of clothing from Angelica Uniform Group of St. Louis, Missouri, began dropping off boxes and boxes of clothes. Warehouse manager Terry Thompson had his hands full storing and "hiding" the overflow. Each prison stored all they could in their Clothes Houses. When filled, Hursey authorized Thompson to rent storage trailers to be brought to the prisons to store the rest. When all these clothes and trailers started arriving, it finally got my attention. In December 1991, I met with my Deputy Secretary C. Monroe Waters to start an internal investigation of the department's purchasing practices. But it was too late. The next month, January 1992, I had to order a State Bureau investigation of the ordering and purchasing practices of Hursey and his department. Rick Hursey resigned the same day he was suspended—making me the brunt of a myriad of jokes and the target of a lot of anger and distrust.

An overstock of $6.5 million in goods was stuffed into warehouses all over the prison system, with another $5.8 million of clothing, shoes and boxer shorts on order which we did not need, could not store, and could not pay for. Stored inside a central warehouse were enough triple-X brown shirts to last for the next 113 years—with another 49-year supply on order.

Another storage facility was holding a 165-year supply of triple-X boxer shorts. We had in a holding tank a 27-year supply of green shirts and 15-year supply of size 13 steel-toed safety boots. It was a mess, and my detractors were enjoying every minute of it.

Besides the overstocked clothing fiasco, it was discovered that Coin Tel, Inc. had been paid $138,339 in maintenance that it never performed and awarded numerous contracts without a bidding process. A company called Variety Sales had been given divided orders to avoid the required sealed competitive bidding procedure as well.

Variety Sales turned out to be owned by Coin Tel, Inc. president Wiggins and his family. By Hursey's direction, Coin Tel was also being paid almost $50,000 a month in commissions on phones owned, installed and serviced by Southern Bell—commissions that had been going to the Department of Corrections. Basically, Coin Tel did not manage or service the payphones that the Department of Corrections leased from Southern Bell. Yet they were receiving a 38 percent commission for absolutely no performance.

To add further suspicion, an attempt by Rick Hursey to divide purchases from Wimyer Industries was discovered. Wimyer's president was Raymond E. Wisely—Rick Hursey's landlord at the time.

I was angry and felt betrayed. I trusted those I shouldn't have. The media called it a scandal, and my head was wanted on a platter.

THIRTY-EIGHT

The Resignation

The brutal crucifixion of an innocent and loving Jesus Christ was a scandal. Having a 165-year supply of triple-X boxer shorts in a warehouse was an embarrassment but certainly not a scandal. Yet my administration was now blemished. The inappropriate actions of a few were causing all employees under my direction to be scrutinized, ridiculed and treated like the criminals in our charge. And I was portrayed as the don.

My heart was breaking as Governor Martin's name was being pulled through the mud with mine. He was no more to blame for the bulging warehouses or the unscrupulous purchasing practices of a few unethical folks than my own mother was. Yet someone had to take the blame, and the guy at the top is usually that someone.

I knew that just firing those responsible would not satisfy my enemies. And I refused to fire innocent folks—which was being called for by the press—a blanket firing of everyone who ever touched a purchase order or walked through a warehouse. The only thing that would satisfy the critics and deter them from scratching, clawing and biting at Governor Martin's jugular was if I disappeared along with the guilty.

I had to pray about my next move, so I found myself in a place that was calmingly familiar—on my knees next to Richard Payne.

Walking up the steps to Richard's office felt like I was trudging through sludge. I was like an old wagon whose wheels were wobbling and creaking under its heavy load. Stacked full of sorrow and anger, I felt like I had let Jim Martin down. He had done nothing but trust me, accept me and encourage me. He had picked me to bring compassionate leadership to the state's broken prison system and here I was bringing shame instead. All the good we had done together would be forgotten if my next move wasn't God-led.

Richard was in a meeting when I got there, but his secretary sent me on in. "I've got a lot of problems going on, Richard, and I think I'm going to resign." Suddenly everyone was on their feet. We were six months from the revival.

"What about Project Macedonia? What will we do?" Richard's forehead immediately scrunched up and I could tell he was already kicking himself for what he had just said.

"I've come here to pray so I'll know what to do."

Everyone in the room embraced me. They had read the headlines, too. This wasn't the first day they'd prayed for me over this.

"I'm sorry, brother. That was a selfish thing for me to say. I was just... just..."

"That's okay Richard. I understand."

"No! It's not okay. I've just realized that we've been putting our faith in you and not God. I'd even say we've loved you more than God. You've opened the doors, brother, but I can see now that this project must not hinge on you. It must depend on God's grace."

Richard and his staff had been working on Project Macedonia for almost two years. Training volunteers, raising funds, enlisting local churches and signing up celebrities and entertainers for the platform was a full time job. And it was just the tip of the iceberg that had to be chipped away. Enlisting prison chaplains, wardens, officers and others in the system to volunteer was the huge chunk just below the surface, and we were counting on my position giving us an edge on that. But we both realized that day that God's edge was deeper, stronger and more powerful. My resignation would not stop His work.

As soon as we closed our prayers, I knew what had to be done. "I'm heading over to the governor's office to resign."

"Are you sure you don't want to try and weather this? You haven't done anything wrong." Richard had his arm on my shoulder.

"No. I know what I've got to do. Besides, it's clear to me now that if I stay, everything about Project Macedonia will be centered on me and not what God will do in the prisons. It's time for me to go."

I went straight back to my office and called Jim Martin, but the governor was in Washington and wouldn't be back until that Friday. It was a long few days.

At the end of the week, I was knocking on the front door of the governor's mansion. Jim was waiting. After some brief pleasantries, we got down to business. "I want you to go back and fire all the people who were responsible for this mistake. That means most of your staff."

I looked at the man I had proudly served for seven years. He was a good man and a good leader. He was hurting for me and wanted to help make it right.

"Governor Martin, I love you and appreciate you, but if any blood is to be spilt, let it be mine. Let me take total responsibility."

"Aaron, there is no culpability on your part, but the person who had the responsibility should not have been in that position. This is a matter of ridicule, not a question of your integrity."

The governor was right. The management controls in my department had not worked. The oversight, the checks and balances, the chain of responsibility simply failed.

I, personally, had done nothing wrong. But at the end of the day, I had the wrong people on the job.

Governor Martin's assistant, Nancy, who was in the room with us, broke down and started crying. "I can't stand it! Secretary Johnson is one of the best men I know."

"It's alright, Nancy," I said. "Governor, if I step down, all of this scandal will follow me."

"Aaron, you have disciplined the inmates in a way that has not been characteristic of the secretary's position. You have shown great concern for the decent treatment of inmates." My friend's voice was thick with emotion. "From wanting them to have clean clothes and respectable health care to being concerned that they learn to read for themselves and to their children. I did not choose the wrong man to be my secretary of corrections."

"And I thank you for that. But it is time for me to go."

The next day, February 28, 1992, we called a press conference and my friend, Governor Jim Martin, announced my resignation. Most newspapers reported or indicated that I was fired.

When I resigned my command, we had 20,427 inmates incarcerated, 98,000 offenders on probation or parole, 94 prison units, 14,000 employees and an operating budget of $450 million. But lawmakers had still not allocated $87.5 million of the $200 million promised, and the system had just exceeded the legal limit on prison capacity for the seventeenth time.

THIRTY-NINE

The Blessing

There is no other way to say it: I hid out for a while. After my resignation became public, I took two months by myself to think and lick my wounds. Mattie stood by me and understood my need to go off somewhere. As usual, she kept the home fires burning and fielded phone calls. My children, although young adults by this time, were hurting for me and drew as close to me as I would allow. My church family stood on the ready to console me. But first, I simply needed to be still.

While I sat alone, I kept seeing my name in print coupled with words like "scandal" and "mismanagement." Those words were daggers—bloody daggers that kept being stabbed into my gut and heart over and over again. My emotions were on this huge spinning wheel, which at any given spin would land its sharp pointer on my anger, my shame, my hurt, my betrayal or my disappointment, making my whole body shudder.

One minute I'd beat myself up at my naïveté. How could I have not seen what was going on under my nose? The next minute the betrayal of those I trusted felt like two huge hands around my neck slowly choking the life out of me.

But the shame was the worst. I'd be lying in bed and suddenly see Jim Martin's strained face the day he announced my resignation. Or I'd close my eyes and Mattie's smile, ever steadfast, ever supporting, never withheld, would hover over me—a smile I felt I no longer deserved. And I feared what my public humiliation was doing to my children, Dezette and Jamale.

What I learned in my seclusion is that God will only let you wallow in your self-pity for so long. If you're truly His, then He gives you your thirty minutes to weep, mourn, lament, kick, shake your fist and eat all the wrong things you can, but then enough is enough.

Like a lightning flash on the darkest of nights, God blinded me into attention with a precious memory.

"Brother, Daddy wants to see you today." It was a Sunday morning and my oldest sister was on the phone with a message from my father.

Willie Lee Johnson was a farmer at heart. He would work in the fields all day sharecropping and then come home at night, grab his old lantern and go out to his hogs and cow. Daddy had a special relationship with those animals. But his kids? That was another matter.

I rarely remember my father at the supper table with us. He preferred to eat alone after we were done. Our only time with him was cropping tobacco. He had us up on Saturday by three a.m. and worked us until the sun went down. There was no play with my daddy.

He was a small man—no more than one hundred and twenty pounds. Very, very clean, as I remember, and he meant for us to be clean as well. Because he kept to himself, we said he was selfish. I was pretty sure he loved me, but how I longed for his words—words that would never come.

"Okay," I said to my sister. "I'll come after I get through with church service today."

Five minutes later she called back. "Brother, Daddy wants to see you. You don't understand. He wants you to come right now as soon as you can."

My father was in the Wilmington hospital and had been there for several days. I had seen him a couple of days before, but I now feared he had taken a turn for the worse. So I had one of the members who was a minister take charge for me, and then I called the chairman of the deacon board and told him I had an emergency, that I had to go see my father.

My mother had died several years earlier from a heart attack. She was in church, of course. Where else would Cassie Johnson have died? She was praising the Lord in song when her heart just decided it was time to lay it down. Aunt Annie was by her side.

As I drove the two hours to Wilmington, I tried to figure out what I would say to my father. I had been at the bedside of dying loved ones many times before, either family or church members, and the Lord had always given me something right to say. But God was quiet that morning.

When I walked into his room, Daddy looked up and smiled. "I knew you would come. I knew you had worship service today, but I knew that if I called you, you would come."

Daddy had never looked at me that way before. Always, whenever we were in a room together or sitting in the yard with the family or cropping tobacco, he'd sort of look in my direction but never right at me. It was like he thought if our eyes ever connected, I'd learn something about him he didn't want me to know—like his eyes would tell on him.

"I've got something to say and I didn't know how long I would last." Daddy didn't have good personal skills and conversation seemed to scare him, like a snake or spider would scare others. But on this Sunday morning, it was as if he had saved all of his words for now.

"I want to tell you that I love you and you've been a good son. And I just want to thank you for all you've done."

Daddy had finally found his words, but mine seemed to be playing hooky. I did manage to place my hand over his small, gnarled fingers, hoping my touch would tell him what my heart was feeling.

Then he said, "I want to apologize to you. I know there were many times when you first started out preaching as a young boy that I should have been there with you. Whenever you went out to preach, I should have been with you. I should have been your number one supporter, your cheerleader." Daddy's almond eyes never left my face as they willed me to stay with him. "I only remember one time being there with you, sitting in a pew listening and wondering where all that good in you came from. Son, I wish I'd been there to encourage you. But all I can do now is ask you to forgive me."

His words took great effort and seemed to be seeping his strength out onto his hospital bed like a bleeding wound. My father was trying to right his wrong and in doing so, he gave me two gifts—the healing of a childhood scar that only his proclamation of love could heal, and the passing down of one of the greatest gifts a father can give a son—his blessing. And it was a blessing as sure as Abraham's was to Isaac and our Heavenly Father's was to His Son that day he came up out of the swirling waters of the Jordan. There may not have been a gliding dove or parting clouds when my father spoke, but I was blessed all the same.

"I want to apologize to you," he said again in a quiet voice.

"You have, Daddy."

"No. I didn't know what it was like to be reared by a mother and father. I didn't know how to be a father because I never really had one."

I didn't know my daddy's story. And if Mama knew it, she never told us children.

"It wasn't until recent years," he continued, "that I really understood what it meant to be a father. And I wanted to tell you that. I don't know if I'm going to live or not, but I want you to tell your other sisters and brothers what I told you, that I didn't know how to be a father."

His face seemed to be melting into his pillow like chocolate ice cream on a hot day. I could feel that he was leaving me. I tried to get him to rest a bit, but he wouldn't.

"The only thing I knew how to do was work and put food on the table for you. But to sit down and talk with you, and hug you and kiss you and play with you—I didn't know how to do that. Because I never had it done."

I stayed with Daddy most of the day. It seemed that when he found his voice it became a fountain bubbling and longing to share its gushing waters with the thirsty boy sitting on its edge.

My father spent the afternoon telling me his story of a young boy of eleven losing both his father and mother within six months. He and his two younger siblings were sent to live with two old aunts who were cruel and hateful, who made him work and pay for his siblings' clothes and food.

"When my parents died, it killed something in me that I've been trying to overcome the whole of my life. But now I feel the presence of my mother and father, and very soon, I'm going to be with them." Daddy smiled when he said that.

My father said all those words to me in August 1984, just a few days before he went to heaven. But the memory of them flashed back to me in a blinding strike as I felt the tip of God's finger lightly graze my heart.

Here I was, wallowing in pain and pity, and all the time I was a man who had received his father's blessing! Not just his earthly father's blessing, but his Heavenly One, as well. How had I forgotten that? How had I let that slip from me?

I was *not* worthless. I was *not* an embarrassment. I *was* loved. And I *was* forgiven—had been all along. I had work left to do, for I was a man carrying around a tremendous blessing.

So, I left my hiding place and went back to Mattie and my children. The first Sunday I stepped back into the pulpit, my Mount Sinai family stood up as one and with cheers and tears, they welcomed me home.

FORTY

Revival

As we walked toward each other, it was like I was greeting a long-time friend. Our eyes met, then our arms stretched out, and before we knew it, we had embraced. No introductions or formal handshakes were required. Charles Colson and I were instant brothers. Our hearts connected through our belief that God was very active behind bars—despite them and sometimes because of them. "Aaron Johnson, you're the type of secretary of corrections I've been praying for for the last eighteen years!"

Richard Payne had brought Chuck to my office in Raleigh not too long after our sojourn to Reston. The founder and chairman of Prison Fellowship needed no convincing that Project Macedonia was a God-thing, and he wasted no time wrestling with whether they should or shouldn't do it. The call to bring the Gospel to North Carolina's prisons was heard by ears open to God's prodding. Planning and strategizing began immediately.

I announced at my quarterly chaplain's meeting in Raleigh that I had authorized Prison Fellowship to bring a unique evangelistic revival into our prisons. Hardly a blip showed up in the newspapers the next day. No atheist or civil liberty groups made a peep.

While superintendents, wardens and chaplains at each prison were encouraged to take the lead in this ten-day revival, Prison Fellowship and its vast resources were at their disposal. Each individual chaplain could design his own events and use his own local ministers and pastors, or he could call upon Prison Fellowship, which had a format and plan in place. Plus, Prison Fellowship was recruiting local churches and volunteers to help with this massive undertaking.

As the plans began to formulate, it all fell into place. You could practically feel God's hand turning the knobs to closed doors and soothing the creased foreheads of skeptical chaplains and wardens. Some prison chaplains feared that Prison Fellowship wanted to replace them with their own volunteers—which wasn't true. Unfortunately, the revival was being planned during a time when surrounding states, in an effort to save money, let go of their paid chaplain positions and replaced them with volunteer chaplains. A handful of my chaplains refused to cooperate. In the end, 98 percent of my chaplains and wardens worked with Prison Fellowship to answer the Macedonian call.

A few days after my resignation, I went to see Jim Martin. He assured me that Project Macedonia would not be jeopardized by the recent events. In fact, he congratulated me on how well this project was coming together and how important an event it would be for our prison population. We were both amazed by how under-the-radar Project Macedonia was, how the press had let it alone. My resignation was probably the best thing that could have happened. The media no longer cared what I did or where I went. God, indeed, moves in mysterious ways.

I had one more person to see to make sure that Project Macedonia would not be sabotaged at the last minute: my replacement. V. Lee Bounds was an old Democrat workhorse who had little love or respect for me. When he accepted the governor's offer to take over my position for the rest of my term—approximately ten months—he was returning as secretary of corrections after an almost twenty-year absence. A retired criminal justice professor, Bounds ran the state prisons for two former Democratic governors. When Governor James Holshouser, Jr., the first Republican elected governor since Reconstruction, took the reigns, Bounds clashed with him over prison policies and resigned. When he once again stepped back into that role after my resignation, he was seventy-three.

"Mr. Bounds, I wanted this meeting to make sure that Project Macedonia will not be in jeopardy. I do not want anything I've done to harm or take away from the good this revival can do."

Sitting across from the acting secretary of corrections in my own former office in front of my own former desk was awkward, but I would have walked on coals if it would mean that Project Macedonia could go on as planned.

"*Reverend* Johnson, I assure you that I will not hinder this program in any way. In fact, I have been an advocate for many years of this kind of community support to help the Department of Corrections meet its responsibilities to the people in our custody."

"I appreciate that," I said, ignoring how he emphasized my pastoral title like it was supposed to take me down a notch or two. "You can expect a call from Richard Payne very, very soon." I had to smile thinking about what that meeting would be like.

"I assure you that I will do all in my power to prevent any loss of momentum in the progress of Project Macedonia." Then Mr. Bounds leaned in and said, "And of course, we all think it's best that you have nothing to do with the revival."

I knew that wasn't true. I had had phone calls and notes from several superintendents inviting and asking me to be part of Project Macedonia at their prisons. But Mr. Bounds was making it abundantly clear: I was not welcome to participate.

The secretary shook my hand and then sent me on my way. That was my last official act as secretary of corrections and my last contact with anyone related to the prison system about Project Macedonia.

The flesh part of me was hurt. I so wanted to be able to step out into the yard at a prison during the revival and proclaim Jesus Christ. I wanted nothing more than to stand in a circle of inmates and pray with them. I wanted to walk back through those dirty beige walls and greet Sonny Craig and my brothers at the Church on Life Row. But this revival was not about me or Richard or even Prison Fellowship. It was about shedding the light of Jesus into the darkest parts of one's life. It was about allowing the healing fingers of God to erase as much hurt as was there. God could do that without Aaron Johnson hanging around.

I thought I would just hide away until Project Macedonia was over. My ministry at Mount Sinai had taken on a more personal feel. I no longer felt content just to be a pulpit man or a congregational pastor. Because of the way God had been using me over the years, my relationship with Mount Sinai was often one of delegation and distance. That would no longer satisfy my church family or me. My heart was being pulled into a one-on-one calling. Relationships were what mattered. It was like I was reacquainting myself with my church family. Like a prodigal husband and father, I was having my heart reopened to the love and goodness of those around me. How precious they all were, and I wanted nothing more than to be the pastor they needed.

Of course, Richard wasn't going to let me totally fade away. "We need you, brother! We've got to have matching funds from here in the state or this thing ain't gonna happen."

Prison Fellowship had set up a speaking tour with Charles Colson, Prison Fellowship founder and chairman, and me to blitz the heart of the state. It was a whirlwind week as we were flown from city to city by the same pilot who had first taken me to Reston. I remember one day Chuck and I had breakfast in Wilmington, lunch in Raleigh and supper in Charlotte—all the while meeting and talking with prospective donors.

Chuck is an amazing speaker and persuader. He's brilliant. He could have had a tremendous career after Watergate. Instead, he chose to give his life to a ministry for criminals—to individuals whom the world really looks down on. His passion for these souls is without question. Because of his commitment, the blitz throughout the state helped Prison Fellowship raise over one million dollars.

Richard Payne and his team rarely came up for air as they planned events, trained volunteers, and recruited national and local celebrities to participate at the various prisons. Myles Fish, vice president for field operations for Prison Fellowship and a good friend of Chuck's, became the vice president of field operations for Starting Line, the theme name chosen for Project Macedonia. Organizers thought that a sports title would probably appeal most to the inmates. Since the summer Olympics had recently been completed, the theme felt timely and the tagline, "Come to the Starting Line and make a decision to run the race with Jesus Christ," would appeal. Myles ran those eleven days with the precision of a military general but with the success that only knees-to-floor prayer can accomplish.

Getting commitments from entertainers was a full-time job. Wading through the line of folks it takes to actually get to each celebrity was time consuming, and then coordinating their schedules to make them fit the Starting Line agenda was like rubbing up against sandpaper.

Coordinating transportation from airports to hotels to the correct prisons was a feat unto itself. Buses were rented and drivers and cars rambled across the state delivering volunteers, platform speakers, athletes, and entertainers here and yon. Even Tom Pratt's wife, Gloria, and their son, Stephen, ended up driving some entertainers around the countryside looking for a particular prison.

Volunteers going into the prisons were trained on the dos and don'ts of prison visitation. Don't give out your name or telephone number. Don't make promises you can't keep. Don't ask why a person is in prison. Do dress properly—especially the women. Do be careful about physical contact. Do be aware of con games. Do be natural… and so on.

One of my favorite lines in the training manual read, "Starting Line has been created especially with one large group in mind—the 80 percent of inmates who might never set foot in anything religious sounding. Most of them are unchurched and basically untouched by any flesh and blood models of Christ's love and compassion. They need to see lives that are true testimonies of God's power to heal and transform. Lives like yours."

When I read that, I couldn't help but think of how the Church on Life Row would have hooted and hollered with joy had they known what was about to happen.

I also remember Richard standing in front of a group of volunteers a few weeks before the kick-off and exhorting them: "When you're going into the prisons, I don't want you standing in any corners. I want you to reach out to someone and share Christ with someone, whether he's a corrections officer or an inmate. Share your life with him, and it will change your life as it changes that person's." How I thanked God for putting Richard Payne in my path.

Time after time, whether it was recruiting entertainers, drivers, speakers, volunteers, supplies or donors, or tackling prison logistics or fighting misunderstandings, the Lord continually shut the mouths of lions. As I watched, mainly from the sidelines, I was humbled and awed. God forged the path toward the kick-off date of September 24, 1992.

On that day, when the first Project Macedonia Starting Line team passed through the security check into the yard, a total of 2,730 volunteers had been recruited and 125 platform personalities lined up to take the stage. A specially formed basketball team comprised of major college basketball players, dubbed the Spirit Express, was ready to take the court and challenge prison teams. They walked through the security check with a sack of basketballs and hearts ready to give testimony. The inmates loved them.

In eleven days, 345 evangelistic events were held in 95 North Carolina prisons. By October 4, the last day of Project Macedonia, more than 75 percent of the entire inmate population had heard the Good News of Jesus. Starting Line partnered with Bill Glass evangelistic teams, which took on eight prisons in the Fayetteville area themselves and conducted several events with their own one hundred volunteers.

The American Bible Society donated fifteen thousand copies of the New Testament with Psalms and Proverbs for distribution. And forty individuals from Prison Fellowship's home office volunteered for the project, taking a bus together from Reston to Raleigh.

But probably one of the most effective efforts was the seven hundred prayer partners who signed on to pray specifically for certain prisons. The prayerful petitions began weeks before the event and did not stop until the last weary, hugged-out volunteer stepped back on the bus.

It was a glorious, life-changing, heart-changing, holy ground experience. And not a single one of us involved would ever be the same again.

FORTY-ONE

Presidential Advisor Turned Inmate Turned Preacher

*T*hree days into Project Macedonia, Chuck Colson and Richard insisted I attend the revival with them at Piedmont Correctional Center near Salisbury. I had been warned to stay away, but it was Sunday and I couldn't resist this opportunity to finally worship inside the prison walls. And besides, Colson had invited me.

Those participating in the project began arriving at Piedmont before noon. Getting so many civilians checked in through security took time. I stood in line waiting my turn to walk through the metal detectors, mixed in among all the other Starting Line volunteers. Huddled together in the intake lobby at Piedmont, we had to lay out our wallets, take off our belts and shoes and show our IDs. From Chuck Colson on down, there were no exceptions—all had to obey the rules. I was sure the officers knew who I was. To their credit they never said a word.

While the bulk of us were escorted across the yard and into a sweltering gymnasium full of two hundred inmates to begin the program, Chuck was ushered to lock up, to those inmates doing time in solitary confinement. With only a four-inch slit to converse through, he talked and prayed with each inmate who would allow it. "Do you remember Watergate?" he asked. Of course, most of the offenders didn't. Most were only children when Richard Nixon and his Republican Party embarrassed our nation with their unethical and immoral shenanigans. "I was President Nixon's assistant," he began, and in a few short sentences he told his story. "Now I go to prisons. I gave my life to Jesus. You can get to know Him in here."

At two o'clock the Spirit Express challenged the Piedmont prison team to a basketball game. Of course, an unusually large crowd turned out for that and the gymnasium filled up. As the players warmed up, I noticed other volunteers beginning to filter through the bleachers, introducing themselves and choosing inmates to sit beside.

I watched from the sidelines as businessmen, teachers, ministers and Christians from all walks of life began praying with inmates one-on-one. Conversations began drifting through the stifling air. I heard phrases like, *"Praise God!" "I'm afraid." "Please, pray for me." "I ain't seen my family since...."* *"Jesus don't know me." "Jesus does know you."*

Tears started burning my eyes as I stood and watched this miracle of fellowship, praise, repentance and salvation. As the voices floated over me, I felt the last remnants of the pain of the previous seven months shrink while the remaining scars of shame faded away, as if Jesus himself had applied a cool cloth.

The hot September afternoon did nothing to quash the excitement around the game. From the tip-off, those in the bleachers cheered non-stop as the ball swooshed the hoop time and time again. Smiles and laughter transported us all beyond those fences and razor wire.

At half time, the entertainers with us, such as Peter Penrose and Arthur Hallett, began to congregate. Their concert was scheduled to follow Chuck's presentation to the inmates. It was the celebrities' presence that had stimulated such a large turnout. Music has a way of reaching the soul, softening the heart and forging conviction. Project Macedonia/Starting Line had been extremely fortunate in recruiting such a talented lineup.

Halftime was Chuck's cue. He walked to the top of the foul line and stopped and gazed over the crowd. I looked at this man standing all alone on the basketball court in his white shirt with his horn-rimmed glasses and short-cropped hair. He looked more like an accountant than an ex-inmate. I found myself doubting for a couple of seconds if he could actually catch and keep his tattooed, hard-living crowd's attention.

I worried needlessly.

"My fellow sinners," he began, "those of you who have been caught and those of you who haven't." The prison officers shuffled their feet a little bit. With those few words, he had them—he had the whole room. Then Charles Colson began to do what he does best, break down the Gospel in just the right way so that anyone in the room can understand its meaning and its personal calling to them. It's one of his gifts.

"The sole figure in the Bible guaranteed entry into heaven was one of the thieves crucified alongside Jesus. When you get to heaven, one of the men you'll see standing next to Jesus will be that thief.... The twelve most powerful men in the world couldn't keep a lie about Watergate, but the Apostles died without ever denying Jesus.... Watergate changed a lot of my perspective and values in life... and it started this ministry. All I know is that what happened to me was for a purpose. I'm grateful. I discovered the objective of life, which is to know and enjoy God.... Thank God for Watergate.... It doesn't take guts to pump iron. It takes guts to live your life for Jesus Christ."

And so it began, a revival like no other that was born in the redeemed hearts of a few believers living on death row.

FORTY-TWO

The Prize

"… but one thing I do: forgetting what lies behind and reaching
forward to what lies ahead, I press on toward the goal for the prize of
the upward call of God in Christ Jesus." Phil 3:13-14 (NASB)

Yancey County Correctional Center was tucked away in a small crease in the North Carolina mountains. Its presence was nearly forgotten by just about everyone, in particular the media. Its population of eighty or so inmates did their time without much notice. Family members visited, but that was about it. However, on a warm September afternoon in 1992, it became the dearest place on earth to me. The superintendent and the prison's chaplain greeted me like old friends. They escorted me into the yard along with singer Jesse Dixon and a few other Starting Line volunteers.

"Welcome, Mr. Secretary. We're so glad you came," said the warden as he shook my hand.

"I'm not sure I should be here. This revival doesn't need me to be getting in the way, and if the press gets wind of this…."

"You see any reporters around here? They don't give us the time of day. No one knows you're here and by the time they find out—if they ever find out—who cares."

Chaplain Blount shook my hand as well and said, "You are simply a pastor who has been invited to bring us hurting souls at Yancey a message. There isn't a person in this institution that doesn't want you here."

The superintendent had called me a few weeks before Starting Line was to kick off and invited me to be the platform speaker at their revival. I had told him of my decision not to take a public role in Project Macedonia, fearing that the media would make a big deal of it. The superintendent knew that Secretary Bounds had strongly suggested that I disappear during these eleven days, but he wouldn't hear of it. He and Chaplain Blount kept after me until I agreed. The fact that Yancey County Correctional was located practically off the map helped make the decision easier.

The event was very low key. Jesse Dixon did a fine job entertaining the small number of inmates who had gathered in one of the dormitories. The few volunteers who had accompanied us were seated among the inmates, introducing themselves and offering prayers and friendship.

When I finally stood up to speak, every face in the room staring back at me seemed like one of a friend. And for the first time and the last time, I preached the Good News of Jesus Christ behind the walls of a North Carolina prison.

"Pastor Johnson, could I speak to you?" asked an inmate after my sermon. I was milling around greeting prison staff and residents when this inmate tapped me on the shoulder.

The man had a hard time looking me in the eye. We walked to one of the corners in the room for more privacy. "I did some terrible things when I was out there, things I'm not proud of."

"Have you given those things over to God? His forgiving grace is for all us, you know."

He shifted his balance from one foot to the other. "Yes, sir. I have. But you see, I'm going to be paroled in a couple of weeks and I'm scared."

How many times during my years as secretary had I heard those words? Being locked away in prison is like cocooning in a way. You're taken from your environment, your old vices, your peers, your family, and rehabilitation can either get a foothold or it can run right off your back like water.

Those who grab hold of Jesus have a better chance of shaking the evils that have enslaved them for so long. But even then, the prospect of walking through that gate a free man can be terrifying. The paroled man knows better than anyone the dangers of the dragon's fire that awaits him on the outside. His fear of becoming its victim once again can almost paralyze him.

"I do not want to hurt anyone ever again. Please, please! Can you pray for me?"

By this time, the man's tears had soaked his shirt and he was trembling. I wrapped my arms around him as our heads leaned together. I prayed out loud for his soul and strength. I asked for God to protect him and surround him with those who would help him make good choices.

But, I couldn't stop there. Wrapped in the embrace of this hurting man, I began to also pray for myself. I asked for God's wisdom in my ministry. I asked for His protection for my family. I asked Him to give me more faith and patience, and I asked Him for more courage to walk through the shadows unafraid.

My soul filled with gratitude. As I hung on to this brother, I felt my heart open up like double doors.

With a trembling voice, I thanked my God for the inmate who had his arms wrapped tightly around me. I thanked the Lord of Creation for years of guidance and faithfulness. My soul jumped for joy for His gift of a loving wife and good children. I thanked my Heavenly Father for a church family who had embraced me unconditionally for most of my adult life. I thanked Him and His Holy Spirit for sparing my life all those times that He could just as well have taken it. I praised Him for His goodness in placing in my life my teachers, my mentors and all those people with whom He had brought me face-to-face as only He could. I thanked Him once again for my own father and his blessing to me. And my chin fell to my chest as that brother and I gave thanks together for Jesus… sweet, sweet Jesus, the Son of the Most High God.

As my breath caught in my throat, and my knees weakened and shook, I thanked God Almighty for my mother, her unshakeable love, and our promise of sweet reunion. And finally, with a smile on my face and a release that was God-breathed, I thanked the good Lord for His mysterious ways—and for the blessing of clothing this inmate and those after him would enjoy for the next fifty years or so.

As I exited the dorm that evening, I felt that familiar tug in my chest. A pinpoint meeting was coming on—I was sure of it. I heard distant doors unlocking and could almost see new paths being lit up. God was at it again.

When the gates of Yancey County Correctional clanged behind me for the last time, I heard myself as that little boy in Willard, calling out as I did so many times around the woodstove, *"Seek ye first the Kingdom of God… ."* It was time to move on.

As I sat in my car looking back at the prison and its dormitories, I heard another voice that evening. Mingled amidst the rustling leaves overhead, a quiet voice filtered through my wounded heart and healed the last lingering bit of hurt.

"Well done," came the whisper in the wind. *"Well done."*

EPILOGUE

As I sat in a small, empty classroom across the table from Reverend Aaron Johnson, we were both in tears.

"Deb, it was like you were there," he said. Only a few feet from his former office at Mount Sinai Missionary Baptist Church, we had just read together the last chapter of this manuscript as a three-year journey came to an end. Hours and hours of interviews have been transcribed and incorporated into this story. Research took me to Fayetteville, Raleigh, Greensboro, several state prisons, a federal prison, and the back roads of Pender County. Through Aaron's storytelling, I have been escorted through a side stage door to the Civil Rights Movement. Through Aaron's eyes and ears, I saw and heard Dr. Martin Luther King, Jr. personally exhort the young Aaron to join in the growing nonviolent revolution. Through the power of story, I experienced the horrific lynching of a black man. As Aaron told of his encounters with the Ku Klux Klan, the Black Panthers and myriad angry mobs, I felt the heat of hatred scorch my own face.

Because of Aaron's willingness to tell his story, I now know what it is like to stand eye-to-eye with the president of the United States and with a death-row inmate. Aaron's heart revealed how it feels to be ridiculed and praised, to fail and be redeemed. But mostly, Aaron's story has taught me how to trust and hope in the call of God—no matter where it leads.

The day before we completed the last edits on this book, I sat in a pew in a country church near Fayetteville where Aaron is serving as interim pastor. I watched my friend gingerly step to the podium. As the chorus sang behind him, his white hair reflected the multicolored stained glass of the surrounding windows. I could not help but think of the young Aaron I met through photographs who first stepped to the pulpit at Mount Sinai those many years ago—his wide smile full of promise and hope. As I watched him hang his cane on the side of this temporary pulpit, that same welcoming smile flashed.

As he opened his Bible, I noticed that its edges had long lost their gold trim and its pages were lop-eared and messy. His prepared lesson unfolded from the thin pages, but it was unnecessary. Aaron did not need notes. My guess is that his sermon that day had been written for him by a far Holier Hand. Gathering himself up with raised hands, Pastor Johnson proclaimed in his ever-present strong voice, "If you do not yield to the love of God, then something must be wrong with you!"

You may be asking yourself what made a white, middle-aged woman think she could tell the story of an enigmatic black pastor with any authenticity? What experiences do they share? Could the pastor find anyone less qualified to piece together his life story, a story centered on the black experience? What was he thinking?

Well, Reverend Johnson wasn't thinking. He had no thoughts whatsoever of having anyone tell his story. Not that he was opposed to it; it just didn't cross his mind that anyone would be interested. While his has been a remarkable life filled with duty, sacrifice, courage, choices, family, service and leadership, he feels that anyone could have lived it had they been called to it. He sees nothing worthy of any kind of special attention. After all, this is what one does when called by God. The service is in the doing of it, not the telling of it.

Eventually he did sit down with me several times in person and on the phone as we began peeling the layers away. Today we both explain our odd pairing as one of those God things, in Aaron's words, "one of those pinpoint meetings that God excels at when you least expect it."

Of course, Aaron's ministry did not end when he stepped down from his state corrections post. Nor did Project Macedonia end with the revival in North Carolina's ninety-four prisons. In the spring of 1993, Aaron Johnson and the Prison Fellowship team were invited to south Texas to lead a similar project. By the end of 1993, Project Macedonia/Starting Line had also conducted an evangelistic program in prisons in Oregon and New Mexico. In 2000, approximately thirty other national ministries, all with a prison ministry component, joined this evangelistic effort and the project name was changed to Operation Starting Line. To date, Operation Starting Line has brought the revival spirit to prisons in more than twenty-seven states. The collaboration continues to grow and now includes more than forty ministries.

While Aaron never again stepped foot into a North Carolina prison as a platform speaker for Operation Starting Line, he continued to travel to other prisons across the country exhorting inmates to trust in the Lord with all their hearts.

His ministry at Mount Sinai Missionary Baptist Church continued for forty-five years and ended in December 2005 with his retirement. His son, Jamale A. Johnson, was called into ministry and has followed in his father's footsteps as pastor at Mount Sinai. My last visit with Aaron finished where it began, in the same Mount Sinai classroom in which we conducted our first interview in March 2006.

Reverend Aaron Johnson may be officially retired, but he is talking about starting a new ministry—a ministry of healing, he's calling it. A ministry of comforting the sick, the shut-in and the downtrodden. Those called by God never retire, not really. They simply catch their breath, get down on their knees, and listen for the next assignment.

Young Americans, African and otherwise, owe Reverend Aaron Johnson and others like him—the many others whose stories are still untold—a debt. He was a pathfinder, a stone-kicker and at times a sacrificial lamb for the cause of human justice. He put his life, his reputation and his heart on the line for righteousness. He is one of my heroes. Now that you've met him, I hope he is one of yours.

Deb Cleveland, November 2009

5334032R0

Made in the USA
Lexington, KY
29 April 2010